D1175246

The
PEKINGESE

ANNA KATHERINE NICHOLAS

Title page: *Left to right,* six months old Mama's Beauty O'Honeybear (Ch. Muhlin Most Royal-Ch. Papa's Penny O'Honeybear); with eight months old Macho's Encore O'Honeybear (Ch. Muhlin Macho-Hanez' Farrah O'Honeybear).

Cover photo by Michelle Perlmutter.

Distributed in the UNITED STATES by T.F.H. Publications, Inc., One T.F.H. Plaza, Neptune City, NJ 07753; in CANADA to the Pet Trade by H & L Pet Supplies Inc., 27 Kingston Crescent, Kitchener, Ontario N2B 2T6; Rolf C. Hagen Ltd., 3225 Sartelon Street, Montreal 382 Quebec; in CANADA to the Book Trade by Macmillan of Canada (A Division of Canada Publishing Corporation), 164 Commander Boulevard, Agincourt, Ontario M1S 3C7; in ENGLAND by T.F.H. Publications Limited, Cliveden House/Priors Way/Bray, Maidenhead, Berkshire SL6 2HP, England; in AUSTRALIA AND THE SOUTH PACIFIC by T.F.H. (Australia) Pty. Ltd., Box 149, Brookvale 2100 N.S.W., Australia; in NEW ZEALAND by Ross Haines & Son, Ltd., 82 D Elizabeth Knox Place, Panmure, Auckland, New Zealand; in the PHILIPPINES by Bio-Research, 5 Lippay Street, San Lorenzo Village, Makati Rizal; in SOUTH AFRICA by Multipet Pty. Ltd., Box 235 New Germany, South Africa 3620. Published by T.F.H. Publications, Inc. Manufactured in the United States of America by T.F.H. Publications, Inc.

Contents

About the Author

Since early childhood, Anna Katherine Nicholas has been involved with dogs. Her first pets were a Boston Terrier, an Airedale, and a German Shepherd Dog. Then, in 1925, came the first of the Pekingese, a gift from a friend who raised them. Now her home is shared with two Miniature Poodles and numerous Beagles.

Miss Nicholas is best known throughout the Dog Fancy as a writer and as a judge. Her first magazine article, published in *Dog News* magazine around 1930, was about Pekingese, and this was followed by a widely acclaimed breed column, "Peeking at the Pekingese," which appeared for at least two decades, originally in *Dogdom*, then, following the demise of that publication, in *Popular Dogs*. During the 1940s she was a Boxer columnist for *Pure-Bred Dogs/American Kennel Gazette* and for *Boxer Briefs*. More recently many of her articles, geared to interest fanciers of every breed, have appeared in *Popular Dogs*, *Pure-Bred Dogs/American Kennel Gazette*, *Show Dogs*, *Dog Fancy*, *The World of the Working Dog*, and for both the Canadian publications, *The Dog Fancier* and *Dogs in Canada*. Her *Dog World* column, "Here, There and Everywhere," was the Dog Writers' Association of America winner of the Best Series in a Dog Magazine Award for 1979. Another feature article of hers, "Faster Is Not Better," published in *Canine Chronicle*, received Honorable Mention on another occasion.

In 1970 Miss Nicholas won the Dog Writers' Association Award for the Best Technical Book of the Year with her *Nicholas Guide to Dog Judging*. In 1979 the revision of this book again won this award, the first time ever that a revision has been so honored by this organization. Other important dog writer awards which Miss Nicholas has gained over the years have been the Gaines "Fido" and the *Kennel Review* "Winkies," these both on two occasions and each in the Dog Writer of the Year category.

It was during the 1930s that Miss Nicholas's first book, *The Pekingese*, appeared in print, published by the Judy Publishing Company. This book, and its second edition, sold out quickly and is now a collector's item, as is *The Skye Terrier Book* which was published during the 1960s by the Skye Terrier Club of America.

During recent years, Miss Nicholas has been writing books consistently for T.F.H. These include *Successful Dog Show Exhibiting, The Book of the Rottweiler, The Book of the Poodle, The Book of the Labrador Retriever, The Book of the English Springer Spaniel, The Book of the Golden Retriever, The Book of the German Shepherd Dog, The Book of the Shetland Sheepdog, The Book of the Miniature Schnauzer, The World of Doberman Pinschers,* and *The World of Rottweilers.* Plus, in another T.F.H. series, *The Maltese, The Keeshond, The Chow Chow, The Poodle, The Boxer, The Beagle, The Basset Hound, The Dachshund* (the latter three co-authored with Marcia A. Foy), *The German Pointer, The Collie, The Weimaraner, The Great Dane, The Dalmatian,* and numerous other titles. In the KW series she has done *Rottweilers, Weimaraners,* and *Norwegian Elkhounds.* And she has written American chapters for two popular English books purchased and published in the United States by T.F.H., *The Staffordshire Bull Terrier* and *The Jack Russell Terrier.*

Miss Nicholas's association with T.F.H. began in the early 1970s when she co-authored for them five books with Joan Brearley: *The Wonderful World of Beagles and Beagling* (also honored by the Dog Writers Association), *This is the Bichon Frise, The Book of the Pekingese, The Book of the Boxer,* and *This is the Skye Terrier.*

Since 1934 Miss Nicholas has been a popular dog show judge, officiating at prestigious events throughout the United States and Canada. She is presently approved for all Hounds, all Terriers, all Toys and all Non-Sporting; plus all Pointers, English and Gordon Setters, Vizslas, Weimaraners, and Wirehaired Pointing Griffons in the Sporting Group and Boxers and Dobermans in Working. In 1970 she became only the third woman ever to have judged Best in Show at the famous Westminster Kennel Club event at Madison Square Garden in New York City, where she has officiated as well on some sixteen other occasions over the years. She has also officiated at such events as Santa Barbara, Chicago International, Morris and Essex, Trenton, Westchester, etc., in the United States; the Sportsman's and the Metropolitan among numerous others in Canada; and Specialty shows in several dozen breeds in both countries. She has judged in almost every one of the United States and in four of the Canadian Provinces. Her dislike of air travel has caused her to refrain from acceptance of the constant invitations to officiate in other parts of the world.

6

The first time I saw "Peter" was at the Thousand Islands K.C. Dog Shows at Brockville, Ontario, in August 1982. This stunning puppy, proudly owned and handled by Nigel Aubrey Jones in co-ownership with R. William Taylor, was the sensation of the several days of shows, winning Best Toy Puppy each time, and I believe Best Puppy in Show on two of those occasions. Everyone was predicting the brightness of his future. And they were correct, for Peter became American and Canadian Ch. St. Aubrey Beeswing of Elsdon, Top Toy Dog in America for 1985, now owned by Edward Jenner.

Ch. Toydom Ch'ien Yuen, a famous historical Pekingese owned by the late Mrs. A. C. Williams whose daughter, Vandy Williams, has most kindly shared the photo with us.

Essdee So Tiny So Precious was very special to all at Toimanor Kennels. Note the outstanding type for so tiny a "sleeve" Peke! Owned by Stan and N. Audrey Drake, Toimanor Pekingese, Fayetteville, Arkansas.

Chapter 1

Origin of
The Pekingese

The Pekingese is without a doubt one of the oldest breeds of dog in the world. Even a casual study of ancient Chinese history makes that fact apparent as one finds the acceptance and popularity of the various "Lion Dogs" reaching back through many centuries, widely referred to and depicted in literature and art.

The ancestors behind our Pekingese, for which we have specific information, are the Imperial Palace dogs of Peking; the small, revered, lion-hearted dogs guarded zealously by special attendants, who were well aware that harm to one of their tiny charges would be paid for by the death penalty. Needless to say, they fulfilled their instructions with care!

It was the Dowager Empress Tzu Hsi who especially honored and respected these tiny dogs. The clarity of her understanding of them was uncanny; she obviously expended thought and affection on her pets.

Empress Tzu Hsi and the other ladies of the court were particularly partial to the "Sleeve Pekingese" because they were so easily carried in the wide sleeves of the ladies' kimonos. She liked their variety of colors, with which she would complement the colors she might be wearing each day. We understand that black and all of the colors were popular. She did not care much for white Pekingese, as white to the Chinese is indicative of mourning.

9

Eng. Ch. Singlewell Jay's Dream, by Ch. Jay Trump of Sunsalve (great-grandson of Ch. Wee Sedso) ex Donelco Sheeza Dream. Mrs. P.M. Edmond, Four Marks near Alton, Hants, England.

That is the factual story of the background of the Pekingese. But there is another one as well, for the romantically inclined, to which one may, or may not, give credence.

It is told that many centuries ago, a lion met and lost his heart to a marmoset. Obviously they were incompatible, owing to his great size. In order to have his beloved, it is said that the lion sacrificed his size, but not his courage and great heart, so that they might form an alliance. The believers say that the ancestors of the modern Pekingese were the offspring of these two.

Chapter 2

History and Development in England

It was during the year 1860 that five Pekingese made the trip from China to Great Britain. They were taken by British troops after the storming of the Imperial Palace during the Boxer Rebellion. These five are the direct ancestors of modern Pekingese in England, and of many others who have been exported from British kennels.

Two of these early Pekingese were presented to the Duchess of Richmond and Gordon. The dogs were the foundation of Goodwood Kennels, founded by the Duchess and carried on for more than 30 years by her sister, Lady Algernon Gordon-Lennox, a breeder of early English champions. Admiral Lord John Hay bought the third dog, Schlorff, who lived to be 18 years old. He also purchased a black and white bitch, Hytien, whom he presented to his sister. The fifth, a parti-color bitch named Looty, was presented by General Dunne to Queen Victoria.

It was not until 35 years later when Loftus Allen, commanding a ship in the China trade, returned to England with a gray brindle dog, Pekin Peter. Purchased from a taxidermist in Shanghai, the dog was a gift for his wife, Mrs. Minna Loftus Allen (who became a famous breeder and an author on Pekingese). With this bitch, Mrs. Allen became England's first Pekingese exhibitor; and Pekin Peter, the first of the breed shown there, was entered in 1894 in the "Any Variety Not Exceeding 90 Pounds" Class at Chester.

Mrs. H. Kingston purchased Pekin Peter from Mrs. Allen; bred to a Goodwood bitch, he became the grandsire of the famous red Pekingese, Goodwood Chun, for whom the color was named. Mrs. Allen then received two more Pekingese from China in 1895. These both were black, Pekin Prince and Pekin Princess.

In 1896, Mrs. Douglas Murray purchased a notable pair of Pekes: Ah Cum and Mimosa, year-old reds sent by an official attached to the Royal Palace. Several of the Goodwood matrons were bred to Ah Cum, and it was one of these who produced the first of all Champion Pekingese, Goodwood Lo.

Importations continued to follow. Several accompanied Mr. George Brown, for many years a Vice-Consul in China, back to England. A bitch bred by Mr. Burns from Chinese stock founded the Brackley strain for Mrs. Browning. Chang and Lady Li, presented by Minister Li Hung Chun to Major Heuston in 1898, founded the Greystones. And in 1900, the last of the Palace dogs to come to England did so; namely, Glenbrane Boxer and a bitch called Quama, both imported by Major Gwynne.

The Kennel Club recognized the breed in 1898. A Standard of Points for Pekingese was drawn up by the Japanese Spaniel Club that same year. Mrs. Allen's suggestion that the Pekingese Club become a separate organization from the Japanese Spaniel Club was proposed that year.

Probably the world's most renowned breeders of Pekingese were Mrs. C. Ashton Cross and her three daughters: Aimee, Cynthia and Marjorie. Shortly before 1900 their Alderbourne Kennel was established; a kennel which remained active until the mid-1970s when Cynthia, by then the sole survivor, passed away. Alderbourne Pekingese are known, have lived, have prospered, and have been beneficial to the breed throughout the world where show Pekingese are raised. I doubt that there is a breeding kennel of top-flight Pekes to be found where one or more of the hundreds of famed Alderbournes does not appear in the pedigrees.

Manchu Kennels started in 1897. Probably the most important of all breedings in early British Pekingese history was that of Manchu Wei Wei (Champion Manchu Cheng Tu–Champion Palace

Miss Vandy Williams has loaned us this photo, which surely brings back fond memories to the author and to other long-time Pekingese fanciers. *Left to right:* Mrs. Alex Williams, founder of the Toydoms and Vandy William's mother; Jimmy MacFarlane (Silverdjinn); and Miss Marjorie Ashton Cross, co-owner of the Alderbournes.

Shi) to Manchu Tao Tei (Champion Goodwood Chun–Champion Gia Gia). It was this breeding which produced Champion Chu Erh of Alderbourne and Sutherland Ouen Teu Tang, the dogs who are the background of Alderbourne and Sutherland Avenue Kennels and all the magnificent dogs who have followed in those and other lines.

Activity was growing fast in the English Pekingese world. Literally dozens of memorable Pekingese made their contributions to the present. The period of Pekingese in England prior to World War II saw the breed steadily climbing the ladder of quality and popularity. Some memorable people and dogs from that period include the already mentioned established kennels plus notable newer breeders of that time: Mary de Pledge and the Cavershams (later in partnership with Mrs. Warner Hill), whose dogs are conceded by experts to have been awesomely outstanding; the Remenhams, breeders of notable champions, owned by Dr. and Mrs. John A. Vlasto; the Sherhills, owned by Miss M. Allen; the Chinatowns, Mr. and Mrs. Weil; the Iwades, owned by Mrs. I. Stowell Brown (Mrs. Foster Burgess at that time); W. Hindley "Willie" Taylor and his memorable Kyratowns; Lady Holder with the Hartleburys; Mrs. Hugh Duberly with the Sanells—all were fantastic breeders of very noteworthy dogs, as was Sybil Whitehead with the Ifields.

At the close of World War II, the Yusens were going strong for Miss S.A. Higgs, as were Alderbourne, Caversham, Kyratown, and the Coughtons for Lady Isabel Throckmorton, just to name a few who helped get things started up again.

MICKLEE

The Micklee Pekingese, active since 1946, are world famous for the quality and accomplishments of their dogs. Joyce and Jack Mitchell are the owners of Micklee, which is located at Denholme in Bradford. This kennel has bred and owned 16 English champions, in addition to having won more than 132 Challenge Certificates.

The top dog at this kennel is the fabulous Champion Micklee Roc's Ru Ago. He was the Top Toy Dog in England for both 1984 and 1985, and received Reserve Best in Show at Crufts during the latter year.

Ru Ago has three all-breed Bests in Show, as well as Best in Show at the Welsh Kennel Club all-breed Championship event; he also has 11 Group wins. He has 23 Challenge Certificates and 22 Bests of Breed to his credit (beaten for one of them by his sister, Champion Royale).

As a sire, Ru Ago is proving himself of inestimable value. Currently a son of his, Ru's Romayo, has earned at least one of his Challenge Certificates and has qualified for the Pup of the Year competition.

14

ROSAYLEEN

Rosayleen Kennels, owned by Mrs. Eileen Newman of Ilminster, Somerset, started their show career with the purchase in 1974 of Isto So Dee Sed of Singlewell from Mrs. Edmond who quickly won two Reserve Challenge Certificates for his new owner.

Mrs. Newman next selected a bitch in whelp to Sancliffe Kibbee at Mrs. Copley's kennel, namely Sancliffe Robinette, whose daughter Rosayleen Carousel, when mated to Mrs. Horn's Champion Belknap Eldorado, produced Rosayleen Brabinge (Junior Warrant Reserve Challenge Certificate), who figures strongly in Mrs. Newman's breeding program.

Robinette was bred for her next litter to a lovely little dog who was seldom shown (Sancliffe Kibbee ex a Drakehurst-bred bitch), producing Rosayleen Roulette, successful as a winner but who did not enjoy the shows. Champion Jay Trump of Sunsalve really hit the jackpot! Their litter produced Champion Rosayleen Casino Royale (Top Stud Dog in Our Dogs Pedigree Petfood competition in 1985), sire of so many important winners, including Champion Rosayleen The Gaffer of Sunsalve, who is co-owned and shown by

Eng. Ch. Rosayleen Casino Royale, outstanding representative of Mrs. Eileen Newman's Rosayleen Pekingese.

Mr. Terry Nethercott. The Gaffer was Top Puppy in 1985 and now has five Challenge Certificates, two Reserve Challenge Certificates, and a Reserve in the Toy Group at Manchester 1986 before even reaching 19 months of age.

Champion Casino, mated to a daughter of So Dee Sed, produced Mrs. Newman's Rosayleen Carolina Moon, Junior Warrant winner, who won the Reserve Challenge Certificate at the L. and P. Championship Show this year; and Rosayleen Harvey Moon who is now in America with Mr. Don Sutton.

Jay Trump has produced the abundant coat for which Mrs. Newman's dogs are known, particularly when bred to Sungarth bitches, some of which were acquired by Mrs. Newman from the late Mrs. B. Prior. Champion Casino, mated to Sungarth Rachel, has produced Rosayleen Big Deal and Rosayleen Royale Command, both winning well in Puppy Classes in championship events. Big Deal has captured three Best Puppy awards and Royal Command two at just nine months of age.

SINGLEWELL

The Singlewell Kennel prefix was born in 1948, with, at that

Eng. Ch. Rosayleen The Gaffer At Sunsalve, co-owned by Mrs. Eileen Newman, Rosayleen Kennels and by Mr. Terry Nethercott, Hayes, Middlesex, England.

Rosayleen Croupier, by Ch. Rosayleen Casino Royale ex Sungarth Rachel, age eight months. Mrs. Eileen Newman, owner, Rosayleen Pekingese.

time, Wire Fox Terriers, Bulldogs, Dachshunds, Sealyham Terriers, Labradors, and several other breeds including Pekingese. Pekingese had always been the favorite companions of the family, however, and over a few years' time, all others were forsaken while the Pekes grew in strength and completely took over.

Mrs. Pamela M. Edmond is the owner of Singlewell Pekingese, who are located at Four Marks near Alton, Hants. Her mother had always had a passion for animals, dogs in particular, which Mrs. Edmond has very obviously inherited. So in 1950, when they bought two Pekingese bitches from Mrs. Hunter Richmond (whose prefix, Peperstiche, was based on mostly Caversham lines), they started the absorbing hobby of trying to breed the perfect Pekingese. The elusiveness of this exploit probably never occurred to them at that time, but, as Mrs. Edmond says, "We are still trying."

The Caversham-Peperstiche bitches were litter sisters by Champion KuKu Kuki of Caversham (Champion Ku-Chi of Caversham–Freda of Caversham, his litter sister). The dam's line was a total outcross, which made possible an outcross to the Alderbourne line, thus getting a degree of puppies with the characteris-

Eng. Ch. Singlewell Prunella was the first black champion Peke in England after a period of 11 years. Owned by Mrs. P.M. Edmond, Singlewell Kennels.

tics of *both* Caversham and Alderbourne. A bitch puppy of this line was born in 1954, by Tulyar of Alderbourne, who was registered Singlewell Talullah. Bred to Champion Tul Tuo of Alderbourne (also by Tulyar), Talullah produced four gorgeous puppies; sad to say, all died of hardpad, which was a real hazard in those pre-inoculation days.

When Miss Cynthia Ashton Cross heard of this misfortune, she kindly offered a free return service to Tulyar, so they tried again, and Mrs. Edmond's mother was able to raise two of the puppies (both bitches) by hand for her daughter. Again there was misfortune in this breeding, as Talullah herself died following a Caesarean delivery. One of the puppies was a lovely solid golden girl whom, in consideration of Cynthia Ashton Cross's kindness to her, Mrs. Edmond named Singlewell Charity.

In due course, Charity was mated to Champion Berar of Ifield, a grandson of Champion Caversham Ku Ku of Yam. From this mating she chose the golden boy, Singlewell Sunny Bear, who was to win many Bests in Show and Bests of Breed at top Open shows but was passed over for the high awards at championship shows, as he never grew ear fringes. He was, however, an unqualified success as a sire. It was his daughter, Morella, who gave the kennel its first champion, Singlewell Sun Chu, by Champion Toydom Sunshen Chu T'Sun, who gained his title in 1966.

In 1960, Mrs. Edmond had started a separate black line with a dog her mother had purchased, Singlewell Samurai Black Monarch. He was 18 months old and had never previously been shown. Soon he was winning well and holding his own among all colors at a time when there were very few blacks being bred. Since a suitable mate could not be located, Mrs. Edmond decided to try a daughter-to-sire breeding, using his daughter, Singlewell Brunette, who was well outcrossed on the dam's side. She produced one male who was Singleman Batman; and the black color gene was so well fixed by this mating that Batman produced only *black* puppies, regardless of the color bitch bred to him. He sired Singlewell Batling, a reserve Challenge Certificate winner who subsequently became an American champion. Champion Prunella owed her color to Singlewell Samurai Black Monarch. She was the first black champion in England for 11 years.

Meanwhile, Champion Singlewell Sun Chu sired 14 Champions overseas and English Champion Dawshill Sun Willow. A daughter of Sun Chu, namely Singlewell Sea Shell, was the dam of Cham-

Singlewell Heeza Fella, one of the outstanding Pekingese from England's famed Singlewell Kennels.

pion Singlewell Wee Sedso, whose sire, Honourable Mr. Twee of Kanghe, had the superb head that Mrs. Edmond and her family so greatly admired.

Champion Singlewell Sedso has sired stock in which the Edmonds take deep pride. His name can still be found on many noted pedigrees today, through his son, Sungarth Kanga of Toydom, and Champion Singlewell T'Sai Magic, dam of Champion Singlewell Magic Charm, Champion Singlewell Some Magic, and Champion Singlewell Sensation.

Mrs. Edmond continues by noting, "We cannot complete the story of Singlewell to date without mentioning the purchase of two very important bitches." These are Moye of Jenntora in 1970 and Donelco Sheeza Dream in 1976. The former was a gorgeous red bitch who never grew sufficient coat to be shown successfully, but who gave her super conformation and type to her offspring. She was by Ku Ying of Jamestown, and was therefore mated to the young dog International Champion St. Aubrey's Singlewell Ku Donovan. This produced a dog puppy, Singlewell Yung Donovan, who was the sire of Donelco Sheeza Dream.

Sheeza has produced such superb stock for Mrs. Edmond as Singlewell Heeza Fella, Champion Jay's Dream, Champion T'Sai Magic, and American Champion Singlewell Jason.

SUNSALVE

Sunsalve Pekingese are owned by Mr. Terry Nethercott at Hayes in Middlesex. The kennel was started in 1967 with a bitch from Toydom Kennels. Mr. Nethercott's first champion was Sungarth Hi-Jinks of Sunsalve in 1974, a son of Champion Yanchy Ah Yang of Jamestown ex Aconite.

The "star" of the kennel is the stunning Champion Jay Trump of Sunsalve (Toydom Trump Card–China Bird of Court Hill). Jay is the sire of 37 champions, ten of which are English champions, the other 27 overseas. This marvelous dog has been Top Pekingese Stud Dog in Britain for the past four years.

Other noted Pekes at Mr. Nethercott's kennels include Champion Josto Madam Gaye At Sunsalve, Champion Sunsalve My Love (both Jay Trump daughters), Champion Rosayleen The Gaffer At Sunsalve, the latter owned in partnership with Mrs. E. Newman, and Champion Josto Airs And Graces, both Jay grandchildren.

20

Eng. Ch. Sungarth Hi-Jinks at Sunsalve, owned by Mr. T. Nethercott, Hayes, Middlesex, England.

TIYANG

Tiyang Pekingese are owned by Roy Littlewood at Bury, Lancashire. This is a small kennel but one that has contributed well to the breed through the outstanding quality of the dogs produced here.

Currently in the limelight is English Champion Tiyang Wine and Roses. A clear red with black mask, she is by Champion Penane Kung Fu from Amelia of Sungarth At Tiyang. The producer of two litters, each consisting of five puppies, Wine and Roses left the show ring for awhile to attend to these matters, then returned to competition and to the completion of her championship.

Tiyang Kennels began in the early 1970s. They have also gained fame as the breeders of Champion Tiyang Pu-Zin Louie of Etive, who made title in 1978.

Miss Adele Summers with a Toydom Pekingese on her arm, enjoys a bit of conversation with England's Queen Mother Elizabeth. The members of England's Royal Family are known throughout the world for their love of animals.

TOYDOM

The Toydom Pekingese Kennel was founded originally by the late Mrs. A.C. Williams in 1920—almost like a fairytale! She had always wanted a Pekingese, and coming from a family who had always had gundogs and racehorses, this caused quite a stir. In fact, she kept her first Peke hidden from her family in her bedroom, especially from her famous racehorse-trainer father, Sir John Renwick, who, as it turned out when the "infiltration" was eventually discovered, was the first to be won over by the little Peke.

Mrs. Williams's first two Pekingese litters were bred from this little girl. She then sold the puppies, since she felt they were not quite good enough to show, and saved the money until the time she would see the Peke she wanted to buy.

Acquiring her new Peke, she was told that it had been sold to her only because it would not show. Her reaction to this was to stay away from shows for awhile, during which time Mrs. Wil-

22

liams worked with and trained the "shrinking violet," until she felt her ready to hold her own in show ring competition. This she did with ease, coming out at an important championship show where she promptly gained the challenge certificate and soon thereafter completed her championship.

Mrs. Williams built up the Toydom Kennels over many years, making up numerous champions, including Champion Toydom Manzee, who went through to his title undefeated in any of his classes, and his handsome son, Champion Toydom Manzee Tu. In addition, there were Champion Toydom Chien Yuen from the earliest days, Champion Toydom Chien Mein, Champion Toydom San San, Champion Toydom Man Lu, Champion Toydom Lo-Lees, Champion Toydom Pun-Kee Jewel of Elfann, Champion Toydom Sambo of Harborough, Champion Toydom Sheraton The Duchess, Champion Toydom Nanette, and her famous parti-color Champion Toydom Ts'zee, who was Best of Breed at Crufts in 1956 and won 18 Challenge Certificates during his show career.

Relaxation time at Toydom! Miss Adele Summers *(left);* Miss Vandella Williams *(right).* The Pekes are English Champions Toydom Modesty Forbids and Toydom Modesty Permits on Miss Summers' lap; Ch. Toydom Dutch Courage *(center).* Ch. Toydom A Touch of Class and Ch. Toydom Erotica with Miss Williams.

Her last champion, who won his title in the 1960s, was Champion Toydom Sunshon Chu Tsun, present in many pedigrees of recent Toydom dogs.

The kennel at that stage was slowly winding down, due to Alex Williams's full-time commitment to daughter Vandy's equestrian pursuits, although she was active in judging engagements (including Crufts) and committee work, which included being Chairman of the London and Provincial Pekingese Club, and being a committee member of the Ladies Branch of The Kennel Club.

After her mother's death in 1973, Vandy Williams started showing the Pekes again with partner Adele Summers, and the kennel really came into contention when Sungarth Kanga of Toydom arrived.

Kanga, mated to Micklee Zanda of Toydom, produced the first Toydom champion of the "new" generation, Champion Toydom Erotica, while Kanga and Doro Dorothello Gay Loretta Wong

Ch. Toydom TsZee, Best of Breed at Crufts in 1956. The winner of 18 Challenge Certificates. Owned by Mrs. A. C. Williams.

Magnificent Pekingese from England in the 1930s. On the *right,* Eng. Ch. Toydom Manzee who holds a wonderful record in the breed having gained his title unbeaten in all his classes. With him is his son, Ch. Toydom Manze Tu. These were two of the outstanding Toydoms owned by Mrs. Alex Williams.

(who was Jamestown linebred) produced one of Toydom's premier stud dogs, Toydom Trump Card, and his sister, Toydom No Secrets, winner of one Challenge Certificate and two Reserve Challenge Certificates.

In his first litter Trump Card sired the great Champion Jay Trump of Sunsalve, Top Sire in the Breed in 1982, 1983, 1984, and 1985; and Champion Toydom A Touch of Class, Best of Breed at Crufts in 1982.

No Secrets, in her turn, mated to Champion Belknap Eldorado, produced another champion, the striking Modesty Forbids, a Toy Group winner and the sire of three English champions to date, namely Champion Toydom Modesty Permits, Belknap Bravo, and Belknap Blush.

Another champion in the kennel is a Kanga son, Champion Toydom Dutch Courage. Toydom dogs have sired ten English champions and numerous champions overseas.

Both Adele Summers and Vandy Williams judge the breed at championship show level, taking assignments at home and abroad, with appointments in the United States, on the Continent, and in Scandinavia. Both are members of The English Kennel Club, and serve on the Committee of the Pekingese Reform Association—Adele as Vice President and Vandy as Secretary-Treasurer.

Ch. Tiko of Pekeboro, the English import who stands behind the Mar-Pat line of Pekingese. Tiko, by English Ch. Tang Tiko of Alderbourne, sired 13 champions and has many titled grandchildren. Owned by Martha Olmos-Ollivier and Patricia Miller, Gardena, California.

Chapter 3

Pekingese in the United States

Americans enjoyed the favor of friendship from the Dowager Empress Tzu Hsi of China, thus it is our good fortune that a number of her beloved Lion Dogs were therefore presented as gifts. The best known of these was a black dog called Chaou Ching Ur, given to Dr. Mary H. Cotton. This little dog was to become the first Pekingese bitch to complete her title in our country.

Mrs. Alice Roosevelt Longworth was another recipient so honored—hers was also a black dog. J. Pierpont Morgan was gifted with a lovely pair of parti-colors. A golden parti-color came to the famed artist Miss Carl while painting a portrait of the Empress at the Summer Palace. Miss Uchida and Mrs. Conger were also given puppies.

Mrs. Eva Guyer and A.J.S. Edwards, both Philadelphians, were America's earliest Pekingese exhibitors. Peking I, a Chinese import, appeared in the ring at Philadelphia in 1901, placing second in the Miscellaneous Class under 25 pounds. Wu Ting Fang, a homebred sired by Chutney and bred by Mr. Edwards, won a blue ribbon at Wissahickon in 1904.

Pekin Chang and Pekin Pu Taiy, bred by Lady Gooch and owned by Mrs. Benjamin Guinness, were the first Pekingese to compete in the New York area. The show was the Westminster Kennel Club event.

Tsang of Downshire made his initial appearance at Cedarhurst, New York, in 1905. Owned by Mrs. Mandy, he was a son of Hai Tung (by Goodwood Put Singh) ex Mi Chou of Downshire; he was destined to become America's very first Pekingese champion. The best puppy sired by him was Champion Ki of Downshire, a daughter of Sueng Pao Ki of Alderbourne. In her one litter, Ki produced the undefeated Champion Huhi, owned by Miss Lydia Hopkins.

The Westminster Kennel Club gave Pekingese their own classification for the first time in 1905. Six competed belonging to Mrs. Guinness and one, Hsia Li, owned by Miss Helen Brice. It was around this same period that J. Pierpont Morgan showed Cragston Sing and some other Pekingese, thus taking his place as an active member of the Fancy.

Ai Gee Kennels, owned by Mr. and Mrs. Alfred Goodson, joined the Fancy in 1910 with an importation from Mrs. Sealy Clark, Champion Broadoak Fatima, later sold to and finished by Mrs. Paul Sorg. Mrs. M.E. Harby, Mrs. Richard McGrann, and

The great Ch. Coughton Sungable of Perryacre winning Best in Show on his debut here in the United States. Co-owned by Mrs. Elaine Rigden, who is handling, and the late Mrs. Ralph G. West. This little dog became one of the breed's truly important winners during the 1960s.

Another Best in Show for the imported Ch. Coughton Sungable of Perryacre, surrounded by his smiling owners, Mrs. Ralph G. (Amanda) West and Mrs. Jerry (Elaine) Rigden, the latter handling. Battle Creek K.C., August 7, 1965.

BATTLE CREEK
KENNEL CLUB
AUGUST 7 1965
BEST IN
SHOW

Mrs. A. McClure Halley were others who became active in the Pekingese world of that day.

The Pekingese Club of America was founded in April 1909 by Dr. Cotton, Mr. and Mrs. Mandy, Mrs. Guinness, Miss Anna Sands and Mrs. Lydig. The inaugural show for the club was in 1911, with Mrs. Guinness, then Club President, judging the entry of 94. Winners at this initial Pekingese Club of America Specialty were: Tsang of Downshire, Winners Dog, and Broadoak Fatima, Winners Bitch.

It was at the third PCA Specialty, in 1912, that the club's two magnificent perpetual trophies made their appearance—the J. Pierpont Morgan Trophy for Best of Breed and the James Gordon Bennett Trophy for best in the American-bred Classes; both were to be won five times for permanent possession. Coincidentally they were both won outright in 1937: the Morgan Trophy by Mrs. Richard S. Quigley; the Bennett Trophy by the Misses C. and M. Lowther.

Literally dozens of breeders played their part in the development of the Pekingese in America. The author recalls, affectionately, the greats of the 1930s–1950s period. Orchard Hill was

29

The late Mrs. Madelaine H. Austin, whose Catawba Pekingese were so justly renowned, photographed with two of them back about 1940. These are Ch. Tang Hao of Caversham-Catawba *(right)* and his daughter Ch. Cherie of Huntington-Catawba, two of Mrs. Austin's successful imports. She also was the owner of the first record holding Best in Show Pekingese, Ch. Che Le of Matsons-Catawba. Photo courtesy of Mrs. Austin's daughter, Mrs. Philip S.P. Fell.

where Mrs. Richard S. Quigley owned well over 100 champions, a large majority of which were homebreds from the quality dogs she so frequently imported. Her greatest homebred was Champion Jai Son Fu of Orchard Hill, but there were many others, both homebred and imports, who deserve acclaim and recognition.

Mrs. James M. Austin, at Catawba Kennels, had the first consistent Best-in-Show-winning Pekingese in the United States in her Champion Che Le of Matsons-Catawba, who scored an amazing (for those days) 30 Bests in Show at a time when Pekingese hardly ever received the recognition of a top award.

Then there was Champion Chik Tsun of Caversham, an imported dog owned by the Charles Venables, who was the all-breed Best in Show record-holder from 1960 until some 20 years later.

AUDRIANNE

Audrianne Pekingese, at Mentor, Ohio, are owned by Miss Audrey A. Atherton, who has not been without a Peke since she acquired her first one in 1952.

It was around 1960 when she reached the decision that she would like to raise and show Pekingese, and she then set out to find some good Pekes of excellent English breeding on which to found her kennel.

One of these was Champion Cho Sen Fo Lisa, by the English import American Champion Wardene Sun Fo ex American Champion Choo Cee of Marglo. Lisa had been bred by Mrs. Edna Voyles, owner of Cho Sen Kennels, very famous in the Pekingese world. In her first litter, for which Miss Atherton had selected Mrs. Rose Marie Katz's Champion Wei Tiko of Pekesboro and Roh Kai as the sire, Lisa produced three champions, Audrianne's Wai Tiki, Wei Star, and Wei Choo Cei. Later, bred to other studs, she also produced Champion Audrianne's Rich Romance and Champion Audrianne's Academy Award. Throughout the years, Audrey Atherton's love of Pekingese has remained steadfast. She can well take pride in the beauty and quality of her dogs who bring her so much pleasure.

In 1986, Audrey retired after 33 years with Ohio Bell. The silver lining to having given up this position is that now she will have more time to devote to being with the dogs, which will enable her to increase her former custom of breeding one litter each year to doing so a bit more frequently.

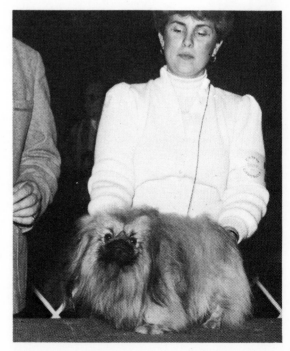

Ch. Lon-Du Dragon Mite, by Ch. Rodari the Dragon of Lon-Du ex Ch. Mi Flaming Maimie of Lon -Du, was born March 1984. Bred by Arlon D. Duit. Owned by Miss Audrey A. Atherton, Audrianne Kennels, Mentor, Ohio.

Although the majority of her winning dogs are colors, Audrey Atherton also has a very special interest in breeding, owning, and showing black Pekes and white Pekes.

The Audrianne whites include Audrianne's Choir Cameo, Oriental Olga, Champion Olga's Jill of Popa's, and Audrianne's Gloria Gardenia, all bitches. The males include Champion Audrianne's Snow Shih Tsun, Crown Challenger, Rodari Snow Dragon, and the white brace (as far as Miss Atherton is aware, this is the only winning *white* Pekingese brace in the United States), littermates Audrianne's Choir Caper and Choir Chime, the latter two by English import American Champion Chintoi Choir Boy ex Audrianne's Oriental Olga.

Audrey and Mrs. Norma Jean Popa have an unwritten contract to help each other to produce *better* whites, the goal being something truly *great*. For those who are unfamiliar with white Pekingese, they are stunning little dogs, very striking and eye appealing. Care of them is difficult, as the white coats soil easily from everything from newspaper print on up and down, but the satisfaction of having a gorgeous white to love and enjoy makes it seem well worthwhile.

Blacks, too, are featured at Audrianne—excellent ones. They include Champion Audrianne's Midnight Magic and Lon-Du Dark Dragon. The latter was purchased in 1985 from Arlon Duit and has not gained his title, as he dislikes the dog shows. Audrey plans to try to change that way of thinking, however, now that she will be home and will have time to really work at socializing him.

During 1975, Audrey purchased two lovely colored bitches from Mrs. Robert I. Ballinger Jr., who have been great assets to her kennel, blending very nicely with her original English stock.

Audrianne champions are numerous now. They include the males American and Canadian Champion Audrianne's Kerr's Kristi Kopi, American and Canadian Champion Saimaifun's Mighty Macho and War Lord; and the female Champions Audrianne's Candy Carnival, Lon-Do Dragon Mite, Crown Special Edition, Claymore Jezebel and Charm, Audrianne's Cinnebar Cinnabel, Kandy Kristibel, Kitty Kristibel, and Might Melody. These make up the foundation on which future Audrianne generations will be bred.

Am. and Can. Ch. St. Aubrey Goofus Brescia winning Best of Breed at Philadelphia in 1967, at his American show debut under Mrs. Ramona Van Court. Handled by Nigel Aubrey Jones for the partnership of Aubrey Jones and Taylor. Brescia became a famous winner in the U.S. and was later sold to Mrs. Nathan Allen and Mrs. Mildred Imrie.

BRIARCOURT

Briarcourt Pekingese are a small, hobby kennel at Yardley, Pennsylvania, owned by Mrs. Joan M. Mylchreest, who purchased her first show bitch, Champion St. Aubrey Phantasy of Elsdon, from the famous kennels of Nigel Aubrey Jones and R. William Taylor in Montreal, Canada.

When bred to her grandsire, American and Canadian Champion St. Aubrey Laparata Dragon, she produced three champions. In her second litter, bred to Champion Briarcourt's Rule Britannia, she produced two more to gain titles, one of these being Champion Briarcourt's Excelsior, now owned by Bob Jacobsen, Sing Lee Pekingese, who has won ten Bests in Show at this time. It is unfortunate, considering the quality of her offspring, that Phantasy was only able to have these two litters.

Champion Rule Britannia has proven to be an excellent sire for Briarcourt. He is from an Australian bitch, Camsue Kaylee, and by Champion St. Aubrey Sunburst of Elsdon, a double great-grandson of Laparata Dragon. Britannia, in addition to having sired Champion Briarcourt's Excelsior, is also the sire of the sensational Champion Briarcourt's Coral Gable, owned by David

33

Fitzpatrick, who is a multiple Best in Specialty Show winner and a Group winner at just 18 months of age. Coral Gable's dam is Mrs. Mylchreest's beautiful Champion Mahjong Mavina Gable.

This was another outstanding litter for Briarcourt, as a result of a linebreeding to Australian Champion Gilgai Stormy Boi, a well-known producer for the Mahjong Kennel.

Mrs. Mylchreest attributes a great deal of her kennel's success to this Mahjong Kennel, owned by Brian Wilson of Melbourne, through the bitches she has imported from there which have "nicked" very well with her sires. The goal at Briarcourt is continuation of this linebreeding program in order to keep the type that has so far proven tremendously successful.

BURKE'S PEKINGESE

Burke's Pekingese are owned by Mary L. Burke and are at Vancouver, Washington.

Among her homebreds is the dearly loved and very successful Champion Burke's Boi Boi Star of China, born July 1978, sire of many champions and still being used. Among his progeny, from Max' Precious Luv, is Champion Namon Lawrence Rohme, a handsome dog who seems to be quite a favorite with the judges.

Champion Burke's Rosy Star of Palacer gained title with five majors. He is by Palacer Wang Li ex Koitown L'Dragon Twinkles, bred by Justine Smith, owned and handled by Mary L. Burke. Promising youngsters at Mary Burke's kennels include Burke's Deli D'Lite China Star, by Champion Koitown Wee Tonni Tiger ex Champion Han-bee's D-Lite of Shangshu, a homebred; and Burke's Jo-Lee of Peri Peke, by Champion Burke's Boi Boi Star of China, bred by Pat and Ed Sourman.

CARDEE

Cardee Pekingese are owned by Carol Dee Blakesley at Yakima, Washington. American and Canadian Champion Bar-Mee's Imperial Lu Chou, C.D., born November 1978, was purchased from Gregory M. Robinson for Mrs. Blakesley's daughter as her 4-H project. Bethel Blakesley trained Chou for show as well as for his obedience degree.

Bethel and Lu Chou entered the AKC obedience ring, and in five trials Lu Chou had earned the C.D. title. His highest score from a possible 200 points was 196—very nice going.

Ch. Briarcourt's Royal Cathay, by Ch. St. Aubrey Laparata Dragon ex Ch. St. Aubrey Phantasy of Elsdon, taking points in 1983 *en route* to his title. Bred, owned and handled by Mrs. Joan Mylchreest, Yardley, Pennsylvania.

At age two years, Chou was entered in conformation at the Rose City Pekingese Specialty, handled by his breeder Gregory Robinson. He went Best of Winners that day for a five-point major. Needless to say that following so good a start, it did not take Lu Chou long to finish, and he even has a Group first from the Open Class while on the way to championship, which was won the day his title was complete. Lu Chou is now retired, siring puppies of handsome quality.

Champion Cardee's Lil Teddy Hsiung was born May 1980. He finished in five shows, winning Groups and an all-breed Best in Show, the latter at Mount Bachelor K.C., June 1982, judged by Mrs. Elaine Young. He is a descendant of the great Champion Ku Chin Tom-mi of Seng Kye.

Teddy's show career was cut short due to illness. He is now retired and siring outstanding puppies.

Ch. Tea Pot's O'So Tickee Tu, bred by Steven and Karen Vaughn, owned by Gregory Robinson and Carol Dee Blakesley, Yakima, Washington. Carol Dee Blakesley handling.

Champion Cardee's Samson of Kalila, born June 1983, is one of the new hopefuls who finished his championship prior to reaching his second birthday. As a special, he now has several group placements to his credit. Samson is descended from Champion Linborne Lombardo.

The newest champion at Carlee is Champion Tea Pot's O'So Tickee Tu, born June 1984. He is a descendant of Champion Trademark of Mike Mar.

A favorite bitch at Cardee is Cardee's Silly Sally of Lu Chou, born November 1982. She is the daughter of Champion Lu Chou, C.D., and she has proven herself as a mother with some exciting puppies. She is about to set out on the road towards titular honors.

Finally there is Cardee's Bid A Bunch of Bar-Mee, daughter of Champion Cardee's Lil Teddy Hsiung, also a proven matron with quality puppies, whom it is expected will finish soon.

36

CARLOTTA'S PEKINGESE

Carlotta's Pekingese are in Biloxi, Mississippi, where their owner, Carlotta Curtis, following the death of her husband a few years back, decided to play an active part in the breeding and showing of both Pekes and Shih Tzus, the two breeds which had been liked and admired by both Curtises.

It was in 1982 that Mrs. Curtis decided that within two years she would own both a male and a female Pekingese champion and a male and a female Shih Tzu champion. As she says, "a complete novice in such matters, I figured that I could make four champions by snapping my fingers—but quickly learned that there is a bit more to it." After realizing that she had lots to learn, Mrs. Curtis decided to drop her Shih Tzu ambitions and concentrate on the Pekes, which she has dearly loved since she was only ten years old. It was in 1942 that her husband purchased her first Pekingese as a gift immediately following their marriage.

Over the years, during their Air Force travels, the Curtises had various pet Pekes, but it was not until years later that Mrs. Curtis, looking for a hobby set out to assemble a small kennel. Her first purchases were several dogs from Dud-Lee's Kennels. From one of these came her first homebred champion. Then in 1985 she purchased the lovely bitch, Fourwinds Lyndon's Lyntosia, who has already had a highly successful sweep of the match shows in preparation for her point show career.

Mrs. Curtis owns an old-fashioned six-bedroom house, where a large downstairs bedroom has been made into a kennel. Thus the Pekes truly are home-raised.

Based on her original Dud-Lee stock, plus several "Fourwinds" which combine the Toydom lines, Mrs. Curtis is off to a good start and we wish her success.

CARRHAVEN

Carrhaven Pekingese are owned by Houston and Peggy Dillard Carr and located in Franklin, Tennessee. This kennel is one of long duration and great success, the Carrs having lately finished their 100th champion, in, to quote Mrs. Carr, a 34-year period.

Pride of place at Carrhaven must go to American and Canadian Champion St. Aubrey Yorklee Fanfare Royale, who was bred in the United Kingdom by Mrs. W. Chapman.

Fanfare is a son of Yorklee Mistique Moonbeam ex Yorklee

Bright Star. This little dog retired the Jack R. Watts Challenge Cup at the Delta Pekingese Club at New Orleans, on which a kennel mate, American and Canadian Champion St. Aubrey Ken Wong Moon Shadow had helped, previously taking two legs on this cup.

Fanfare has been shown 67 times in the United States and Canada, winning Best of Breed on 62 occasions. He has been Best in Specialty Show on 22 occasions, and has scored 32 Group Firsts. He has also taken the Best in Show award at all-breed events on an impressive 17 occasions. During 1979, he was No. 9 Toy Dog in Canada and No. 2 Pekingese in the United States. As a stud dog, Fanfare has sired 15 champions.

American and Canadian Champion St. Aubrey Ken Wong Moon Shadow, in addition to his two legs on the Watts Challenge Cup, has brought home a total of more than 20 Best in Specialty Show awards, with a total of about this same number of Toy Groups in the United States and Canada. A nine-pound dog, he is the sire of three champions, and he is a son of Champion Etive Copplestone Pu-Zin Juilees.

Champion Carr's Moon Shadow Carbon, by Champion St. Aubrey Kenway Moon Shadow ex Knolland's Dream Whip, is the Carrs' 100th Peke to gain title.

CEE-KAE

Cee-Kae Pekes are owned by Chuck and Kim Langley of Galt, California, who have been into showing the breed since about 1978. Their foundation bitch, Manticore Fuffiglia, was purchased from Fran and Ray Alcock and Ken Winters that year, coming to her new owners bred to Champion Manticore Don Fano. The ensuing litter consisted of three bitch puppies, two of whom became Champion Cee-Kae's Don's Fuh Fuh and Champion Cee-Kae's Ying Hee. The third from the litter was lost tragically prior to embarking on a show career.

The Manticore line is primarily Jamestown, the main stud being International Champion Fu Yong of Jamestown. Champion Fuh Fuh was bred to Champion Cherangani Kitakin of Ralshams, giving the Langleys their first home-bred champion, Cee-Kee's Silver Rocket, who in turn sired for them Champion Cee-Kae's Suzie Me Lei.

Suzie was Best in Show at the Pekingese Club of Central Cali-

Manticore Fuffiglia, by Mandra Gora Fuffigno ex Manticore Magic Fire, bred by Mr. and Mrs. R. Alcock and Ken Winters in Canada; owned by Kim Langley for whom she is the foundation bitch at Cee Kae's Pekingese, Galt, California.

fornia Specialty in the winter of 1985. In 1986, the same honor was gained by the Langleys' Champion Ai Gee Bentley of Cee-Kae.

The Langleys have been successful in breeding their bitches to the Cherangani and Ai Kou lines. Suzie's grandsire is Champion Cherangani Bombardier, owned by Jean M. Thomas of Ai Kou fame.

Cee-Kae is small kennel since both owners are employed. They usually have about nine to twelve dogs. Four of these are champions and one is on its way.

CHAMBRAE

Chambrae Pekingese at Racine, Wisconsin, are the very successful hobby of Christine L. Hann, who has dearly loved the Pekingese breed all her life. As a very young girl, she was in the habit of stopping to play with a parti-color Peke she passed daily on her way home from school. Like most kids, she wanted a dog, but was told she couldn't have one until she had a place of her own.

Ch. Chambrae Jack Daniels, a young "star" of 1985. Bred, owned and handled by Christine L. Hann, taking Reserve Winners as a youngster at the Alabama Specialty.

In February 1966, Christine married, and four months later bought her first Pekingese, a parti-color bitch. Her breeders told Christine of a magazine named *Dog World*, to which she promptly subscribed, and quickly found herself becoming interested in "the world of purebred dogs."

Christine Hann's first Peke was Ta-Yo of Tao-Peke-No (3/28/66–12/77), from the Caversham-Coronation lines. She was bred back to her grandsire, Champion Coronation T'Sun Shee, producing one bitch puppy. Although these two were never more than loving pets, it was they who started the Chambrae Kennel.

Being increasingly anxious to have a show dog, but still not knowing exactly what to look for in one, Christine visited the Kentucky Colonel Kennels, purchasing what she thought was a show dog out of Champion Cho Sen's Robin of Pierrot. It was upon entering her first show that she discovered the dog had only one testicle, which is, of course, a disqualification. Mrs. O'Daniel was hastily contacted, had another dog, guaranteed to be show quality, which Christine purchased and then she was on her way.

This dog became Champion Kentucky Colonel Aristocrat, by American, Canadian, Mexican, Bermudian Champion Mandarin's Kentucky Colonel ex Kentucky Colonel's Ameroid. Affectionately known as "Colonel," he and his new owner learned a lot together, especially Christine in learning how to groom and show. In 1973, Colonel finished his championship. Specialed in only a short period of time, he was No. 10 Pekingese, Kennel Review System, in 1973, winning 14 Bests of Breed and eight Group placements, including a first. His owner's proudest moment, however, was when, at the age of ten years, he won Best in Show at the North Central Illinois Specialty from the Veteran's Class!

In the latter part of 1968, Mrs. Hann imported a lovely blonde bitch. This was Changkim Moon Princess, by English Champion Cheryl's Atom of Chintoi ex Changkim Ping-E-Poo. In 1973, this became Christine Hann's second champion. "Sally," as she was known, produced two champions and the four-and-a-half pound sleeve, Loner's Tiny Tuff Stuff.

Champion Apricot Delight of Chambrae, by Champion Changkim Dominic ex Champion Changkim Moon Princess, was specialed six times, winning the breed twice, a Group third, one of Opposite Sex, and one Specialty Best of Opposite Sex. She was the dam of a champion.

In 1970, Changkim Moon Dust was imported from Australia. Samantha, by Australian Champion Shalwyn Gerhard ex Changkim Moon Imp, (daughter of Champion Copplestone Pu Zee), was pointed but never finished her title. She did, however, produce a champion.

Champion Aristocrat's Sherry Flip, born in 1970, was a particolor out of Champion Kentucky Colonel Aristocrat ex Champion Changkim Moon Princess. She was pointed and sold to Dorothy Holman in Pennsylvania, who finished her and later re-sold her to Mrs. Hann and Francis Councill. Sherry was bred to Champion Muhlin Black Magic, producing Champion Loveland Lic'Rice of Chambrae, a black. Lic'Rice was sold to Jackie Wipperling in California, for whom he became a champion.

Champion Black Tia of Chambrae was the start of the Chambrae black line which has won such high acclaim and many prestigious honors. Born December 1974, she was by Champion Muhlin Black Magic ex Changkim Moon Dust. Tia completed her title in

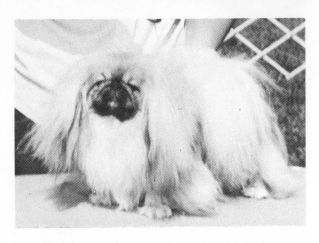

Ch. Apricot Delight of Chambrae, another of the owner-handled homebreds from Chambrae Pekingese.

1975, having gained many honors along the way. As a special she won ten Bests of Breed, 16 Bests of Opposite Sex and five Group placements. She probably holds the record for Best of Opposite Sex honors at Specialty events, having many of them, including the Pekingese Club of America March Specialty under Mrs. Geraldine Hess. Probably the most thrilling moment of her career was under breeder/judge R. William Taylor, who awarded her Best in Specialty Show at the Pekingese Club of Southern New Jersey Specialty in 1981, she was bred only twice, producing just one puppy daughter each time, both of which became champions.

Champion Tiffany of Chambrae, by Champion Kentucky Colonel Aristocrat ex Champion Apricot Delight of Chambrae, became a champion in July 1976. She was bred once, from which there were no surviving puppies. Sadly, this lovely bitch died at age six years from an unknown virus.

Champion September Morn of Chambrae (Aristocrat–Tia) finished during 1977, going Best of Winners five times and Best of Opposite Sex over a bitch special. She was bred to Champion Black Cavalier of Chambrae, producing Black Satin of Chambrae, who has been shown but prefers being Mrs. Hann's house pet.

Champion Black Chiffon of Chambrae, born in 1977 (Colonel–Tia), went through to title without delay. At her second show, the Derbytown Pekingese Club Specialty, she was Best in Sweepstakes, Winners Bitch,and Best of Opposite Sex over three bitch specials from the six-nine month puppy class for a five-point major under English judge Mrs. G.A.G. Williams. Out just once in specials, she took Best of Breed and third in the Toy Group. A litter of five puppies from her included two which gained their titles.

It was in July 1977 that Champion Muhlin Boogaloo was born, bred by Patty Mullendore (by Champion Muhlin Mai O Mai ex E'Jean's Hichie Echo Chik of He'Lo). Mrs. Mullendore sent "Boog" to Mrs. Hann to be shown, and in April 1978 these two ladies became co-owners of him. He completed championship in June 1979, his majors including two gained at Specialties. Out only a few times as a special, he had eight Bests of Breed and two Group placements. He was the sire of many champions, and his death in 1984 was a loss to the breed.

Boogaloo sired, from Champions Black Chiffon of Chambrae, a stunning dog in Champion Black Cavalier of Chambrae. On his second ring apperance he won a three-point major and at his third show, the Derbytown Specialty, followed in his dam's paw-prints by winning a five-point major there as she had done. But the really big day in his show career was the one on which he won a Best in Show at an all-breed event in 1982. It is felt that Cavalier holds the record as the most winning black in Pekingese history. His career as a special included 92 Bests of Breed, 67 Group placements of which 19 were firsts, four Specialty Bests in Show, and an all-breed Best in Show. He is the sire of two champions plus a number of others who are major pointed.

Cavalier's litter sister, Champion Black Velvet of Chambrae, gained her title in May 1981. She was a Best of Breed and Best of Opposite Sex winner over specials.

Champion Jamaican Rum of Chambrae, January 1979, was by Knolland Mandingo (son of Champion Batling Spats of Freeland), ex Amaretto of Chambrae, a full sister to Tai, co-owned with Patricia Mullendore. "J.R." gained his title in June 1981. Specialed a few times, he won nine Bests of Breed and five Group Placements.

The newest Chambrae title-holder is Chambrae Jack Daniels, by Meh-Ling's Aristocrat's Image ex Chambrae Black Lace (a Black Cavalier daughter). "J.D." won two Best in Sweepstakes and finished with three majors and a Best of Breed over specials. It is hoped that when he matures he will become the next Chambrae star.

After nearly 20 years in Pekingese, Mrs. Hann still prefers that hers remain a small, select kennel of owner-handled Pekingese. Though there have been very few litters bred at Chambrae, there have been 14 champions finished, 11 of them homebred.

CHAR-MIN

Char-Min Pekingese were started in 1968 by Minnie Wisdom of Poplar Bluff, Missouri, with the birth of a litter of five puppies belonging to her sister, Anna L. Brown. As a token of appreciation to Minnie for the hours she put into seeing the puppies safely into the world, Minnie was given one of them, which she named Jo Dee.

The puppy thoroughly convinced Mrs. Wisdom that it would be fun to raise and show Pekingese; thus she started thinking of a suitable "wife" for him, and of a kennel name! The latter problem was solved by her husband, Charles, who said, quite sensibly, that a combination of their two names (*Char*les and *Min*nie) would be very suitable. She promptly agreed to the designation Char-Min.

The bitch puppy was chosen, purchased from McJ.J. Kennels and was named Tonya Star of Char-Min. This bitch was bred to Ruby Dudley's noted Champion Dud-Lee's Little Joe, by whom she presented the Wisdoms with Little Joe's Natike of Char-Min. Other foundation stock included two sons of Champion Ku Chi Tom Mi of Seng Kye.

Minnie Wisdom's first top stud dog was Bel-Mar Talisman, sire of four champions, three from the nice bitch Char-Min Yu Lan of Dud-Lee's.

Others which she added to her kennel were Champion Connie's Ku Tong of Dud-Lee's, Champion Dud-Lee's Lil Timothy's Kris, and Champion Dud-Lee's Tomette's Master King, all of whom have produced champions for her. But Master King did especially well, having sired ten champions for Minnie. Among them was Char-Min's Master King's Khi-Lyn, who produced Best in Show winning Top Pekingese of 1983 and 1984, Champion Char-Min's Jason of Toimanor. He was sold as a young puppy to Audrey Drake and Janet Oxford, and was campaigned with such spectacular success by the late Max Kerfoot. Another Master King son, Champion Char-Min's Master King's Flint, is the grand-sire of the lovely bitch, Champion Elpha Sun Arrhythmia, the Top Pekingese bitch in 1983 and 1984.

Minnie Wisdom is also the breeder of Char-Min's Miss Amy-Lou, Top Producing Pekingese Bitch of all time, we understand.

Twenty-two Pekingese Champions have been bred at Char-Min plus others who have been purchased elsewhere; included are several Best in Show and multi-Group winners and Specialty Best in

Ch. Dud-Lee's Black Sequins Glo at age six months was Best Puppy at Pekingese Club of Texas Specialty Shows, September 1984; Best of Winners at the Alabama Specialty two months later; and finished title with Best of Winners at the Derbytown Specialty. Pictured winning at Crab Orchard K.C., October 1985.

Show winners. A fairly new addition to the stud force, Champion Windwyck's Tic-Mark of Char-Min, has sired at least six champions for her.

Minnie Wisdom states "I feel that my greatest accomplishment as a Pekingese breeder is Champion Char-Min's Jason of Toimanor." I am sure that a breeder could not take other than tremendous pride in having produced so magnificent and so successful a dog, and we most heartily congratulate her on having done so!

The present young star at Char-Min is a homebred black bitch, named after the "Showetime Video" owned by the Wisdoms' son. She is Char-Min Showetime, and needs just a three-point major to finish.

Also in the limelight is Dud-Lee's Black Sequins Glo, bred by Ruby Dudley, who made some splendid puppy wins, completed title, and now will be the new Char-Min campaigner in specials. Wycross Kioko Andrew should finish soon as should Char-Min's Tom-Mi of Shir-Lees.

45

CHINATOWN

Chinatown Pekingese are owned by Mrs. Walter M. Jeffords Jr., New York City and Andrew's Bridge, Pennsylvania, who has loved and owned the breed over more than 15 years. Her first was a handsome little English dog who was handled for her by Mrs. Edna Voyles. Then came the fateful day when she saw Michael Wolf with his British import Dagbury of Calartha, and the rest has been history.

The dogs owned by Mrs. Jeffords and Mr. Wolf are covered in the Mike-Mar Kennel story. Mrs. Jeffords, since starting her own breeding program, has truly done herself proud with Best in Show winners, multiple Group winners, and an imposing list of champions, all homebred, all handled personally or by Hernan Martinez and Jaime Celis.

Champion Fu Manchu of Chinatown was the first of Mrs. Jeffords' dogs to make a notable show record under the new Chinatown kennel identification. He was sent to California in John Brown's care, and when he returned home to Pennsylvania he had a notable list of successes on the books.

Fu Manchu scored even more notably as a sire than in the show ring, as his champion progeny includes Mrs. Jeffords's most memorable homebred to date, the multi-Best in Show, many times Group winner and Best of Breed winner (including Westminster 1983) Champion Randolph of Chinatown. Randy's career has been an exciting one, as Hernan or Mrs. Jeffords herself have led him to victory in some of the stiffest Toy competition to be found; in addition, his Bests in Show have been at some half dozen quality events.

Another of Mrs. Jeffords' Chinatown homebreds, Champion Ching, is also a Best in Show winner and a sire of outstanding progeny. Ching was sired by champion Mi-Twee Jai Kee of Lon-Du from Fortune Cookie of Chinatown.

The younger generation at Chinatown includes Cholly of Chinatown, Winners Dog and Best of Winners at the Pekingese Club of America Specialty Show in March 1986 under British judge Miss Shipley; Lola of Chinatown, a tremendously promising young bitch, Best of opposite Sex in the Pekingese Club of American Sweepstakes; Tangerine of Chinatown, another gorgeous bitch who took Winners at Westminster; and so very many more. Mrs. Jeffords already has an enviable list of Chinatown champions to

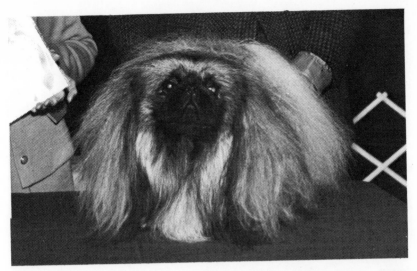

Ch. Shinnecock of Chinatown is one of the 5 Pekingese Best in Show winners bred and owned by the Chinatown Pekingese of Mrs. Walter Jeffords. Pictured winning one of his many Toy Groups on the way to all-breed Best in Show. Shinnecock is a Westminster winner and a Specialty winner as well. Handled by Hernan Martinez.

her credit; and from what we have seen, it is easy to predict many more of the same in the future. For Mrs. Jeffords is a true *breeder* at heart, and it is interesting to note the capable manner in which she decides what she wants in her kennel, and then goes about the process of producing it from her own stock.

CHU LAI

Chu Lai Pekingese are owned and loved by Pat and Charles Farley, located in Norton, Massachusetts, who purchased their first Pekingese in February 1967. Nikki was a tri-colored parti male who was bought from Beverly Green of Greenbriar Kennels. It was Nikki who taught the Farleys the many delights of Pekingese ownership.

In December 1970, the Farleys acquired their first bitch, Chu Lai's Little Sissi Su, who also came from Greenbriar out of Fourwinds and Dah-Lyn bloodlines.

Sissi was bred to Nikki, producing the first Peke puppy to be born at Chu Lai, who was named Chu Lai's Dan Dee Ting. Owing to the kind advice and guidance of Miss Emily Jean Hennessey

(Cedarwood Pekingese), this puppy gained his championship in less than seven weeks, winning five Bests of Breed over specials, and taking Group placements while still in the classes. "Ting" was campaigned as a special in the New England area, and won more than 50 Bests of Breed plus numerous Group placements prior to his retirement, with a Best of Breed in an entry of 30 Pekes under William Bergum, where he had also placed third in a very strong Toy Group. He had just turned eight years old.

When Ting's dam, Sissi, came back into coat, she, too was shown, becoming the Farleys' second champion.

Several months later, Sissi was bred to Michael Wolf's Champion Bracewell Giacomo, which produced two males, one of which was stillborn. The other became Chu Lai Sissi's Sir Oliver. Sadly to report, after whelping her litter by Caesarean section, Sissi died. Oliver was never shown due to an eye injury, but later produced the well-known parti-color bitch, Champion Chu Lai's Painted Lady, who finished in record time.

Chu Lai Pekingese are always owner-handled, and during the summer of 1981 the Farleys finished five champions: Chu Lai's Painted Lady, Chu Lai's Casanova, Chu Lai's Duster, Yang Kee Sammy Chin (co-owned with breeder Marjorie Ruggiero), and the black and tan Black Bandit of Chu Lai (with four majors); the latter by taking Best of Winners at the Pekingese Club of America Specialty in conjunction with Ox Ridge.

Eighteen champions have been finished by the Farleys, with several more pointed and on their way.

During a four-month period, May-August 1983, Pat was hospitalized and had major surgery. Three weeks after her second major surgery she was back in the ring to finish her bitch, Champion Chu Lai Que's Fu-Jin. Her doctors thought that she was crazy, but Pat had put all her points on her along the way, and wanted to be the one to finish her. Maybe the doctors did not understand, but I am sure any of us involved in the dog show world would—completely! Bar-Hers Buddha of Chu Lai, co-owned with Elizabeth Whitford of Pleiku Pekingese and bred by Barbara Herbster, is the sire of several of the young dogs the Farleys now are showing. The newest arrivals at Chu Lai are the two adorable English puppies from Toydom and Sunsalve, who are co-owned with Betty Whitford, and Briarcourt's Cedric and Briarcourt's Sunburst Sonata co-owned with Ruth MacDonald.

Chu Lai Pleiku Masterpiece winning a 3-point major in 1985. Bred and owned by Patricia and Charles Farley and Elizabeth Whitdorf. Handled by Charles Farley.

CLAYMORE

Claymore Pekingese, owned by Mrs. Robert I. Ballinger, of Palm Beach, Florida, started out in 1970 when Mrs. Ballinger purchased her first Pekingese puppy from Karen Franzoso. She named the puppy Tiger Butter (after an orchid, which she also raises) of Claymore, the latter being the name of her home outside of Philadelphia.

Tiger Butter was bred to Champion Keio-Ko Yuan of Pencedar, producing, in 1971, Mrs. Ballinger's first Pekingese litter. Among the puppies was a very nice bitch who became Tiger Mist of Claymore and who, in very limited showing, was Reserve Winners Bitch at the Pekingese Club of Southern New Jersey Specialty.

Also in 1971, Mrs. Ballinger obtained a fine quality male, Pasha of West Winds, from Mrs. Horace Wilson.

Soon after starting Pasha at the shows, Mrs. Ballinger went to Crufts in search of additional basic breeding stock. The two stars of that trip were her Yu Yang of Jamestown son, Dorodea Yu Sam TSun, called Robin, and the beautiful Volksmana Mi Queen, called Ondine. She then continued showing, always handling the dogs herself, and doing some limited breeding—Claymore never has been a large kennel.

Pasha became the first of Mrs. Ballinger's champions, finishing in July 1972. Tiger Mist of Claymore was bred to Louise Snyder's

Ch. Claymore's Cinnamon Bun, owner-handled by Mrs. Robert Ballinger, winning one of his several Bests in Show. On this occasion under Derek G. Rayne.

lovely import, Champion Fairy Prince of Kanghe, producing the first homebred Claymore Champion, Prince's Tiger Eye, who was Reserve Winners Dog at the Pekingese Club of America's March Specialty in 1973 from the puppy classes; he finished his title at Westminster.

Tiger Eye was the sire of Champion Claymore Dulcinea, who was Best of Opposite Sex at Westminster in 1983 and 1984, owned by Miss Deborah Sprouse. Dulcinea was third generation of Claymore breeding, and is the dam of Miss Sprouse's Champion Rosewood's Sea Dragon.

When Pasha was bred to Mrs. Ballinger's double Fu-Yong granddaughter, Mandragora Cloisonne, Mrs. Ballinger bred what she feels up to this time was her best show dog, Claymore's Cinnamon Bun. Born January 1973, Cinnamon Bun was a most correct and handsome dog whom the judges were quick to appreciate. He finished his championship during 1974, as did Robin, Tiger Eye, Ondine, and Claymore Night Owl (by Tiger Eye from Cloisonne).

Cinnamon Bun was going strong that year, rising to No. 2 Pekingese in the United States with over 50 Group placements and three Bests in Show. But then tragedy struck, as this dearly loved and very outstanding little dog developed an intestinal obstruction exactly one week following his third Best in Show, and despite immediate surgery, did not survive.

Despite the onset of a muscle disorder, Mrs. Ballinger continued to show, and she bred an occasional litter. She had finished Cinnamon Bun's son, Champion Claymore Oriental Spice, in September 1976, and finished Sabrina Fair of Claymore (by Pasha from Ondine) in early 1977. Sabrina had been Winners Bitch at the September Specialty of the Pekingese Club of America in 1976. In August 1977, she finished Champion Claymore Lilith (by Tiger Eye from Ondine).

Owing to a worsening of her health, Mrs. Ballinger sold almost all of her Pekingese in early 1979, keeping Pasha and Ondine. Among those sold to show homes were four future Claymore champions: Neptune, Jezebel, Dulcinea, and Audrianne's Claymore Charm. In 1977 Mr. and Mrs. Ballinger moved to Florida.

Happily, by 1983 Mrs. Ballinger had regained her health and returned to the Pekingese ring with Knolland Slowboat to China, whom she finished in November 1983. Slowboat was bred to daughter of Champion St. Aubrey Bees Wing of Elsdon ex Knolland The Queen Bee, and this produced a new show dog for Mrs. Ballinger in September 1985. Claymore Four Leaf Clover has a solid background of quality behind him, his parents being Slowboat and Queen Bee, who both are grandchildren of Champion St. Aubrey Laparata Dragon.

Mrs. Ballinger has now visited England again, looking for a

quality dog and bitch. From the Toydom Kennel she obtained her delightful daughter of English Champion Toydom Modesty Permits, Toydom Accepts With Pleasure. "Plezzie" had 14 points, including a major by ten months' age.

While at Bath, Mrs. Ballinger also saw, and purchased, through Vandy Williams of Toydom Pekingese, the beautiful son of English Champion Toydom Dutch Courage, Dratsum Captain Courageous by Toydom. Captain Courageous started his American career by taking two Bests of Breed.

Having three bloodlines that she likes very much (Laparata, Toydom, and Belknap), it seems very likely that Mrs. Ballinger will have some really lovely homebreds set to go again in the near future. Mrs. Ballinger has finished six homebred champions, finished four others from other breeders, and bred four others which were finished by their new owners.

CLOUD NINE

Cloud Nine Pekingese are owned by Margaret H. Stamey of Winston-Salem, North Carolina, and the author feels quite certain that this name was selected for the kennel as that is what she was on when she finally got her first Pekingese!

As a five-year-old, Margaret had adored Shirley Temple, and as Shirley had several Pekes, of course that was the breed for Margaret, too. The first of her Pekingese, when she was ten years old, was a black and tan male from Tien His breeding. The second, a bitch, was a wedding present, followed by others to insure that the Stamey household always had a Peke.

Margaret Stamey's daughter became involved with Afghan Hounds in 1970, and the two of them had been actively showing that breed until Margaret acquired her first show Pekingese, from Michael Wolf, in 1982.

Champion Mike-Mar's Dutch Master has been a joy to his owner, fun to show and to live with. He has the true Pekingese temperament, considering himself on equal footing with any Great Dane. He completed his championship, taking many Bests of Breed and Group placements, and is a Group First winner, too. "Mr. Bump," as he is known to friends and family, retired soon after Mrs. Stamey's second purchase from Michael Wolf joined the family. This one is Mike Mar's Destiny, who is just starting a show career.

DUD-LEE'S

Dud-Lee's Pekingese began in 1959, when Ruby and Bill Dudley acquired their first Pekingese, "Goldie," for their daughter's 12th birthday. "Goldie" was far from a top show specimen, but she became the household pet who started Ruby and Bill on a long involvement with the breed.

Over the past 26 years, the Dudleys' Creston, Iowa, kennels have housed 85 homebred Pekingese champions, among them several Group winners, at least one all-breed Best in Show winner, and some Specialty Best of Breed winners. The Dudleys have bred, raised and conditioned these dogs themselves; Ruby almost exclusively handles the grooming along with personally handling their dogs to their titles and as specials. Bill's principal job has been the driving (no small item!) and seeing to it that Ruby and her dogs make it to the shows safely and on time, traveling many thousands of miles (as dog show exhibitors do) each year.

Champion Zodiac's Joe was the first champion owned by the Dudleys, finishing in June 1966. He provided foundation for this kennel, and is behind the early champions there. Ruby won her first Toy Group with him at an Iowa show in autumn 1966.

In 1969, Mrs. Dudley purchased the marvelous winner and producer, Best in Show International Champion Ku-Chin Tom-mi of Seng Kye from Irene Ruschaupt. Besides numerous Bests in Shows and Specialty Shows, he had sired several champions at time of purchase. He went on to sire 16 champions, and was a Top Producer in 1971 for five champions within that year.

Champion Tommi Masterpiece Sing Lee, son of the above dog, was acquired by the Dudleys from Mrs. Ruschaupt in 1971. He, too, proved to be an invaluable asset, giving the Dudleys 12 champions, including several Group winners and the famous Best in Show winning Champion Masterpiece Dud-Lee's Zodiac, whom Mrs. Dudley considers to be one of her best homebreds. Zodiac, widely admired by some of our most respected judges, finished quickly for Ruby Dudley, winning eight Toy Groups plus other placements and his first Specialty Best of Breed at the North Central Illinois Pekingese Specialty in 1973. Later that year he won his first all-breed Best in Show.

In July 1973, the Dudleys took Zodiac and their bitch Champion Khi Lyn's Tometta of Dud-Lee's to dog shows in British Columbia, Canada. Zodiac finished in the first three shows winning

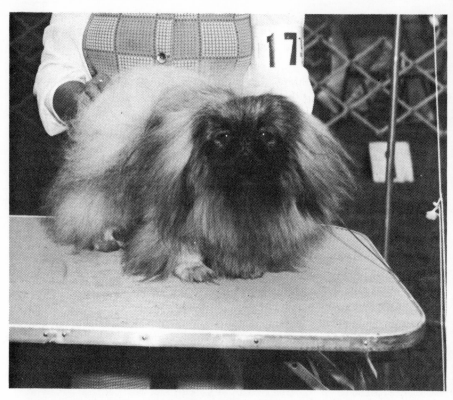

Ch. Dud-Lee's Little Timothy was sire of five champions and a consistent winning and placing Toy Group dog. By Ch. Ku-Chin Timothy of Tom Thumb ex Dud-Lee's Kim Fo Yu of Char-Min.

Toy Group first and third along the way. Champion Tometta also gained title while they were doing these shows, becoming a double champion at 12 months old. She went on to produce four champions herself, among them the Group winning Champion Dud-Lee's Tometta's Fascination.

During February 1974, Mrs. Dudley took Zodiac to Westminster. There Mrs. Jeffords and Michael Wolf saw him, fell in love with him, and persuaded the Dudleys to leave him with them. He won a Best in Show his first time out under their ownership, added several more, plus some Specialty Shows and more than 50 Group firsts.

When Mrs. Dudley returned home to Iowa, she and Bill Dudley found themselves missing Zodiac enormously. But she soon picked out another homebred, Champion Ku Chin-Tom-mi Tu of Dud-Lee's, sired by the Best in Show International Champion Ku-Chin Tom-mi of Seng Kye. He became a Toy Group winner and sired several handsome champions for the Dudleys.

Then, by chance, Mrs. Dudley was able to get back a little male she had sold as a puppy. This was Champion Dud-lee's Little Timothy. Although he did not care to be shown, Mrs. Dudley persuaded him that dog shows are not all that bad, and in nine weeks she had won on all but a single occasion and had made some nice Group placings along the way, taking Group first at the ninth show. He did some more good winning after that; he also sired five champions.

Next came the little red dog whom Ruby Dudley describes as her "most favorite of all," Champion Dud-Lee's Ku-Lyn's Masterpiece, sired by her Champion Tom-mi Masterpiece, thus carrying on a line of memorable show dogs and producers. He was a champion by 11 months, placing in the Toy Groups from the classes on several occasions. He was campaigned by Ruby Dudley in 1975, 1976, and 1977. He became No. 1 breeder-owner-handled Pekingese in the Top Ten Pekingese for 1976 and 1977. His dam was Top Producing Bitch in 1975 with three champions that year, Kennel Review System, and was awarded the Phillips System Silver Certificate for Top Producer Bitches with six champions in 1975.

Masterpiece has sired 12 champions for the Dudleys and is still hale and hearty at age 12 years. His No. 1 Producing son is Champion Dud-Lee's Ku-Lyn's Fabulous One, with nine champions already finished and more pointed and on the way.

Ruby Dudley's next great winner was a son of Ku-Lyn's Masterpiece, American and Canadian Champion Dudley's Ku-Lin Masterpiece, whose dam was another of the best producers, Dud-Lee's Marla Lil' Tims Star, a daughter of Champion Dud-Lee's Little Timothy. Ku-Lin was a Christmas gift, having been born on Christmas 1976. He, too, made his presence felt in the Toy Groups while still in the classes, then became a Canadian champion quickly, and No. 1 Peke in the United States, Pekingese News System, in 1979. He amassed close to 50 Group placements, including eight Group firsts. In 1979 and 1980 he was No. 1 Pekingese, breeder-owner-handled, and he placed high in the Top Ten both years. He is the sire of champions.

Ruby Dudley has bred on the average of five champions each year since she started showing in 1968, and for several years was the Breeder With Most Points for Pekingese.

On Valentine's Day 1983, the Dudleys drove to the Jacksons' Fourwinds Kennels, where they purchased Champion Fourwinds Cassius. He was a proven producer of quality for the Jacksons, and has already given the Dudleys six champion offspring, including the current lovely bitch, Champion Dud-Lee's Cassius Sheeza Dream. Recently, another visit was made to Fourwinds for a male to use with Cassius daughters. For this they selected a young puppy sired by the English-bred Champion Pendenrah Lysander of Sunsalve.

They have also acquired a young son of Champion Char-Min Jason of Toimanor, who is named Toimanor Jason of Dud-Lee's. Nine Dud-Lee bred champions finished their titles in 1985.

ELPHA SUN

Elpha Sun Pekingese are the joint project of Duane Doll and Joe McGinnis, who, in April 1979, over brunch at the Muehlenbach Hotel in Kansas City, discussed their mutual dissatisfaction (boredom) with their careers, and decided to get down to seriously breeding Pekingese. Within two months the property called Snow-Capa in Lakeland, Florida, was purchased, Duane's original Pekingese bloodlines re-purchased, and Elpha Sun was born.

Although Duane Doll had been showing Pekingese for 12 years, he had no real breeding program as such until his move to Florida in 1979. In partnership with Joe McGinnis, they founded their Elpha Sun strain in memory of Duane's mother, Elpha Clark Doll.

Based upon the heavily Caversham laden Bel-Mar line of Mary Davis, Elpha Sun Pekes were awarded 126 AKC championship points, all from the puppy class in its third year; all were on breeder-owner-handled homebreds. This was the first time that any Pekingese breeder in the United States had won over 100 points in any single calendar year.

Among the Pekingese stars at Elpha Sun are its fabulous producers, such as Char-Min's Miss Amy Lou, Top Producing Bitch in the history of the breed at this time, with nine champions and five more on the way to their titles being major pointed. This incomparable bitch produced these champions by three different stud dogs: Champion Char-min's Master Flint, American and Ca-

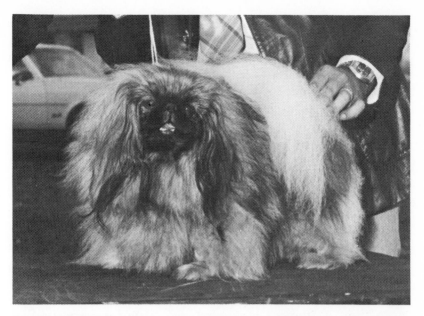

Ch. Koty-Ke of Sutton Place, 1981 Top Producing Stud. As of May 1986, his progeny included 10 champions; two Group winners; and the No. 1 bitch, 1983 and 1984, Ch. Elpha Sun Arrhythmia. Owned by Dolland McGinnis. Here placing in a strong Variety Group.

nadian Champion St. Aubrey Laparata Dragon, and Champion Koty-Ke of Sutton Place. Additionally, Amy Lou is grandmother of four champions and is great-grandmother of one who finished on the same weekend as did her ninth champion.

Then there is Top Stud dog, Champion Koty-Ke of Sutton Place, whose tenth champion has recently finished, Champion Kiss Mee Yoo Fool of Elpha Sun. The latter, incidentally, has herself produced four champions in Elpha Sun Arrhythmia, Elpha Sun The Advocate, Elpha Sun Arriviste, and Elpha Sun Kissandra.

The exquisite Champion Elpha Sun Arrhythmia, No. 1 Pekingese Bitch in the Nation for 1983 and 1984, was bred and is owned, shown, and *very* much loved by Duane and Joe. At age three years, she has 40 Group placements, ten Group firsts, and a Specialty Best in Show. Temporarily retired for breeding, she proceeded to free-whelp three lovely puppies.

Champion Kiss the King of Elpha Sun, one of the Koty-Ke ex Miss Amy Lou champions, was a Group winner the first time specialed. There are numerous others with outstanding achievements as well, not to mention the assorted "young hopefuls" who are awaiting their opportunity to continue carrying the Elpha Sun banner high.

Duane and Joe are contributing a great deal to Pekingese through the quality of their dogs and the success of their breeding program. They are, however, contributing in another way, as well, and in a fabulous manner, with the highly successful Pekingese magazine known as *The Orient Express*. Once again over brunch (this time at Disney World), the two decided that there must be such a publication. Being men of action, not of surplus words, the announcement went out within ten days and *The Orient Express* was on its way.

Over the first few months the boys, being perfectionists, felt that the magazine quality was very poor and they decided that something must be done to upgrade it in a manner worthy of our Pekingese. Within two months a wing was added to the house, typesetting equipment was purchased, and Joe went back to school to learn how to make magazines. To this day, Duane handles all the bookwork and Joe does all editing, typesetting and layout for the magazine.

The Orient Express continues to live up to its original premise: a vehicle for the preservation, protection and advancement of the breed. It is succeeding! So are Duane and Joe succeeding as publishers, for what had once been a single publication now includes some half-dozen breed specialty magazines, plus an all-Toy publication. Who knows what may follow next at their Lakeland, Florida, address!

PEKINGESE OF ELEGANCE

Pekingese of Elegance are owned by Leon and Donna Wolfgang, who are situated at Brookville, Pennsylvania. Donna has been seriously breeding and showing Pekingese since the mid-1970's and "loving every moment of it," to quote her words. There have been lots of ups and downs, she adds, but the finishing of a dog such as her puppy, now Champion Picasso's Bosco of Elegance, in a whirlwind of success from the puppy classes with several Bests of Breed over champions, then on to a Group first plus several Group placement, surely tips the scale heavily in favor of the ups. Bosco created a sensation from the moment he first set

Ch. Lee Wang's Rascal of Elegance, by Ch. The Earl of Elegance from a Ch. Wild Venture of Lotusgrange daughter, was the first homebred champion for Leon and Donna Wolfgang. Elaine Rigden handling in 1981 for the breeder/owners.

paw in a show ring. The completion of his title came both quickly and in a spectacular manner!

Donna Wolfgang, in discussing her experiences with Pekes, tells us that her real experiences with the world of purebred dogs began when she took a pet bitch to Ruthe Painter to be bred—and Mrs. Painter flatly refused to breed her due to her poor quality. Sensibly, Donna took this criticism well, especially after Mrs. Painter began pointing out to her what a real Pekingese should look like. Mrs. Painter followed through her criticism with the constructive gesture of offering Donna the opportunity to own an exquisite little dog, Champion The Earl of Elegance Panore, known to his friends as "Stuffy." Thus began a whole new life for Donna and her very understanding husband, Leon, as Donna became increasingly enthusiastic over the Pekes. Later, Donna purchased a half sister and also a daughter of Champion Wild Venture of Lotusgrange from Mrs. Painter. And so she was on her way!

During February 1985, Donna Wolfgang made her first trip to England and to Crufts. There she purchased her first English Peke from May Robertshaw: Lotusgrange Apollo, who was sired by Lotusgrange Alexander. It is expected that his potential as a sire will be fulfilled and that he will fare well in the show ring.

FOURWINDS

Fourwinds Pekingese are owned by Mary Ann and Bob Jackson at Seneca, Illinois, who originally established their kennel on bloodlines from Orchard Hill, Dah Lyn, and Langridge. From the earliest days, the Jacksons and their Pekes have met with considerable success. Their first champions were Champion Malita of the Shades, in 1954, and their first homebred to finish (also gaining title that same year), Champion Ju Jai Me Tu of Fourwinds.

It was in 1974, after some 20 years' success in the breed, that the Jacksons made their first trip to England, which was tremendously enjoyed. They found the huge number of entries in the breed impressive, as was the quality at the British shows. A highlight of this trip was their visit to Mrs. Jean Eisenman, owner of the Jamestowns. Although she was keeping only a few dogs at the time, the beauty of the Jamestowns well lived up to their expectations; thus they were thrilled when they succeeded in persuading Mrs. Eisenman to allow them to purchase one of her favorites among the younger dogs, which returned with them to America.

This was Jamestown Jean's Dream, who became a champion for the Jacksons in short order. He was a double grandson of English Champion Yu Tang of Jamestown.

During this same trip, Mary Ann and Bob also selected a promising black puppy, Singlewell Howz Dat, from his breeder, Mrs. Pam Redmond. This youngster, the first *black* champion to be finished by Fourwinds, gained his title with aplomb. His daughters have proven to be excellent producers, thus he is behind several of the current champions.

Returning to England in 1977, the Jacksons met Vandy Williams and Adele Summers, who had re-established the Toydom Kennel. There they selected two puppy bitches who were the first of the modern Toydoms to come to America, Toydom Gay Flirt and Toydom Tempting Touch. They were daughters of Sungarth Kanga of Toydom, who was destined to become one of England's truly important sires. Flirt became a champion soon after her ar-

60

Ch. Kalaframa Jays Joseph at Toydom, Best of Breed and Group 3rd; and Fourwinds Trumps Up, Best of Winners to finish. Owner-handled by Mr. and Mrs. Robert M. Jackson, Fourwinds Pekingese

rival here; and Touch won several points. But most of all, both have produced Fourwinds champions.

During the 1977 visit, there was a puppy dog by Kanga who really appealed to the Jacksons. He was not for sale, but Mary Ann and Bob were unable to forget him, and after a successful puppy show career in England, he finally became theirs. Toydom the Dramatist, as he was named, was a small, breed specialist type Peke, and he won his title in top competition, including a five-point major at Chicago International, after which he captured two Specialty Bests in Show.

Along with The Dramatist, the Jacksons also brought back on this occasion Chintoi Choir Boi, who utterly charmed them. He was a white Pekingese, never especially interesting to the Jacksons in the past, but *his* striking beauty was more than they could resist and they had to have him. He became one of the very few white Pekingese champions, and is the sire and grandsire of champions.

Another visit was to Ethel B. Partridge and the Pekehuis Pekingese. This dear lady was in her 80s at the time, the breeder-owner of the famed Champion Petula, record-holder for the number of Challenge Certificates won by a bitch. From there they brought home the seven-week-old puppy dog who grew up in America and became Champion Pekehuis Sundaea, who was to take a four-point major and on to Best of Breed over four Group winners at Chicago International. His intelligence and personality have made him one of the Jacksons' most favorite dogs; he is the sire and grandsire of several champions.

During the above period, some good homebreds were also winning titles for the Jacksons, and, as their stud dogs are always available to other breeders, others were also finishing numerous champions by representatives of their kennel.

After several more trips to England, there have been other importations who have worked out well. Champion Mahjon Cassidy T'sun, bred by Pat Drew, was a son of the top winner at the time, Champion Shiarita Cassidy. This youngster had a wonderful puppy career with Specialty and Group wins and is now the sire of eleven champions, plus a dozen or so more with points.

Becoming impressed with the good winning being done in England by puppies sired by Champion Jay Trump of Sunsalve, the Jacksons imported the first by him to come to America, Colhamdorn C'Est Ci Bon of Toydom. He finished in top competition and is the sire of champions, including Champion Fourwinds Lady Farrah, who scored a huge success by going Best in Specialty Show at the Pekingese Club of America from the puppy bitch class over 15 champions for her owner, Wendy Bramson. Farrah's two puppies from her first litter are following in their mother's paw prints by already having completed titles.

A son of Jay Trump, Champion Kalafrana Jays Joseph at Toydom, was the next Fourwinds's importation. He was a champion at nine months, and later a Group and Specialty Best in Show winner. To date he has sired several champions.

Another Jay Trump son doing well for the Jacksons is Champion Pendenrah Lysander of Sunsalve, whom they were able to bring back with them at seven months in 1983, and at seven months he won two Bests of Breed and a Group first on his first weekend out. He is the sire of six champions.

Now, after 35 years in Pekingese, the Jacksons view with pride their record of more than 100 champions owned or sold by their kennel. In addition, many other lovely champions have been sired by their stud dogs.

FRASER-MANOR

Fraser-Manor Pekingese, in Seattle, Washington, are owned by Robin and Bobbie Fraser, the latter a long-time fancier who has loved, bred, and shown Pekes in England, New Zealand, and America since 1940.

When she was a young girl in England, Bobbie's father gave her a Peke for her birthday, and that was the start of a lifelong affection for these wonderful little dogs. Mrs. Fraser has shown her Pekes at Crufts, and remarks that her husband shares her interest and enthusiasm for exhibiting with her here in the United States.

The Frasers arrived in Seattle in the 1970s, starting their kennel with High-Wind's Fu-Jin, purchased from Bernice Sugden in Canada. Fu-Jin's sire was Margold's Rascal, a son of Champion Fu-Yong of Jamestown; his dam was High-Wind's Jennifer Kai-Lee, also from Jamestown breeding. Fu-Jin went on to sire the exciting American and Canadian Champion Bar-Mee's Tea-Cup, an all-breed Best in Show winner, a Specialty Best in Show winner, and the winner of many Groups and Group placements in the United States and Canada. Tea-Cup was hand-raised by Mrs. Fraser, his dam having been killed by a car shortly after his birth.

Late in 1984, the Frasers imported a lovely bitch, Josto Candy Floss, form the well-known English breeder, Mrs. Joan L. Stoker, MBE, of Chard, Somerset. The Josto Kennel is well respected, and Candy is the second bitch the Frasers have acquired from there. Candy started her show career in 1986, winning a total of three majors for 12 points in four shows. On the Evergreen State Specialty weekend, she was Winners Bitch and Best of Opposite Sex at the Specialty itself, and Best of Winners and Best of Opposite Sex the following day at Bremerton.

The Frasers' other Josto bitch was Champion Josto Red Poppy, whom they owned and took through to her title. The Josto dogs are all descended from Jamestown.

A beautifully marked black and white parti-color dog, Fraser-Manor's Tyi-Yen, was the Frasers' first American champion. Sired by Wakham's Fei-Ching, son of the noted Australian and American Champion Linbourne Lombardo, owned and shown by Randy Gemmell of Seattle, Washington. Lombardo's early death from heat exhaustion was a sad loss for both the owner and the breed.

Tyi-Yen achieved his title within a year of his birth. As a puppy, he went Best Puppy in Show and Reserve Winners Dog under

Ch. Fraser-Manor Sam-Yen going Best of winners at Greater Clark County K.C. Owned by Bobbie Fraser, Fraser-Manor Pekingese. Handled by Greg Robinson.

Mrs. Marge Bartley, another respected breeder-judge. Tyi-Yen was sold to Jennifer Sims of Johannesburg, South Africa, who bought him following Mrs. Bartley's comments on his quality when she had judged him at the Canadian Pekingese Club Show. Tyi-Yen has continued to win in South Africa.

In 1981, a lovely six week old puppy bitch, Saimaifun's Pip's Mighty Presh's, was purchased by the Frasers from Canadian breeders Mr. and Mrs. Doug Kleinsorge of Vancouver, British Columbia. Presh's was bred to Wakham's Fei-Chang and has produced several champions, including Fraser-Manor's Tyi-Tyi and Fraser-Manor's Sam-Yen. One of Sam-Yen's puppies is already a champion, owned and shown by Greg Robinson in Yakima. Presh's's bloodlines are Jamestown. She has 13 points and would undoubtedly have finished had not illness necessitated her being spayed. Presh's remains one of the household pets, and is still a lovely Peke with magnificent expression.

Han-Bee's Jackpot Starfire was purchased by the Frasers in 1982, sired by Champion Han-Bee's Jackpot Bingo from Champion Diamond Jim-s Kopi of Han-Bee. These dogs, from the kennels of Beverly Cain in California, are mainly from the Ho-Dynasty dogs so carefully developed here in the eastern United States by Gilma Moss prior to her death. Starfire became both an American and a Canadian champion, a Specialty Show in each of these countries, with many Best of Breed, Group wins, and Group placements. He is used as an outcross stud dog in the Fraser-Manor breeding program, and also to establish coat. His champion offspring include, to date, Champion Fraser-Manor Pixie and Pilchuck's Dragon.

At this time, the Frasers look forward to breeding Champion Fraser-Manor Pixie. This Starfire daughter is from Fraser-Manor Kin-Chin, who as a puppy did some good winning at the Western Canada Pekingese Show under the English judge, Mrs. Bull. Her bloodlines include both Jamestown and Bugatti. Sold prior to completing her points, Kin-Chin never gained title, as the doctor who had purchased her preferred not to continue her show career.

HOPE HARTENBACH

Hope Hartenbach of St. Louis, Missouri, has been a Pekingese owner since 1967 when she purchased her first, strictly as a pet, from a pet shop. This was followed by two other pet females from Virginia Moore and Margie Bartley.

By then, thoroughly in love with the breed, Hope's next purchase was a show quality male from Mrs. Everett M. Clark of Pound Ridge, New York, a dog named Fu-Gee's China Idol of Miralac. Well-pleased with this dog, Hope returned to Lillian Clark for the acquisition of the bitch who was to become her first champion, Wu's China Star of Miralac.

By this time, thoroughly "bitten by the bug," Hope wanted another show dog, which led to the purchase of Champion Mammarick's Alleluia Angel from Richard Mammarello, and of Champion Half Note's Toccata of Su-Con from Jean Carroll. The breeding of these two produced Champion Miss Stardust Melody, who, in turn, bred to Champion The Dapper Darlin of Appin, produced Champion Mr. Sandman of Magic Charms and Champion Charm of Moonglow, both of whom became Group winners; and the pointed Dreamboat of Happy Charms.

65

These bitches were bred to Mrs. Clark's Mighty Mandarin of Miralac, from which came Champion Hope's Crackerjack Surprise and Hope's Mandarin Angel Cake. The combination of Sandman and Angel Cake produced Hope's Almosta Perfect Angel, who turned out to be a priceless producer, numbering among her progeny Champion Hope's Tequilla Sunrise, Champion Hope's Sun-Kiss of Dawn, Champion Hope's Firecracker Sparkler, and Champion Hope's Black-Eyed Susie. Crackers and Susie both finished quickly as puppies and Crackers is already a Group winner.

Hope's Pekingese represent a combination of outstanding old champion lines with the very best of a few choice new ones, basically Caversham and Laparata.

1985 was a very exciting and successful year for Hope Hartenbach and her Pekes in the show ring. In March 1985, she traveled to England, bringing back with her the lovely bitch Champion Tirakau Repeat Design, who finished very quickly following her arrival here. Other new champions for her kennel that year, handled and finished by Brenda Scheiblauer, were Champion Balerina's Dallas Cowboy; Champion Hope's Cardinal Celebration (Winners Dog at the Pekingese Club of America and Derbytown

Ch. Laparata Celestial Prince, originally from Mrs. Snook in England, was handled by Luc Boileau for former owner Edward B. Jenner. Celestial Prince now belongs to Hetty Orringer, Hatamen Pekingese.

Ch. Hope's Sandstorm Weatherman, by Mahjon Mon Ami ex Hope's Almosta Perfect Angel, handsome Pekingese dog bred and owned by Hope H. Hartenbach.

Specialties); Champion Hope's Sandstorm Weatherman; Champion Hope's Just-A-Tuppins; Champion Hope's Firecracker Sparkler; and Champion Hope's Black-Eyed Susie—surely the type of year to bring deep satisfaction to any dedicated breeder!

Champion Hope's KoKo Puff Dragon gained most of his points in 1985; he then started off 1986 with back-to-back majors, finishing at age nine months at the North Central Illinois Specialty. Both he and Crackers were Group placers from the puppy class.

Hope Hartenbach points out that achievement of high honors for her dogs also represents a partial victory for the following breeders whose stock contributed to her success. They are Mrs. Everett Clark (Miralac), Catherine Eadie Adams (Appin) and Pat Drew (Mahjon). Then there are also the very capable handlers who have presented her Pekes so well, thus helping them capture their many honors. These include Hermine Cleaver, Mrs. Lorraine Heichel Masley, Betty Caton, and Brenda Scheiblauer.

HATAMEN

Hatamen Pekingese is a small kennel of only eight Pekes owned by Hetty Orringer at Southborough, Massachusetts. The Hatamen foundation bitches are Knolland Morning Dancer and her litter sister, Champion Knolland Noblesse Oblige. Both bitches were acquired from Mr. Edward Jenner of Knolland Farm fame.

Knolland Morning Dancer was bred to American and Canadian Champion Laparata Celestial Prince, who now also resides at Hatamen. This breeding produced Champion Hatamen Queen of Hearts who was Reserve Winners Bitch from the 9-12 months puppy class at the Pekingese Club of America 1983 March Specialty. She is owned by Mr. Jenner and handled, until finished, by Luc Boileau. Knolland Morning Dancer, known as "The Rose," was then bred to Champion St. Aubrey Romany of Elsdon, this time producing Hatamen Splashdown. This young dog went on to win Best of Breed from the Bred-by Exhibitor Class over a special while still a puppy, and continued to bring home Specialty win firsts.

Champion Knolland Noblesse Oblige is owned and was finished to her title by Hetty's mother, Nancy Higgins. Although shown sparingly, she quickly gathered her points under judges Frank Sabella, Ed Biven, Ann Seranne, Betty Dullinger, and William Bergum. Bred back to her grandsire, American and Canadian Champion St. Aubrey Laparata Dragon, she produced a son, Hatamen High Flaunting. Hatamen Off In A Huff, the other male from this breeding, does not care for the ring but is busy proving himself as a sire.

All Hatamen Pekes are based on the English line of Laparata, and Hatamen's pedigree shows the great one himself, Champion St. Aubrey Laparata Dragon, in their first two generations.

HI WIN'S

Hi Win's Kennel was started in the early 1970s by Hiram Stewart, Kenner, Louisiana.

As owners of a small kennel, it was very important to Mr. Stewart that he learn proper type and structure. Many thanks go to neighboring breeders and loyal friends such as Donna Bergeron, Priscilla Jackson, and Peggy Carr for the major role they played in his foundation learning of the breed.

Through the years, Mr. Stewart has taken on the role of a professional handler of Toy breeds while, at the same time, working to maintain a breeding program of his own. During recent years, he has put titles on more than 20 Pekingese who were either

Ch. Espree by Hi Win's, by Ch. Judcilla's Elite of Hi Win's ex Ch. Acadiana Estee of Hi Win's, taking points at Southeast Arkansas, 1985. This homebred belongs to Hiram Stewar, Hi Win's Pekingese.

owned by him or belonged to faithful friends and clients.

To this date, the bloodlines in Hiram Stewart's own kennel are principally Wellion, Singlewell, and Jalna. With this combination, he has been able to achieve the type and soundness which are so desirable, and reproduce them in succeeding generations. This is the goal which has been his incentive as a breeder for nearly 16 years, and is the one he hopes to be able to retain over future years.

HOTOI

HoToi Pekingese are owned by Leo and Mary Jo O'Leary at Endicott, New York. To date they have owned 11 Pekingese in their small kennel, nine of them champions. The HoToi Pekingese are always owner-handled to their championships. Their bloodlines are based on strong linebreeding to the famous Caversham Kennels in England.

The beginning of HoToi Pekingese was the O'Learys' purchase of Top Hat's Pied Pixie of He'Lo, a black and white female, in

69

May 1976. A granddaughter of the famous black and white parti-color, Champion Spankey's Tux-Ce-Do of He'Lo, Pixie was bred and sold to the O'Learys by Mrs. Ruby Turner Williams in Houston, Texas (a lady who has given Mary Jo inestimable help in learning about the breed and its care).

Pixie won two points shown as a puppy by her novice owner, but most importantly of all, she gave Mary Jo several nice litters, sired by Dag's Dylan of HoToi (son of Champion Dagbury of Calartha), Puz Fondu of Dragonhai, and Champion Sherrie's Samson of Hotoi.

In November 1976, the O'Learys bought Champion Beverlyhill Saton's Sherrie of Se-Je from Karen and Wayne Tyree of Buena Vista, Virginia. Sherrie, a blond daughter of Champion Sunstar Satan of Se-Je (grandson of Champion Dah Lyn Yen Chu) and also descended from Champion Caversham Ku Ku of Yam and Champion Chik Tsun of Caversham, was then four years old and already the dam of one champion bitch, Lori Ann of Tai Shan. She was purchased in whelp to Mrs. Florence Gwynne's Mye Sun Chello, by Champion Linsown Ku Chello who was a grandson of Champion Linsown Ku-Che-Tu. At age 14 years, Sherrie won the Veteran's Class at the Pekingese Club of America 1986 March Specialty.

Sherrie's litter in 1976 produced two puppies who gained titles, Champion Sherrie's Samson of HoToi, a blond male, and Sherrie's Circe of HoToi, a blonde female. Samson became a champion in December 1978, finishing triumphantly with Winners Dog and Best of Winners at the New Jersey Specialty, won several Bests of Breed, but was never specialed due to an eye injury.

Litter sister, Circe, was finished in June 1978, taking Best of Breed on three occasions along the way. She was then retired for breeding and not shown again until September 1983, when she took Best of Opposite Sex, despite her six-and-a-half-years' age, at the Pekingese Club of America Specialty under judge Mrs. Kay Gately.

In January 1984, Circe whelped another litter, the result of a breeding to Su-Con Boxcar, a son of Sungarth Truffle and a grandson of Champion St. Aubrey Laparata Dragon. The litter produced a red male, The Sun King of HoToi; and a silver female, I'm No Angel of HoToi. Circe is now retired from matronly duties and has returned to the show ring. At age nine-and-a-half years,

70

Ch. Sherrie's Samson of HoToi at one and a half years old. A handsome winner belonging to Mary Jo O'Leary, HoToi Pekingese.

she won Best of Opposite Sex at three all-breed shows on the Southern Tier Circuit in Syracuse, New York. She has produced three champions.

The current young homebreds now at HoToi include The Rough Rider of HoToi, a blond son of Champion Pizie's Marmalade Kid of HoToi and grandson of Champion Lori Ann of Tai Shan, who has six points, including a major, from Bred-by Exhibitor Class.

Several of HoToi's champions have won Group placements, among them Champion The Cayene Cowboy, Pixie's Marmalade Kid, his son The Lemondrop Kid, and American and Canadian Champion The Microdot of HoToi.

Leo and Mary Jo started the Colony Pekingese Club of the Southern Tier, based in Endicott, New York, in September 1981. In April 1985, this Club held its first Sanction B Match, followed by the second in October 1985 which drew the amazing total of 90 entries. Presently, the Club hopes soon to advance to holding "A" matches. This is an active and dedicated group doing a good job for the breed through educational programs, handling classes, grooming demonstrations, and a monthly newsletter containing special material to benefit the breeders and the breed.

JOMAR

Jomar Pekingese are the result of Margaret Zuber, who is located at West Monroe, Louisiana, having been given an orphaned puppy of this breed whom she raised on a bottle. He was pet quality, but Margaret promptly fell in love with him and her affections switched from the Toy Poodles, which she had been showing, to Pekes.

She contacted Nigel Aubrey Jones, from whom she purchased a puppy dog grandson of Champion St. Aubrey Laparata Dragon, who was known informally as "Herman." In short order he became Champion St. Aubrey Ting Tong of Elsdon. His new owner was thrilled with him and loved him dearly. What a pity that he was destined to remain only briefly in his new home, as tragically he died at only a year and a half. Even in that short time, he left a legacy of two champions: Champion Xanadu Ting Tong Tu O'Irwin and Champion St. Aubrey Yu Tong of Elsdon.

Margaret Zuber had long admired the Jamestown Pekingese from England, and wanted to go in that direction with her breeding program. From Richard McCallum in Canada she purchased Pekeland Sunset Skies, a daughter of Champion Bellerne's Yu Benito and a granddaughter of Champion Yu Yang of Jamestown. Bred to Champion St. Aubrey Etive Yu Kan, a great-grandson of Champion Yu Yang of Jamestown, she produced Champion Jomar Kaiti Kan.

A lovely male puppy was acquired, sired by Patty Mullendore's Champion Muhlin Mi O Mi, who grew up to become Champion Jomar Teddy Bear. Jomar Kaiti Kan and Champion Jomar Teddy Bear produced Champion Jomar Sunni Bear (a Group winner), Champion Jomar Ruffles and Flourishes (Best of Winners, Pekingese Club of Texas Specialty Show), Champion Darling Litle Abra of Jomar (among the Top Ten Pekingese Bitches), and major-pointed Jomar Pettycoat Pamela, Jomar Fancy Pants, and Jomar Fleur De Lis.

In Texarkana, Arkansas, in the midst of a downpour, Margaret Zuber met Betty Claire Peacock, who was also at this time trying

Ch. Darling Little Abra of Jomar taking a Best of Breed for owners Margaret Zuber (Jomar) and Betty Claire Peacock, Dumas, Arkansas, who is handling.

to get started showing Pekingese. In fact, Margaret Zuber comments, "Betty Claire and I made points for other people for a few years." They formed a lasting friendship, and Betty Claire has handled and helped finish most of the Jomar Pekes, several of which are co-owned by her.

Other Pekingese at Jomar, owned and finished by Margaret Zuber, include Champion Pai Jin Tre of Xanadu, Champion Mike Mar's China Buddah, and Champion Scarlet O'Hara of Xanadu. Champion Jomar Sunni Bear has two major-pointed daughers, Jomar Mariko and Jomar Poppette, owned by Kathleen G. Smith of Monroe and Shirley Dannehower of Baton Rouge, Louisiana.

All of the Pekingese at Jomar have the freedom of the kennel except at feeding time, when separate pens are needed. They all have little hammocks to sleep in, which they all love.

KATERING

Katering Pekingese Kennels at Baring, Oregon, are owned and loved by Gwenn and Trevis Southmayd.

In 1972, this couple acquired their first show Peke, and from the very beginning their particular interest has been in producing outstanding dogs of the black and tan coloring. This dream has now become a reality as there have been several lovely black and tan winners, including Champion Lit'l Gus Go Tu of Katering, who was the foundation behind the black breeding program. He was sired by Champion Tam-Ky-Do of Ongenae ex Jo Dee Do of Ongenae. Then there is Champion Katering's Ho Lee Smoke, who completed his title with ease and is by Katering's Ashes to Ashes ex Gus' Effervescence of Katering.

Champion Sho Me-N-Angel of Katering is a lovely black and tan bitch, successful in the show ring and as a producer. Champion Katering's Ain Chi Dah Ling is also a black and tan bitch of merit, who finished No. 5 in the United States, a daughter of Champion Born Agan O'Jay of Katering ex Fan-Cee- Mani-Kin of Katering.

There are several others pointed, too. Gwenn Southmayd especially comments on her appreciation of the judges who have honored the good black and tan Pekes, as it is well-known that they do not always win easily, and it takes a mighty good specimen to gain approval.

Lately the Southmayds have taken a fancy to the pure white Pekes, and to the parti-colors, and are concentrating now on these along with the black and tan dogs. We wish them equal success with these!

KNOLLAND FARM

Knolland Farm Pekingese are owned by Mr. Edward B. Jenner and have for many years been located at Richmond, Illinois. At this time Knolland Farm is moving to Wisconsin, which is where Ed Jenner, the magnificent Pekingese who live there, and Luc Boilleau who keeps them so beautifully conditioned and presents them so perfectly, will be located in the future.

Ed Jenner has been associated with many breeds of dogs over the years (and still is), and has a very active interest in his horses in Kentucky and various other "beasties," but there is no breed or type of animal which he holds in higher regard, nor loves more

74

Ch. Born Agan O'Jay of Katering, grandson of Ch. Lit'l Gus, finished with three major wins and Group placements. He is a wonderful sire with many progeny in the ring. Owned by Katering Pekingese.

dearly, than the Pekingese. He is a breeder-owner-exhibitor who truly takes pleasure in his dogs for their personalities and the pleasure of their company, and I cannot wait to see the kitchen at the *new* Knolland Farm, as I am certain that, as in Richmond, there will be lovely comfortable nooks for the dozen or so house dogs, mainly Pekes, who make their headquarters there.

There are so many distinguished Pekingese at Knolland Farm that making a choice is difficult. However, it is only fair to say that "pride of place" (plus an award for distinguished service to his breed) is most of all deserved by Champion St. Aubrey Laparata Dragon. This little dog has sired, by his owner's figuring, about 100 champions, and is still an active stud at age 12 years. The best part is the type and quality with which Dragon stamps his progeny. Eight out of ten times, they are instantly recognizable as being sired by him, and the portion of these dogs with outstandingly distinguished show records is impressive.

Miss Jean Grant in Canada was the breeder of this lovely dog of the 1960s, Ch. Temple Bells of Blossomlea, owned by Edward B. Jenner, Knolland Farm Kennels; and Mrs. Elaine Rigden, Wadsworth, Ohio.

Hot on Dragon's heels is the sensational Champion St. Aubrey's Bees Wing of Eldon, a Dragon son, of course, who triumphed during 1985 as America's Top Toy, winning the Ken-L-Biskit Award. "Peter," as this gorgeous dog is called, was bred in Canada at St. Aubrey-Elsdon, and I know that it took powerful persuasion to get him away from there. He, like Dragon, has a stunning list of Best in Show victories to his credit, and, best of all, like Dragon he is making his presence felt as a sire. Like father, like son—these two dogs are carving for themselves an outstanding niche in Pekingese history.

Then there is the homebred Best in Show winner, Champion Knolland Tiger Rag who, several years back, became the first to win the Pekingese Club of America Summer Specialty at Ox Ridge, then to go clear through to the all-breed Best in Show. After this he was retired, having already brought home a memorable collection of choice Best in Show and Group wins, making this one truly the "frosting on the cake."

Ed Jenner is by no means new to the Pekingese world. His earlier Pekes included several well-known winners co-owned with Elaine Rigden, lovely dogs who won well. Edna Voyles and Lorraine Heichel Masley campaigned members of this breed for him as well.

Were Ed and Luc not so busy with the moving right now, I would insist that they give us a list of the total homebred Peke champions; but, knowing that there is little chance of my getting it from them while things are so hectic, I shall just say that there must be a very respectable number, as Knolland Farms shows and wins with great puppies and young homebreds as well as with the specials, being true breeders, not just exhibitors.

LON-DU

Lon-Du Pekingese, at Monticello, Iowa, are owned by Arlon D. Duit, who started in 1975 with a pet eight-year-old white male, and was soon bitten by the show bug. He entered his first show in 1976. The entry arrived late, but even so, Arlon had an interesting time observing the Pekes who were there. Ruby Dudley was exhibiting and needed a helping hand with some of hers at the last moment. Arlon's show experience started that day when he took the lead on one of Ruby's dogs.

Ch. Mi London Fog of Lon-Du at age eight months winning a 4-point major. By Ch. Mi Little Rain of Lon-Du ex Beaupres in Pink (British Junior Warrant winner), London Fog was bred and is owned by Arlon Duit, Lon-Du Pekingese.

Three months later, Arlon was so brave as to try again, this time with a new male he had purchased. When he took second in a class of two, Arlon asked Ruby to go over the dog and tell him her opinion of his chances. She advised him to keep on showing the dog as he would probably gain points, but that she doubted he would finish. Asked why, Ruby Dudley showed him, on the dog, where fine points in the breed were lacking—a most helpful experience for anyone just starting with a breed!

A year later, Arlon was back in the ring with a black granddaughter of Champion Pekehuis Twee's Dan's Sun, the latter by Champion Twee Choo of Caversham. One of his early disappointments with Pekes was that this lovely bitch did not reproduce.

It was then that Arlon met William D. McMillan of Trenton, Missouri, from whom he arranged the purchase of a six-month-old brother and sister by Champion Su-Con's St. Nick ex Champion Gemini's Vikky of Beverlyhill. Mi Vic-Kee of Bilmar, a granddaughter of Champion Nia Ku Tulyar of Orchard Hill, was bred to a grandson of Nia Jai Mi Ling of Orchard Hill, half sister to Tulyar. Arlon 's first homebred champion was the result. Champion Mi Twee Jai-Kee of Lon-Du. This handsome dog won his first major from the author, who was very favorably impressed with him.

Jai-Kee is the sire of Champion Mi-Twee Anna of Lon-Du, and of several champions for Mrs. Walter Jeffords, including the Best in Show winner Champion Ching of Chinatown. Twee Anna, when mated to Black Cavalier of Chambrae, produced the Duits' first black champion, Mi-Black Knight of Lon-Du.

Champion Wild Rain Boi of Panora, bred by Olga Fitzgerald came to Lon-Du in 1977, a grandson of both Champion Yu Yang of Jamestown and Champion Copplestone Pu Zee. Rain Boi is over 12 years old and is still siring. His progeny includes Champion Mi Little Rain of Lon-Du, who in turn sired Champion Mi London Fog of Lon-Du.

Cambalu Lady Margo, a Champion Ho Dynasty Brut daughter purchased from Marjorie Kaye, was to prove a most valuable brood matron. When bred to the Jacksons' Champion Mahjon Cassidy T'Sun, they produced Champion Lon-Du Casanova and Lon-Du Cassandra (pointed). Bred to Rodar's The Dragon At Lon-Du, she produced Champion Lon-Du Dee Lady Di and the stubborn Lon-Du Dee Lady Matilda. Champion Casanova was mated to his half sister (by Cassidy) which resulted in Champion Lon-Du's Valentino, whose first puppies will soon be in the show ring.

Dud-Lee's Tometta's Flame was purchased from Jerry McDonald when three years of age and soon became a champion. He sired Champion Rikke Rick Shaw of Lon-Du and the lovely Champion Mi Flaming Mamie of Lon-Du who, bred to Champion Rodari the Dragon of Lon-Du, became dam of Champion Lon-Du Dragon Mite.

Undoubtedly the star of this kennel is Champion Rodari The Dragon At Lon-Du. Linebred to one of the all-time great sires, Champion St. Aubrey Laparata Dragon, and bred by Mrs. Barbara Melless, Ontario, Canada, "Puff" has put his mark on his offspring, both in the show ring and in the whelping box. The winner of three Bests in Show, plus numerous Group successes. At age three-and-a-half years, he is already the sire of seven champions with eight others major pointed.

MAR-PAT

Mar-Pat Pekingese in Gardena, California, were established in 1954 by two sisters, Martha Olmos-Ollivier (Bingham) and Patricia Miller. They imported Tiko of Pekeboro (not to be confused with Mrs. Katz's Champion *Wei* Tiko of Pekeboro), a son of Champion Tong Tiko of Alderbourne. This dog became the dominant foundation force in their kennel and, following completion of his American championship, he became the sire of some 13 champions for Mar-Pat and for other breeders.

The bitch line for the most part was Sing Lee, and that combination worked out beautifully by producing many winners. Occasionally other lines were introduced, but the best combinations seemed to come through the Sing Lee and Alderbourne.

Since the mid-1960s, the impressive number of 35 champions were bred at Mar-Pat Kennels. Five of these became Best in Show dogs, with a total of 12 who were Toy Group winners. Of these, Champion Tiko was either the sire or the grandsire.

Later, Champion Tiko daughters were bred to Champion Calartha Mandarin of Jehol, a combination which produced several top winners including the Best in Show father and son, Champion Mar-Pat Man D Sun and his son Champion Mar-Pat Man D's Liliput.

Ch. Mar-Pat Mandarin's Star at age six months. Owned by Martha M. Olmos-Ollivier, Mar-Pat Pekingese.

The Mar-Pat Pekes were always known for short backs, which they inherited from the Sing Lees and for profuse red coats from the Alderbournes and Cavershams. A bitch from Mar-Pat, in which Mrs. Ollivier takes special pride, was Champion Mar-Pat's Tiko's Sun Bonnet, owned by Russell Herman, who was the Top Pekingese Bitch until her record was broken in the early 1980s. A very beautiful Best in Show winner, she also produced one champion for her owners.

There are still Mar-Pat Pekes with Mrs. Miller, and a new litter has recently arrived. But Mar-Pat has not exhibited Pekes in several years now, owing to Mrs. Ollivier's busy schedule as a multi-Group judge, which she feels would make showing a conflict of interest. Other breeds for which she is not licensed to judge have been finished, however, by a professional handler. The Mar-Pat line is carried on by others, with a number of winners still gaining their titles.

MRS. MAYNARD'S PEKINGESE

Mrs. Walter Maynard of Southampton, New York, is a very dedicated Pekingese breeder and fancier who has some most outstanding members of the breed in her kennel.

Pride of place here goes to the glamorous bitch, Champion Velspring's Velvetina, who has truly swept the boards in exciting competition during 1985. Her record at this time stands at 72 times Best of Breed (including twice at the Westminster Kennel Club), 30 Group first awards, 30 additional second and third Group placements, and five times Best in Show all-breeds.

Velvetina, as we write, is at home with her owner after a year of campaigning with Bill Trainor; she will be bred sometime soon. Her sire, English and American Champion Belknap Kalafrana Caspar, was also imported by Mrs. Maynard and is more than proving his value as a stud dog, with Velvetina and a number of other young champions already to his credit.

Mrs. Maynard's interest in Pekes extends back over a considerable period of time, to the days when she owned Westwinds (Mrs. Harace Wilson) and Dah Lyn (John B. Royce) breeding. She has

The important Pekingese winner and stud dog, Eng. and Am. Ch. Belknap Kalafrana Caspar, by Ch. Shiarita Cassidy ex Ch. Belknap April Showers, is the sire of the famed multi-Best in Show bitch, Ch. Velspring's Velvetina and numerous other champions. Owned by Mrs. Walter Maynard.

also had the lovely bitch Champion Mike-Mar's Desert Song, who gave her some especially beautiful puppies by Champion King Kon of St. Aubrey-Elsdon.

Now Mrs. Maynard is working primarily with imports from England, and travels there frequently; she has many friends among the leading breeders.

We surely wish her success, and another big winner, with Velvetina's puppies when she is bred.

MI-GEMS

Mi-Gems Pekingese are owned by Mr. and Mrs. James P. Lamb Sr. (Jim and Eleanor Lamb) in West Palm Beach, Florida.

Natives of North Carolina, both the Lambs have always been interested in purebred dogs. As a youngster, Eleanor Lamb was a member and a Junior Officer of the Piedmont Kennel Club. It was there that she took her first handling lesson, and became acquainted with Pekingese. Mrs. Charles Jordon (Pekingese House) a neighbor of Eleanor's grandmother was a member there, too.

Eleanor and Jim Lamb had been acquainted ever since the fifth grade. Both of them at that time wanted to become veterinarians. After high school they were married, and Eleanor became involved with raising "the four little Lambs:" James Jr., Anne, Susan, and John.

In 1960, the Lamb family moved to Florida. Throughout all these years, Eleanor had been involved with one breed of dog or another—but always briefly, and never was she really satisfied, as what she truly wanted were Pekingese.

It was not until her children were grown and had children of their own that Eleanor got her Pekingese, at long last. She was manager of a ladies' clothing store, and enjoyed her work. One morning her assistant came in very much agitated; her sister had a Pekingese who was so mean that they were going to put him to sleep. Eleanor had at that time been looking for a Peke, feeling that the time for her to have one had arrived, and had been unable to find one she really liked and that was what she had wanted to work with. So, not for one moment believing that any Peke could *possibly* be as mean as this one had been described, Eleanor took this dog. "Chuckie" lived to be ten-and-a-half years old, and dearly loved by the entire family. Just once, a few nights after his arrival, Eleanor's granddaughter forgot she had been told to keep her face away from the puppy, and gave him a goodnight kiss, at which he promptly bit her on the lip. Just as promptly, Eleanor had him up for a sound spanking, never saying a word. That is that last time Chuckie ever made an attempt to bite anyone.

By now, the Lambs were more determined than ever to become Pekingese breeders. Eleanor wanted a quality bitch from whom she hoped to raise some home-bred champions. It was in 1979, at the vet's office with Chuckie, that Eleanor noticed a picture of what she describes as "a real Peke." She asked many questions, and that afternoon she purchased not only this little dog but his brother as well.

The dog Eleanor Lamb brought home that day turned out to be her first champion, Ja Mie See Me Tu of Tujaks, U.D. His brother was given to their great-granddaughter. The breeders were Jack and Jackie Carter.

Ja Mie became tremendously attached to Jim Lamb, to the point that Eleanor felt if Ja Mie were ever to be successfully shown, Jim must be the one to do it. Having no desire to show a dog in breed, Jim started Ja Mie on an obedience career.

Eleanor was both happy and frustrated at having finally acquired some Pekes. For, you see, she had three males instead of the females she yearned for, and her young hopeful was definitely her husband's dog. She therefore started making inquiries about Ja Mie's sire, Champion Jamison May Ray of Lyt-ton. She learned that he belonged to Frank Tingley in Charlotte, and, thus, off went the Lambs on a visit to Eleanor's parents, who were still living there, and to Mr. Tingley. Eleanor explained what she wanted, her ambition being that of breeding her own champion. While there she saw, wanted, and purchased a lovely bitch who was half sister to Jamie. On the way home to Florida with her, they selected their new kennel name, Mi-Gems.

This beautiful bitch became Mi-Gems Ting Lee of Lyt-ton, and was the first Pekingese Eleanor Lamb ever showed. She was doing well in the ring, but Eleanor's dream of breeding her own show dogs had not been forgotten. As soon as she was ready, Ting Lee was bred to Champion Micklee Travis. In her first litter of three males and three females, born in January 1981, there were two bitches who produced Eleanor's first champions, and two dogs who became obedience winners with top standings.

On their next trip to North Carolina, Frank Tingley, with

Mi Gems Jamisons Captivator, by Ch. Jamison May-Ray of Lyt-ton ex Ke Kou Kele of Mi Gems, bred by Eleanor Lamb, is owned by George and Mary Hines, Mooresville, North Carolina. He is a full brother to Ch. Mi Gems Golden Chalice and half brother to Ja Mie See Me Tu of Tujako, U.D.

whom they had become good friends, took the time to take the Lambs to Grimesland for a visit to Larry Elks and his Elksway Pekingese. Here they acquired a linebred Jamestown bitch, Elksway Donnah Yang, sired by Champion Wellbarn Dandee ex Champion Pu Ki Piawacket. Bred to Champion Micklee Travis, she produced for the Lambs their first male champion.

Eleanor Lamb will never forget her gratitude to Frank Tingley and Larry Elks for their trust in her and for providing her with these two handsome bitches who made her dream a reality.

Famous Pekingese at Mi-Gem include Champion Mi-Gem's Smidgen of Perfection, who has produced an excellent litter by Champion St. Aubrey Yu Tong of Elsdon; Champion Elksway Enticer of Mi-Gems, by Champion Mickelee Travis Ex Elksway Donna Yang, who gained his title quickly, taking his very first points with a Best of Breed win over three champions, and now has numerous Bests of Breed to his credit; Champion Mi-Gems Golden Chalice, by Champion May-Ray of Lyt-ton ex Ke kou Kele of Mi-Gems; Champion Mi-Gems Honorable Simmet, producing lovely puppies and is, Eleanor feels, the best dog she has owned; and Champion Mi-Gem's Soc It To Um, CD, who took five Bests of Breed from the classes and completed his CD all within the same year. He was sold as a puppy to Jean Crossley and Delores Vance, by whom he is dearly loved and successfully shown.

MIKE-MAR

Mike-Mar Pekingese are owned by Mr. Michael Wolf of Oxford, Pennsylvania, who started with the breed several decades back while a resident of Long Island. Pekes were not the first breed Michael especially loved; his interest in Italian Greyhounds and in Maltese goes still further back. But the one which has remained with him constantly has been the Pekingese, and his achievements in this breed have been notable and memorable.

Michael was busy showing a whole series of outstanding home-bred Maltese when he became aware of, and purchased, the very beautiful American-bred Pekingese dog Champion Dan Lor Dragonseed, with whom John Brown was at that time hitting fantastic heights in the stiff competition of California, where he was piling up steadily increasing numbers of Best in Show and Group victories. This little Pekingese made a spectacular Eastern debut under Michael Wolf's ownership when, at Westminster Kennel Club, his first show following the purchase, he proceeded to go from the breed through to first place in a keenly contested Toy Group. He added two Pekingese Club of America Specialty Shows to his laurels, the September Specialties (which are open to both American-bred and imported dogs, and where the competition always seems to be exceptionally keen), and, among other honors with Michael in the East, five *consecutive* Bests in Show at All-Breed events, bringing his total to an impressive number.

Dragonseed lived out a long and happy life at Mike-Mar, and was always a favorite of Michael's. His descendants have continued to be, and are producing, true quality.

Another purchase made by Michael from California during this period was Champion Mar-Pat Solo's Liliput, a Group winner, a Best in Show dog, the sire of champions.

Champion Hi Swinger of Brown's Den was another American-bred which Michael Wolf purchased, who won for him Best of Breed at a Pekingese Club of America Winter Specialty.

Michael has always been very aware of the Pekingese quality available in England; thus he has imported numerous dogs and bitches for his breeding programs and for show. It was one of these, Dagbury of Calartha, who was to lead to the very successful eight-year partnership between Michael Wolf and Mrs. Walter M. Jeffords, which resulted in Michael's leaving Long Island to take up residence at Mrs. Jeffords', where he could generally pursue their mutual interest in the breed.

Dagbury made his debut at a Bronx County Kennel Club Dog Show, which Mrs. Jeffords had also attended. She had owned a Peke or two herself at this point, and she was literally unable to take her eyes off Dagbury as he went from the Open Dog Class to Best of Breed, first in the Top Group, then on to Best in Show! She truly longed to own this beautiful little Peke, and approached Michael about his purchase, but there was no way Michael would give him up.

Finally, the happy thought was hit upon of their co-owning Dagbury. This led to the formation of the partnership and to the series of exciting winners which followed under the Jeffords-Wolf banner.

There is no one in dogs with a better eye for quality than Michael Wolf and no one with more natural know-how when it comes to presenting dogs at their very best. He and Mrs. Jeffords, during their partnership, owned such spectacular Best in Show winners as Champion Dragon Hai Fanfare (three Bests in Show and nine Toy Groups); Champion Masterpiece Zodiac of Dud-Lee's (eight times Best in Show, 53 Groups); Champion Quilkin the Stringman (11 all-breed Bests in Show, 54 Group firsts, a three-time winner at the Pekingese Club of America Specialty Shows); Champion Yankee Bernard (17 times Best in Show, 52 Toy Group firsts, and a Pekingese Club of America Specialty winner); and whole flock more.

Dagbury did a highly satisfactory amount of winning, including multiple Bests in Show and Group firsts. Another prominent Best in Show winner was a stunning Peke, imported from England, named Bon Bon—a dog who was another notable sire.

Following a very successful eight-year period, Kay Jeffords and

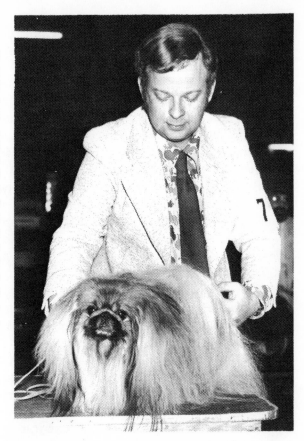

Ch. Dagbury of Calartha at his first dog show in the United States, Bronx County K.C. in 1972. Michael Wolf, who is handling, had just imported this young "star" from England and it was obvious that he was destined for a notable career. At this show Mrs. Walter Jeffords first saw Dagbury, the meeting which led to the formation of the partnership between Mrs. Jeffords and Mr. Wolf.

Michael Wolf ended their partnership by mutual agreement. As time has proven, in neither case did they lessen their interest and activity in the Pekingese world.

The one area at this point where Michael had not yet made an impact on the Pekingese world was as a breeder, and now he decided that the time had come! With a stunning homebred male named Mike-Mar's China Dragon (called "Puff," of course), Michael set out to show the Pekingese world that he could breed them as well as select, import, and present them. This is exactly how it turned out!

"Puff" is a breathtaking Pekingese, and Michael formed a co-ownership on him with Mrs. Alan Robson of Glenmoore, Pennsylvania, who had been interested in a top quality Peke for some time. The heights "Puff" reached included 49 all-breed Best in Show victories; 168 Group Firsts; a Pekingese Club of America victory, and the honor of becoming Top Toy Dog in America for the Ken-L-Biskit Award in 1983. He is now the Top American-bred Peke of all time.

The record "Puff" broke in becoming Top American-bred Pekingese of all-time was the one which had been held by Dragonseed. The latter had 38 Bests in Show, more than 100 Group firsts, Pekingese Club of America Specialty success, and he had gained the Ken-L-Biskit Top Toy Award in 1968!

There are some lovely Pekes coming out from Mike-Mar now, along with the canine stars of other breeds always to be found on Michael's lead. His dog sense takes him into almost every Group, and always with a good specimen.

MORNINGSTAR

The Morningstar Pekingese of Mr. Anthony E. Rosato and Mr. John D. French were established in Indianapolis, Indiana in 1981.

A good deal of study on the principle of genetics and the history of the breed was undertaken before the first Morningstar litter was bred. After careful consideration of pedigrees of many well-known dogs through the years in both England and America, it was decided to base a breeding program on St. Aubrey-Elsdon and Belknap bloodlines. It was also decided to exercise judicious line-breeding and strict selection as the means to form a new bloodline.

Hence, two granddaughters of American and Canadian Champion St. Aubrey Laparata Dragon were obtained, as well as their grandmother, Champion Violette of St. Aubrey-Elsdon. One of these bitches was bred to American and Canadian Champion St. Aubrey Sunburst of Elsdon, which produced Morningstar Sun King, the kennel's top stud dog.

In the summer of 1984, Mr. Rosato and Mr. French relocated in Miami Beach, Florida, bringing with them some 25 dogs. Among these were Champion Cambalu Wee Sed T'Ruffles, a glamorous silver fawn bitch; and Cambalu King Be Morningstar, a grandson of English Champion Belknap El Dorado and son of a top winning bitch, Champion Cambalu Sunburst Serena. Both of these have made valuable contributions to the Morningstar breeding program.

Since moving to Florida, a good many litters have been bred, from which have emerged a number of winning dogs, including Morningstar Lionhart and Morningstar Frangelico, both on their

Morningstar Sun King, by Am. and Can. Ch. Ch. St. Aubrey Sunburst of Elsdon ex Fourwinds Margaux Cantabile, is the top stud dog at Morningstar Kennels.

way to their titles. With them and other young prospects, plus a strong team of well-bred bitches, Morningstar looks forward to a highly successful Pekingese breeding program.

MUGIECHUN

Mugiechun Pekingese in Phoenix, Arizona, are owned by Miss Sakota (Sandy) Wheat, whose interest in owning and showing excellent quality homebred Pekingese began around 1975.

In the beginning, Miss Wheat realized quite soon that her first Peke bitch, Chimie, was not quite up to success in the conformation ring. Her solution to that was to turn to obedience, working for three years in obedience training and competition with Chimie and her daughter. It must have been great satisfaction that her efforts paid off with two C.D.X. degrees on these Pekes, who completed them in 1978.

Ch. Sportsman Jody, the very first Pekingese champion owned by Sandy Wheat, Mugiechun Pekingese. Jody finished title in 1980, handled by John Brown.

Champion Jody was the first to gain a conformation title for Sandy, handled to it by John Brown.

Then, from Nigel Aubrey-Jones and R. William Taylor, she purchased St. Aubrey Royal Star and St. Aubrey Maydrena. These two started out in spring 1981, and later that year both had gained their championships. They are descended from Champion St. Aubrey Laparata Dragon and from a New Zealand imported bitch. These two became excellent producers, and have produced very nicely for Miss Wheat. Since then, another bitch has arrived.

Sandy Wheat enjoys her Pekes tremendously and loves working with them. She has recently been approved to judge the breed, and we have noticed that she is doing so quite frequently and quite well.

MUHLIN

Muhlin Pekingese, a small kennel that has been active since 1970, is owned by Mrs. Patricia G. Mullendore of Oswego, Illinois.

90

To date, Mrs. Mullendore has bred and/or owned 27 champions.

Since 1984, Mrs. Mullendore has functioned in partnership with Diana Mehling (Meh-Ling Pekingese), and both ladies and their Pekes have found this arrangement most enjoyable.

Now relocated in Illinois from Michigan, Mrs. Mullendore is still working full time, and she continues to find the dogs a bright spot in her life. She tells us, too, that she has thoroughly enjoyed her foray into the world of judging with several Specialty Sweepstakes assignments.

Special sources of pride are the Top Producers, Champion Muhlin Boogaloo and Champion Belknap Little Nugget. The late "Boog" has thus far produced 12 champions: Group winners, Specialty Show Best of Breed winners, and an all-breed Best in Show winner. Nugget has produced nine champions and a C.D. degree holder, including multiple Specialty point winners and Specialty Bests of Breed. He himself is a multiple Specialty Best of Breed winner. Each has a child exported back to England by Pat Drew (Mahjon), an honor indeed.

It is hoped that Muhlins and Meh-Lings will be in the Pekingese ring for many years to come.

Ch. Muhlin Molly Brown, by Ch. Muhlin Midas ex St. Aubrey Royal Mee of Elsdon, shown by co-owner Diana Mehling for breeder and co-owner Mrs. Patricia G. Mullendore.

PEKINGESE O'HONEYBEAR

Pekingese O'Honeybear are owned by Annette L. Borders in Abilene, Texas, whose infatuation with the breed began with the gift of one as a puppy on her 17th birthday. Her parents did not like housepets, and although Annette stayed awake most of the night in an effort to keep the puppy from crying and bothering them, they still insisted that she return it. The time she was able to keep that puppy was short, but it was long enough to instill in her a love of the breed that has lasted over the years. When her younger son graduated from high school, Annette decided that the time had come for her to indulge herself by getting the Pekingese she had always wanted, and while she was at it, why not get a really *good* one? Having attended one dog show, she thought that it would be nice to have a dog with whom she could participate and, knowing exactly what she wanted, she started out to locate a red female with a black face. An eight-week-old female she had seen seemed to fit the bill. Annette never got to show her, but found herself more enraptured with the breed each day, and she started to read the standard very seriously and every Pekingese ad or article she could find.

The Manticore Pekes in Canada seemed to have the things she most admired, and Annette got in touch with Fran Alcock regarding the possible purchase of one. After considerable conversation and correspondence, Fran offered her a lovely young Jamestown linebred male being campaigned at the time, Manticore Honeybear. The decision to purchase him was, as Annette puts it, the best she ever made. He was not only beautiful, but was sound, of faultless temperament, and he passed these qualities along to his offspring. Annette herself had never been in the ring before, but Honeybear was well trained and took Best of Breed along with two points his first show. It took a full year to finish Honeybear's championship while his new owner learned to groom and handle a Pekingese, but he taught her well! As he was the beginning, and had brought so much pleasure, it was decided to use his name for the kennel—thus the identification Pekingese O'Honeybear.

Annette's next show dog, and an equally wise choice, was the lovely bitch she purchased from Inez Hankins in Arkansas. This was Hanez' Cherub of Me Mo, whom she had seen as a seven-month-old puppy and had never forgotten. Considering her the most beautiful puppy she had ever seen, Annette found it impossi-

Annette Borders's husband Tom holds his favorite of the Pekes, the lovely Ch. Papa's Penny O'Honeybear. The Borders and their Pekes live at Abilene, Texas.

ble to put this one out of her mind; when she was just over a year old, Annette finally succeeded in acquiring her.

Cherub, somewhere along the way, had decided that she really did not care for dog shows, so Annette bred her to Honeybear just before her second birthday. The results were exciting! There were six girls, four of whom became champions, and the fifth had acquired a major just before injuring an eye. Annette kept three of the girls from this litter; Champion Hanez' Jim Chin O'Honeybear, Champion Image O'Honeybear, and Hanez Farrah O'Honeybear. After producing two litters, Cherub did finish her championship by going Best of Breed over two specials on that same day.

Cherub's third litter was sired by a lovely male whom Annette was showing for Inez Hankins, named Hanez' Hsiao Cho Tu. From this litter, she kept Papa's Penny O'Honeybear, who easily

Rascal O'Honeybear taking Best of Breed from the classes in May 1985. Annette L. Borders, owner, Abilene, Texas.

won her title, taking Best of Breed and Group placements on the way.

Next, the Jamestown line was brought back into the breeding program with two males from Patricia G. Mullendore's Muhlins. These were Champion Muhlin Macho and Champion Muhlin Most Royal. Royal, known as Deja, was bred to Papa's Penny, from which came Annette Borders' very special Group winning girl, Mama's Beauty O'Honeybear.

Beauty was a litter of one, so there was no question that Annette would keep her. From the very first, her owner tells us, she truly had it all. At seven months, she took Puppy Sweepstakes at the Pekingese Club of Texas under judge John Brown and Reserve Winners Bitch from the Bred-by-Exhibitor Class under judge R. William Taylor. At eight months she took a four-point major at the Delta Pekingese Club in New Orleans. At nine months, she took Best in Sweepstakes at the Pekingese Club of Southern New Jersey under judge Michael Hill and first in the Bred-by-Exhibitor Class. She finished her championship, before reaching ten months old, by going Best of Breed over Group winning champions under judge Jane Kay, truly gaining her title in a most spectacular manner. As a special, she has consistently taken Best of Breed in very stiff competition, and has held her own in the Groups with wins and placements.

Annette Borders has spent, by now, a considerable bit of time studying and learning about Pekingese, and she is enjoying the fruits of her efforts a very great deal!

PALADIN

Paladin Pekingese Kennels were founded in New Orleans, Louisiana, in 1961, when Bob and Dottie Schuerch purchased a beautiful Peke bitch sired by Champion Lin Yutang of Westwinds. When it was decided to breed her, they went in search of an excellent male, and soon found themselves favorably impressed by the dogs belonging to Mrs. Betty Von Herr, and especially by her Orchid Lane's Wei-Ku, sired by the famous Champion St. Aubrey

Bob Schuerch with the handsome little dog Wendylou's Ku Kee who taught his owners the fun of show ring competition and was to sire champions for them.

Chickling of Caversham. Breeding their bitch to this dog, they found themselves with a male puppy, whom they named Wendylou's Ku Kee. They had not as yet selected their kennel name, and as their daughter, Wendy, was excited over the dogs, that seemed a good choice, at least for the time being.

When this puppy was a few months old, Dottie and Bob took him over to show the Von Herrs. Dottie says, "I'll always remember the look on Betty's face when she saw him." By the time they had left for home, Mrs. Von Herr had explained all about entering at dog shows, and the Schuerches had picked up her enthusiasm for the idea.

Ke Kee, shown by his very novice owners, went through almost to his championship when an ear infection forced him into retirement, leaving him with a decided tilt to his head. He did, however, make a name for himself as an especially successful sire. One of his sons was American and Canadian Champion Paladin's Peabody Pipsqueak, who gained his American title with ease, then going to Canada to do likewise under Nigel Aubrey Jones, R. William Taylor and Anne Rogers Clark. All three placed "Pippy" Best of Breed from the classes; thus he gained his Canadian title in three straight shows. Dottie comments, "This little dog was one of the highlights in our breeding program, for though we had many champions throughout the years, this one was very special."

Champion Paladin's Sneaky Pete is another favorite of the Schuerches. Although a different type from those normally produced at Paladin, the Schuerches were thrilled with his numerous important wins. He retired with a Best of Breed at the winter Pekingese Club of America Specialty under William Bergum, where he was handled by David Fitzpatrick.

The Schuerches have found their winning dogs especially exciting since theirs is a small kennel of between eight and ten dogs, including the veterans. Thus all receive the love and care on which Pekes thrive, and the owners gain the pleasure of really knowing and enjoying them.

An often-asked question to Dottie Schuerch over the years has been how they came to select Paladin as their kennel name. It is a French word meaning champion or hero, she explains. How appropriate.

Paladin Pekingese, along with the Schuerches, are now located in Ruffsdale, Pennsylvania.

← **Overleaf:**

Ch. Elpha Sun Arrhythmia at three years of age. Her record includes 40 Group placements, 10 group 1sts and a Specialty Best in Show. Retired and bred for the first time at three years, she whelped a litter of three without problems. Always bred and owner-handled by Doll and McGinnis, Elpha Sun Pekingese, Lakeland, Florida.

Overleaf: →

1. Am. Ch. Audrianne's Claymore Charm, Am. and Bda. Ch. Pasha of West Winds ex Am. Ch. Claymore Jezebel. Bred by Mrs. Robert L. Ballinger, Jr. Owned by Miss Audrey A. Atherton, Mentor, Ohio.

2. Ch. Audrianne's Midnight Magic, by Sambeau Ebony Shadow of Beyli ex Tino's Tini Tiko, was bred by Mrs. Frances E. Bright and is owned by Miss Audrey A. Atherton, Mentor, Ohio. Pictured taking Best of Opposite Sex at Erie K.C., June 1981.

3. Ch. Audrianne's Snow Shih-T'Sun, by Popa's Ta'Le Shih ex Presleen Li Ping, bred by Mrs. Sara J. Crown. Finished his title at Progressive Dog Club of Wayne county, April 1986. There are very few white male Pekingese Champions in the US, so owner Miss Audrey A. Atherton, Mentor, Ohio, is especially proud of "Nikki's" accomplishments.

4. Ch. Ber-Gum's Dee Oh Gee, a Group winning male bred, owned, and handled by William and Elaine Bergum, Ber-Gum's Pekingese, Ventura, California.

5. Ch. Topaz Lin of Ber-Gum, a Group winner and the Top Winning Pekingese Bitch of her era. Bred, owned, and handled by William and Elaine Bergum, Ber-Gum Pekingese, Ventura, California.

6. Ch. Briarcourt's Rule Britannia, by Ch. St. Aubrey Sunburst of Elsdon ex Camsue Kaylee, is the sire of Bob Jacobsen's Ch. Briarcourt's Coral Gable. Bred and owned by Mrs. Joan Mylchreest, Briarcourt Kennels, Yardley, Pennsylvania.

7. Brother-sister team take Best of Breed and Best of Opposite Sex at the Pekingese Club of America, March 1986. The dog on *left,* is Ch. Briarcourt's Coral Gable, owner-handled to Best in Specialty Show by David Fitzpatrick; the bitch, *on right,* owner-handled by Mrs. Joan Mylchreest.

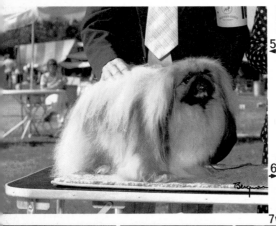

← **Overleaf:**

1. A proud and happy David Fitzpatrick sets his mighty little Pekingese Ch. Briarcourt's Coral Gable in the famous trophy on which he has just made a win. The Lasca McClure Halley Perpetual Trophy has been in competition through the Pekingese Club of America over many decades. The honor of having one's Peke's name engraved on it is a prestigious and highly valued one to all Peke owners, as it indicates that the dog has won the big Winter Specialty Show of the Pekingese Club. In the case of this dog, he has won two PCA Specialities within six months, having completed his championship by going Best of Breed from the classes, while still a puppy, at the September event in conjunction with Ox Ridge.

2. Ch. Briarcourt's Excelsior is now owned by Bob Jacobsen. Taking Best of Winners, breeder-handled by Mrs. Joan Mylchreest, at Westminster 1984. Excelsior has 10 Bests in Show and 45 Group 1st. By Ch. Briarcourt's Rule Britannia ex Ch. St. Aubrey Phantasy of Elsdon.

3. Ch. Ku Chellos Ditto Sing Lee, by Ch. Linsown Ku-Chello (UK import). Bred and owned by Irene Ruschaupt, this handsome dog is behind most of today's top winning Sing Lees. Robert Jacobsen, Sing Lee Pekingese, Point Reyes Station, California.

1. Ch. Koitown Wee Toni Tiger, by Bond's Hi Extra Terrestrial ex Glen Eden's Caro Lee. Bred by Evelyn Sommerfelt, owned by Mary L. Burke, Vancouver, Washington.

2. Ch. Burke's Rosy Star of Palacer, by Palacer Wang Li ex Koitown L'Dragon Twinkles, was bred by Justine M. Smith. Owned and shown by Mary Burke, Vancouver, Washington.

3. Ch. Cardee's Lil Teddy Hsiung, by Bar-Mee's You Chin Nee Chin ex Per-Mar's Sun-Lit Jade, is a multi-Group winner and Best in Show dog. Bred by Agnes R. Wilson and Gregory M. Robinson. Owner-handled by Carol Dee Blakeslee and Gregory M. Robinson, Yakima, Washington.

4. One of the "stars of the future," Ch. Candee's Samson of Kalila, owner-handled here by Carol Dee Blakeslee for herself and co-owner Gregory Robinson. By Ch. Fraser Manor San Yen ex Kan Pei's Kim Ling-Moth. Pictured winning Best of Breed, Inland Empire 1985.

5. Am. and Can. Ch. St. Aubrey Kenwong Moon Shadow. By Ch. Etive Copplestone Pu-Zen Juliard, one of the successful winners owned by Houston Carr and Peggy Dillard Carr, Carrhaven, Franklin, Tennessee.

6. Ch. Cee-Kae's Silver Rocket, bred and owned by Kim and Chuck Langley, Cee-Kae Pekingese, Galt, California. Handled by Lois Frank.

7. Ch. Carr's Moon Shadow Carbon, by Ch. St. Aubrey Kenwong Moon Shadow ex Knolland Dream Whip, winning the Delta Pekingese Specialty Show under judge Ed Jenner. This multi-Best in Specialty Show and Toy Group winner is the 100th champion, over 34 years, for owner Peggy Dillard Carr, Franklin, Tennessee.

8. Ch. Ai Kou Bentley of Cee Kae winning Best of Breed at the Pekingese Club of Central California Specialty, February 1986. Bred by Jean M. Thomas; owner-handled by Kim Langley, Galt, California.

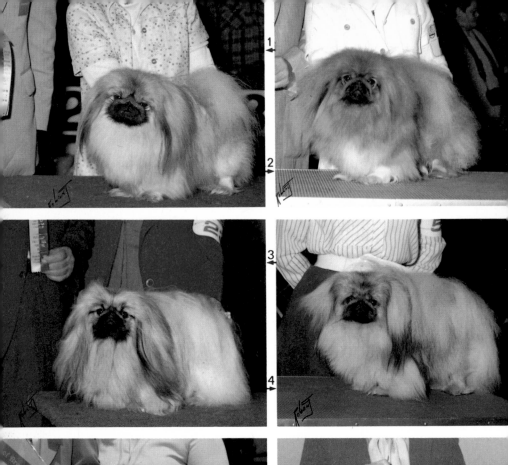

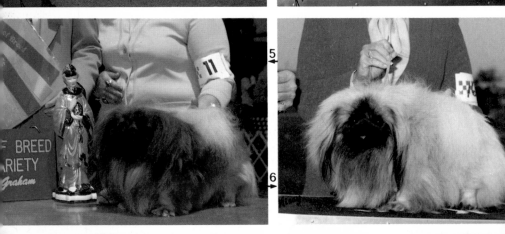

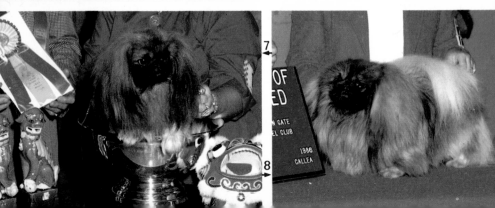

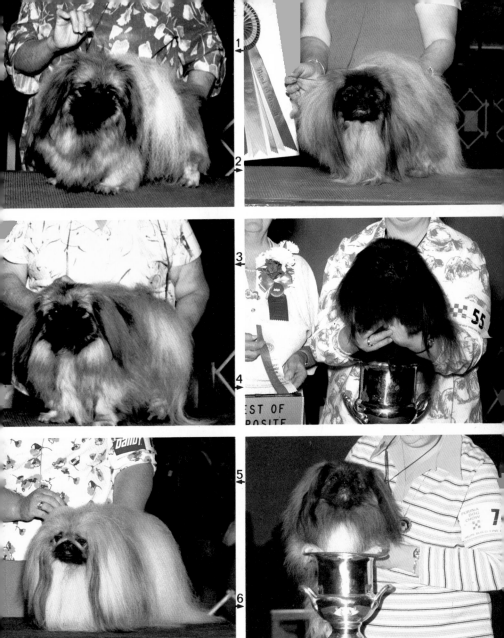

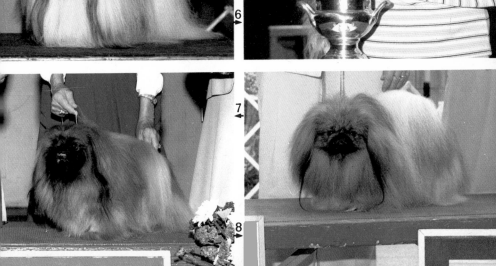

← **Overleaf:**

1. On the way to the title, Carlotta's Po Kee Tow by Ch. Ku Jin Superstar ex Dud-Lee's Lil Joe's Josie, was born in May 1984. Owned by Carlotta Curtis, Biloxi, Mississippi.

2. Am. and Can. Ch. St. Aubrey Yorklee Fanfare, a noted winner in the United States and Canada and sire of 15 champions. Owned by Houston and Peggy Dillard Carr, Carrhaven, Franklin, Tennessee. Pictured winning the Atlanta Pekingese Club Specialty, 1985.

3. Ch. Su Lyn's Maggie of Ja Noo's, by Dud-Lee's Fascinatun Perfectun ex Dud-Lee's Talisman's Su Lyn. Bred, owned, and handled by Carlotta Curtis, Biloxi, Mississippi.

4. Ch. Black Tia of Chambrae, taking Best of Opposite Sex at the Greater Pittsburgh Specialty in 1982, judged by Mrs. Geraldine Hess. Christine L. Hann, Chambrae Pekingese, Racine, Wisconsin.

5. Ch. Jamaican Rum of Chambrae, co-owned by Christine L. Hann and Patricia G. Mullendore, co-breeders. Christine L. Hann handled this Peke to Best of Breed under Ed Jenner. Chambrae Pekingese are at Racine, Wisconsin.

6. Ch. Kentucky Colonel Aristocrat, bred by Lil O'Daniel, owned and handled by Christine L. Hann, Racine, Wisconsin, posing in his trophy following an important Specialty Show victory.

7. Ch. Char-Min's Master Kings Pride winning the Toy Group for breeder-owner Mrs. Minnie Wisdom, Poplar Bluff, Missouri.

8. Ch. Char-Min's Kris of Tea Pot winning a Group 1st at Fort Smith, Arkansas, June 1982 for owner Mrs. Minnie Wisdom, Char-Min Kennels, Poplar Bluff, Missouri.

1. Ch. Char-Min's Troy of Shir Lees winning a Group placement at Southeast Arkansas K.C., June 1984. Mrs. Minnie Wisdom, owner, Char-Min Pekingese, Poplar Bluff, Missouri.

2. Ch. Randolph of Chinatown winning one of his multiple Bests in Show, Elm City Kennel Club 1985. Handled by Hernan Martinez for breeder-owner Mrs. Walter M. Jeffords, "Randy" has many Group wins and placements to his credit, including a Best of Breed at Westminster in 1983. By Ch. Fu Manchu of Chinatown ex Mingulay Rosalind.

3. Cassandra of Chinatown, one of the gorgeous bitches owned by Mrs. Walter M. Jeffords, Chinatown Pekingese, Andrews Bridge, Pennsylvania, and New York City.

4. Ch. Ching of Chinatown, homebred Best in Show winner owned by Mrs. Walter M. Jeffords, Andrews Bridge, Pennsylvania, and New York City. Ching is a son of Ch. Mi Kwee Jai Lee of Lon-Du ex Ch. Fortune Cookie of Chinatown. Born August 1981. Handled by Hernan Martinez.

5. Ch. Chu Lai's Gussie of Ding Ho finishing his title. Bred and owned by Patricia and Charles Farley and Frances Kukla. Handled by Pat Farley. Chu Lai Pekingese are at Norton, Massachusetts.

6. Ch. Claymore Dulcinea was Best of Opposite Sex at Westminster K.C. two years successively. Bred by Mrs. Robert Ballinger. Owned at that time by Miss Deborah Sprout.

7. Ch. Sabrina Fair of Claymore, Winners Bitch at Pekingese Club of America in September 1976. Bred, owned, and handled by Mrs. Robert Ballinger, Palm Beach, Florida.

8. Ch. Claymore's Cinnamon bun, whose more that 50 Group placements and three Best in Show awards brought him to No. 2 Pekingese during his brief show career. His tragic death one week after his third Best in Show was a sad and heartbreaking experience for his breeder-owner-handler Mrs. Robert Ballinger, Claymore Kennels.

107

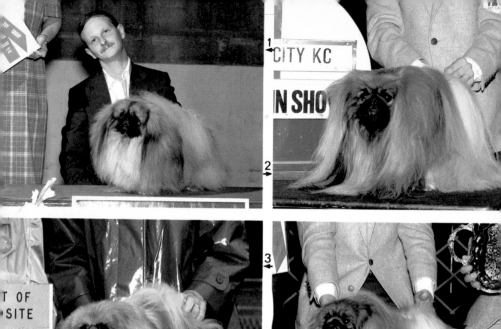

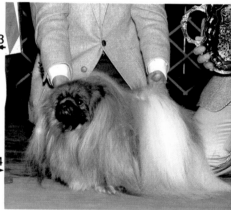

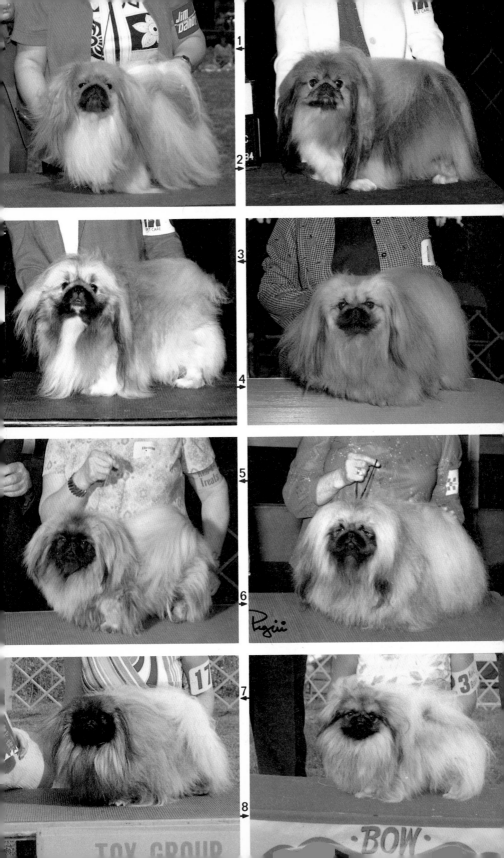

← Overleaf:

1. Ch. Chu Lai's Duster finishing his title with a major in 1981. Handled by Pat Farley; owned by Chu Lai Pekingese, Patricia and Charles Farley, Norton, Massachusetts.

2. Ch. Mike Mar's Dutch Master, bred by Michael Wolf, by Bracewell Giacomo (Ch. Wild Venture of Lotusgrange–Caversham Rebecca of Bracewell) ex the Duchess of Chyanchy (Eng. Ch. Chyanchy Ah Yang of Jamestown–Lady Loanna), is one of the winning Pekes owned by Margaret H. Stamey, Winston-Salem, North Carolina.

3. Mike Mar's Destiny, by Bracewell Giacomo ex Mike-Mar's China Doll, was born October 1983, bred by Michael Wolf, and is owned by and winning well for Margaret H. Stamey, Winston-Salem, North Carolina.

4. Multiple Best in Show Am. and Can. Ch. Masterpiece Zodiac of Dud-Lee's, bred and handled by Mrs. W.L. (Ruby) Dudley until purchased for Mike-Mar Pekingese by Mrs. Walter Jeffords and Mr. Michael Wolf for whom he continued his prestigious career in the East.

5. Ch. Khi-Yu-Ki-Ku's Khi Lyn of Dud-Lee's completed title in eight shows and is the dam of six champions, two of them Group-winning littermates. She is Top Producer, Kennel Review System, 1975 and a Silver Certificate Top Producing Dam, Phillips System. Bred, owned, and handled by Ruby Dudley, Creston, Iowa.

6. Am. and Can. Ch. Dud-Lee's Ku-Lyn Masterpiece, No. 1 Pekingese in 1979, bred, owned, and handled by Mrs. W.L. (Ruby) Dudley, Creston, Iowa.

7. Eng. and Am. Ch. Coughton Sungable of Perryacre making one of his multiple Toy Group wins. Co-owners are Elaine Rigden (handled for herself) and Mrs. Amanda West, Wadsworth, Ohio.

8. Ch. El Acre Wang Lu, bred and owned by Vivian Longacre and handled by Elaine Rigden. El Acre is one of our oldest Pekingese kennels where many outstanding dogs were produced.

110

Overleaf: →

1. Am. and Can. Ch. Bar-Mee's Tea-Cup going Best in Specialty Show as Josto Candy Floss takes Winners Bitch and Best of Opposite Sex at the Evergreen State Pekingese Specialty in 1986. Tea-Cup, *on right*, handled by Miss Sylvia Harben. Both Pekes owned by Robin and Bobbie Fraser, Seattle, Washington.

2. Ch. St. Aubrey Beeswing of Elsdon started his fabulous show career in the United States after a brilliant one as a puppy in Canada, by earning Best of Winners at Westminster in 1983, handled by Luc Boileau for owner Edward B. Jenner, Knolland Farm Kennels. Bred by R. William Taylor and Nigel Aubrey Jones, "Peter" is a son of Ch. St. Aubrey Laparata Dragon ex St. Aubrey Honey Bee of Elsdon.

3. Mary Ann and Bob Jackson (Mr. and Mrs. Robert M. Jackson), owners of Fourwinds Pekingese, their arms full with Ch. Cassidy, Ch. Nicholas, Ch. Gemma and Ch. Cookie.

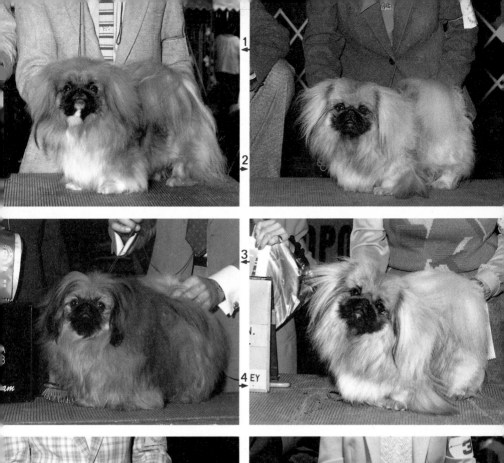

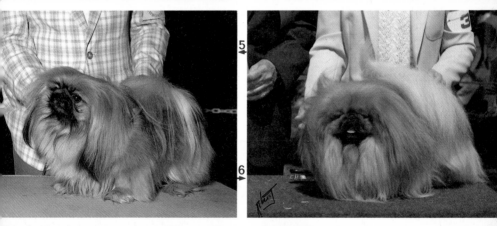

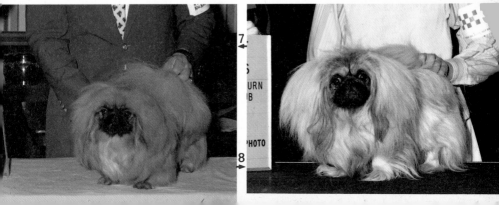

← Overleaf:

1. The homebred Ch. Boni of Elegance, by Ch. Rodari the Dragon of Lon Du ex Tazzaria of Elegance, has numerous Best of Opposite Sex awards to her credit over other champions. Bred and owned by Leon and Donna Wolfgang, Pekingese of Elegance, Brookville, Pennsylvania. Pictured here in June 1985.

2. This is the sensational homebred, Group winning Puppy, Ch. Picasso's Bosco of Elegance who gained title in March 1986. A homebred class dog, Bosco has certainly made his presence felt at an early age. He is by Ch. Pascan Picasso ex Tazzarea of Elegance, and was bred and is owned by Leon and Donna Wolfgang, Brookville, Pennsylvania. Elaine Rigden handles Bosco.

3. Ch. Elpha Sun the Idolmaker, by Am. and Can. Ch. St. Aubrey Laparata Imperial ex Char-Min's Miss Amy Lou. Bred and owned by Doll and McGinnis, Lakeland, Florida. Pictured finishing title at age eight months.

4. This handsome youngster, a Group winner from the clases, completed title in no time flat to become Ch. Picasso's Bosco of Elegance. Bred and owned by Leon and Donna Wolfgang, Brookville, Pennsylvania. Handled by Elaine Rigden. He is a son of Ch. Pascan Picasso ex Tazzarea of Elegance, and knowledgeable experts see a bright future for him.

5. Elpha Sun Tsunami (Amy II), close to title, is by Ch. St. Aubrey Laparata Imperial ex Char-Min's Miss Amy Lou. Owned by Rita Colette of Arleta, California, bred at Elpha Sun by Doll and McGinnis.

6. Am. and Can. Ch. Han-Bee's Jackpot Starfire (by Ch. Han-Bee's Jackpot Bingo ex Ch. Diamond Jim's Kopi of Han-Bee) is a Specialty Show winner in both Canada and the United States with numerous other Best of Breed, plus Group placements, to his credit. Robin and Bobbie Fraser owners, Fraser-Manor Pekingese, Seattle, Washington.

7. Ch. Hatamen Queen of Hearts winning Reserve from the Puppy Class at the Pekingese Club of America March Specialty. Owned by Edward J. Jenner, handled by Luc Boileau.

8. Hatamen High Flaunting taking second major at Lewiston-Ashburn K.C. in 1985. Owned and handled by Hetty Orringer, Southborough, Massachusetts.

Overleaf: →

1. Ch. Jay's Joker of Fourwinds winning Best of Breed, Central Ohio K.C., November, 1984. Owned by Mr. and Mrs. Robert M. Jackson, Fourwinds Pekingese, Seneca, Illinois. Handled by Mrs. Jackson.

2. Ch. Pendenrah Nicholas on the day he completed title, May, 1981, Ft. Wayne, Indiana. Owned by Mr. and Mrs. Robert M. Jackson, Fourwinds Pekingese, Seneca, Illinois.

3. Ch. Hope's Firecracker Sparkler, one of the excellent Pekingese representing Hope Hartenbach, St. Louis, Missouri, in keenest competition. Here winning Best of Breed and Group 1st at Belle City K.C. in 1986.

4. The English importation, Ch. Tirakau Repeat Design, became a champion quickly after her arrival here. Personally selected in England by Hope Hartenbach, St. Louis, Missouri, for her kennel.

5. Su-Con Boxcar winning the American-bred Class, Pekingese Club of America 1984. Owned and handled by Mary Jo O'Leary, HoToi Pekingese, Endicott, New York.

6. The Sun King of Ho Toi taking Winners Dog at Troy K.C. 1985. This is an excellent example of the Pekes that are bred, owned, and handled by Mary Jo O'Leary, HoToi Pekingese, Endicott, New York.

7. Ch. Jomar Sunni Bear, by Ch. Jomar Teddy Bear ex Jomar Kaiti Kan, winning the Toy Group at Calcasieu K.C. in 1986. Handled by Walter Green for owner Margaret Zuber, Jomar Pekingese, West Monroe, Louisiana.

8. Ch. Jomar Ruffles and Flourishes taking points towards the title in October 1983. Owned by Margaret Zuber, West Monroe, Louisiana and Betty Claire Peacock, Dumas, Arkansas.

115

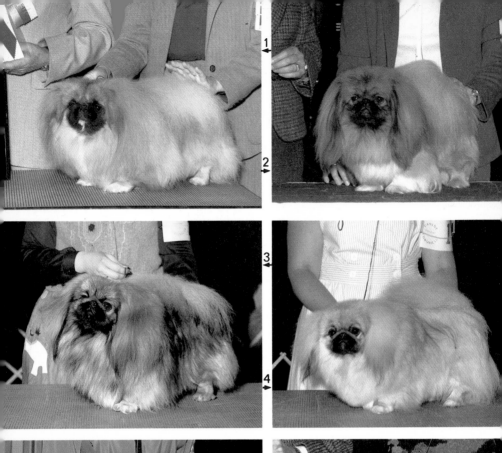

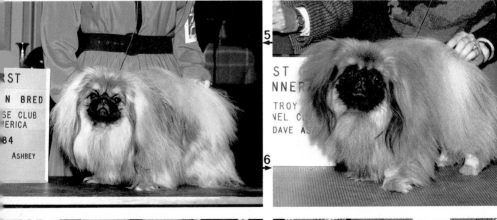

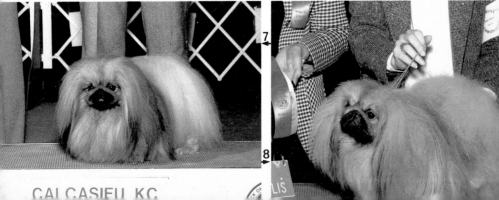

← **Overleaf:**

1. Ch. Judcilla's Elite of Hi Wins, by Jalna's Gabellero O'Judcilla ex Judcilla Acadiana Elegance, was bred by Priscilla Jackson and is handled and co-owned by Hiram Stewart, Kenner, Louisiana. Pictured winning one of his Best of Breed awards.

2. Ch. Hi Win's T'son Tan, by Ch. Welkins Wee T'Sonking ex Ch. Ku Jin Little Miss Muffet, was bred by Hiram Stewart and Catherine Bond. Owned by Hiram Stewart, Hi Win's Pekingese, Kenner, Louisiana.

3. This is The Wun Tu Watch of Katering, who with several points towards his title, should be finished soon. He is by Ch. Kalafrana Jay's Joseph at Toydom ex Lon-Du Cassandra. Owned by Katering Pekingese, Gwenn Southmayd, Boring, Oregon.

4. Ch. Lori Ann of Tai Shan finishing title with a Best of Breed for HoToi Pekingese, Mary Jo O'Leary, Endicott, New York.

5. Wun Tu Ku Ki of Katering gained her first major at just six month of age. By Katering's I'll Take it Black ex Rok-N-Row-Dee of Katering. Owned by Gwen Southmayd, Boring, Oregon.

6. Homebred Ch. Knolland Lady Jane winning Best Puppy in Breed under judge Lillian Snooks, who came to Canada from England to judge this Pekin Palace Dog Association assignment in 1985. Luc Boileau handled for Edward B. Jenner.

7. Ch. Knolland Beeswax, homebred son of Beeswing, winning the Derbytown Pekingese Club Match Show in May 1984. Mrs. Walter Jeffords, owner of Chinatown Pekingese, was the judge. Jerry Voyles presented the trophy. Jerry and his wife Edna have been interested in Pekingese for many years, and Mrs. Voyles, who is now a busy judge, was formerly a professional handler and a Pekingese breeder. Luc Boileau handled this exciting youngster for Edward B. Jenner.

8. Famed homebred multi-Best in Show winner Champion Knolland Tiger Rag following a Best at Michiana in 1982. One of the outstanding homebreds produced at Knolland Farm. Edward B. Jenner, owner.

Overleaf: ⟶

1. Ch. Aubrey Laparata Dragon, an all-time Top Pekingese sire and a multi-Best in Show winner, is here winning Best in Show at Channel Cities. Handled by Luc Boileau for owner Edward B. Jenner, Knolland Farm.

2. The late G.W. Cobb, noted Texas Pekingese breeder and enthusiast, is pictured here with one of his famed winners, Ch. Mr. Tim Bo of Ling Tu. Mr. Cobb was extremely well liked by the Texas Fancy, and his dogs were noted for quality. He is missed by his many friends.

3. A real "field day" for the Lon-Du Pekingese. Mrs. E.W. Tipton awards Best of Breed to Ch. Rodari The Dragon at Lon-Du for Best of Breed as his son and daughter account for Winners Dog and Winners Bitch. Arlon Duit and the Lon-Du Pekingese are at Monticello, Iowa.

1

2

CHANNEL CITY

3

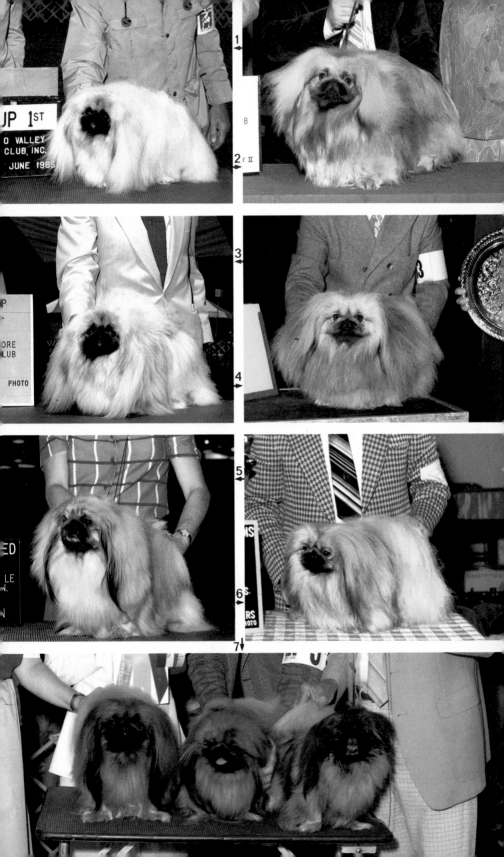

← Overleaf:

1. The multiple Group and Best in Show winning bitch, Ch. Velspring's Velvetina, by English and American Ch. Belknap Kalafrana Caspar ex Colhamdorn Hazel of Velspring, was bred by Mrs. S.N. Stickley and is owned by Mrs. Walter Maynard, Southampton, New York.

2. Here is Michael Wolf's youngster Mike-Mar's China Dragon winning points on his title with Best of Winners from the classes at the Pekingese Club of America Specialty in 1981. Bred and owned by Mr. Wolf, co-ownership in "Puff" was later acquired by Mrs. Alan Robson and with his breeder handling, China Dragon became the Top American-bred Pekingese of all time with 49 Bests in Show and 168 Group 1sts. He was the Ken-L Biskit Top Toy for 1983.

3. Ch. Velspring's Velvetina, the multiple Best in Show winning bitch who has enjoyed so exciting and successful a show career under William Trainor's handling for Mrs. Walter Maynard, Southampton, New York.

4. Ch. Zodiac Masterpiece of Dud-Lee, winner of eight times Best in Show and 53 Toy Groups. Michael Wolf handled for himself and Mrs. Walter F. Jeffords.

5. Ch. Mi Gems Soc It To Um, C.D. winning one of his five Bests of Breed from the classes. Owned by Jean Crossley and Delores Vanek, bred by Eleanor Lamb, West Palm Beach, Florida.

6. Ch. Lon-Du Valentino completed title in 1985. A son of Lon-Du Casanova, Valentino started his career by winning Best Puppy in Match at the Greater Pittsburgh Pekingese Club. Owned and handled by Arlon Duit, Lon-Du Pekingese, Monticello, Iowa. pictured at North Central Illnois Specialty, where he went from the Open Dog Class to Best of Breed, June 1985.

7. *Left*, Ch. Elksway Enticer of Mi Gems (sire) *center*, Ch. Mi Gems Honorable Simmet (son), and *right*, Kay Tee Did of Mi Gems (dam): Best of Breed, Best of Winners, and Best of Opposite Sex, respectively. Owned by Eleanor Lamb, West Palm Beach, Florida, who comments "We didn't win the Group that day. but our group won!"

122

1. "Puff," the China Dragon! This is Ch. Mike Mar's China Dragon, winning Best in Show at Back Mountain K.C. Michael Wolf is breeder-handler of this notable dog whom he co-owns with Mrs. Alan Robson, Glenmoore, Pennsylvania. "Puff" was the Top Toy in the Nation for 1983, and is the Top American-bred Pekingese of all time.

2. Ch. Mudlin Midas at age two years. This Peke by Ch. Belknap Little Nugget ex Temper Midnite Specialness is a multiple Specialty Best in Show winner and the sire of two champions. Bred, owned, and handled by Patricia G. Mullendore, Oswego, Illinois.

3. Ch. Mugiechun Royal Chinbi winning four points to finish title, and Best of Breed over two specials at Santa Ana Valley K.C., September, 1984. Owner-handled by Miss Sandy Wheat, Mugiechun Pekingese, Phoenix, Arizona.

4. Ch. Belknap Little Nugget winning the Pekingese Club of Alabama Specialty in Novermber 1983. By Eng. Ch. Ch. Belknap Eldoradom he is the winner of multiple Specialty Bests of Breed, and the sire of nine champions and one holder of a C.D. degree. Mrs. Geraldine Hess, former President of the Pekingese Club of America, was judge. Mrs. Patricia Mullendore owner, Muhlin Pekingese, Oswego, Illinois.

5. Ch. Prima Fabulous Solo winning a Toy Group 2nd in 1985. Solo is by Ch. Dud-Lee's Khi-Lyn's Fabulous One (sire of nine champions). Bred and owned by Barbara and Bob Streemke; handled by Barbara.

6. Ch. Paladin's Sneaky Pete made a fine show record for his owner, Dottie Schuerch, Paladin Kennels, Ruffsdale, Pennsylvania.

7. Ch. Mama's Beauty O'Honeybear winning the Toy Group at Panhandle K.C. in 1985. Annette Borders, owner, Abilene, Texas.

8. Hanez Jin Chin of Honeybear at eight months old taking Winners Bitch, Best of Opposite Sex and Best Puppy in Show at the Pekingese Club of Texas. Jin Chin (born January 1980) was sired by Ch. Manticore Honeybear. Handled by Annette L. Borders for owner Inez G. Hankins, Pleasant Plains, Arkansas.

123

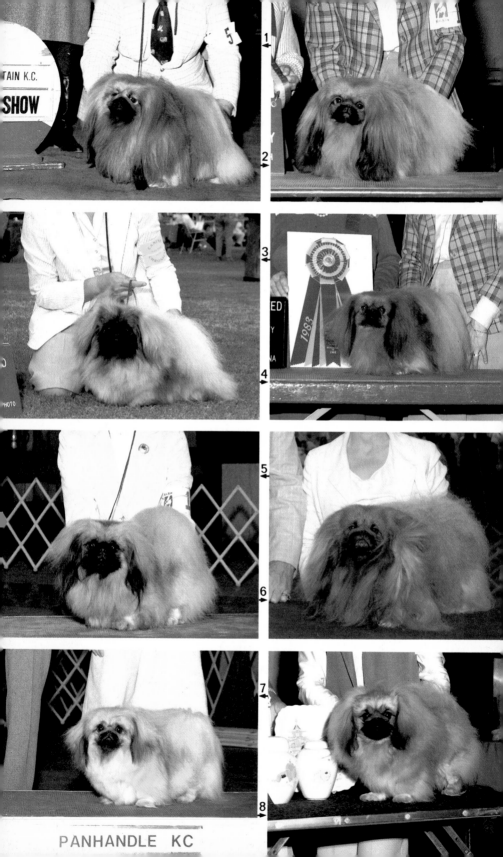

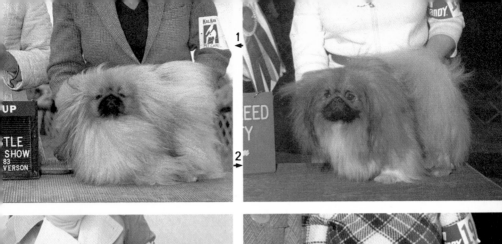

← Overleaf:

1. Ch. Lotusgrange Another Venture has acquired an imposing list of achievements that includes Best of Show all breeds, Best in Specialty Show, and multiple Toy Groups. Mrs. Ruthe Painter owner, Panora Pekingese, Irwin, Pennsylvania. Elaine Rigden handler.

2. Ch. Wild Venture of Lotusgrange, sire of 14 champions, is himself a son of the noted Eng. Ch. Yu Yang of Jamestown. Owned by Mrs. Ruthe Painter, Panora Pekingese, Irwin, Pennsylvania. Handled by Elaine Rigden.

3. Ch. Jon Jo of Etive took a 5-point major, under Jack Watts at a Specialty Show, his first time in the American show ring. The following week he finished and won Best in Show from the classes. Elaine Rigden handled for owner Mrs. Ruthe Painter, Panora Pekingese, Irwin, Pennsylvania.

4. Ch. Beaupres Wonderview Prisca pictured on his first weekend in America gaining points towards his title handled by Elaine Rigden for owner Mrs. Ruthe Painter, Panora Pekingese, Irwin, Pennsylvania. The sire of 16 champions!

5. *Left to right*, R. William Taylor of St. Aubrey-Elsdon fame, judging the Pekingese Club of America Specialty; Mrs. Walter M. Jeffords and Mr. Michael Wolf, co-owners of the winner, Ch. Quilkin the Stringman, who is posing in the Pekingese Club of America's Perpetual Trophy for Best of Breed. Stringman won this Specialty in three occasions. Mr. Wolf handled for himself and Mrs. Jeffords.

Overleaf: →

1. Ch. Peacock Pu Ying Poppit, by Ai Kou Bell Boi ex Ch. Peacock's Lady Keiko of Kade, taking Winners Bitch and Best of Opposite Sex on the way to the title, Birmingham, Alabama, Easter Sunday 1984. Bred, owned, and handled by Betty Clair Peacock, Dumas, Arkansas.

2. Ch. Ai Kou Myrddin Emrys winning Best of Breed, Oklahoma City K.C., April 1982. Handler/owner Betty Claire Peacock, Dumas, Arkansas. Breeder/co-owner Jean M. Thomas. By Ch. Ai Kou Bravo ex Ai Kou O'Mai.

3. Ch. Prisca's Rip Cord of Peke-A-Toi winning Best of Breed at South Hills K.C. in November 1981. Evelyn A. Magun, owner-handler, Peke-A-Toi Kennels, Smithfield, Pennsylvania.

4. Ch. Peke-A-Toi's Venture Domique winning Best of Breed at New Castle K.C. in May 1981, owner-handled by Evelyn A. Magun, Peke-A-Toi Kennels, Smithfield, Pennsylvania.

5. Hope Hartenbach (*left*) with Ch. Balerina's Dallas Cowboy; Lorraine Scheiblauer with Ch. Hope's Cardinal Celebration; and Brenda Scheiblauer with Hope's Just a Tuppence, full sister to Celebration. Here pictured accepting their awards at the Pekingeese Club of America 1985 Specialty from judge Miss Iris de la Torre Bueno. All three Pekes belong to Hope Hartenbach, St. Louis , Missouri.

127

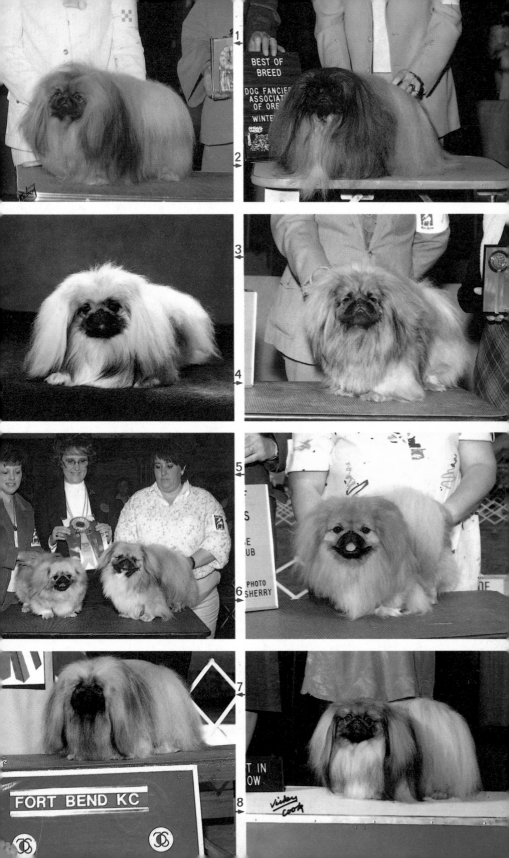

← Overleaf:

1. Ch. Wunsum Ko-Lee of Pickway winning Best in Show in 1979, owner-handled by Mrs. Bessie V. Pickens, Pickway Pekingese, Portland, Oregon.

2. Ch. Japeke Shogun of Pickway in 1986. Handled by Steve Arnold. Co-bred by Bessie Pickens and Marjory Nye White, this great dog has had a very exciting show career.

3. Ch. Mugiechun St. Aubrey Sajoewin, by Ch. Mugie's St. Aubrey Dragonwind ex Ch. St. Aubrey Maydrena of Elsdon. Bred by Satoka Wheat, co-owner with Dee and Richard Creighton, Granby, Connecticut. Ira Nozik photo.

4. Ch. Richdee's Tien-Yin Lilbit, by Ch. Dragonwyck of Yoney ex Nightingale of Shangrilla, has multiple Bests of Breed and Group placements to his credit. Owned by Dorothy and Richard Creighton, Granby, Connecticut. Terence Childs, handler.

5. Ch. Rosewood's Mystic Warrior (*right*), bred, owned, and handled by Deborah Sprouse, Warminster, Pennsylvania. Completing title here at Saw Mill K.C. in March 1986, under breeder-judge Kathleen Kolbert, by going through to Best of Breed from the classes. Tart A' Ki Wi (*left*), age ten months, Warrior's daughter, handled by breeder/owner Bonnie Rahmer, wins her first point and Best of Opposite Sex to her sire.

6. Rosewood's Jade Dragon taking Best of Winners on the way to championship. Bred and handled by Deborah Sprouse, co-owner with William H. Sullivan, Warminster, Pennsylvania.

7. Ch. Briarcourt's Excelsior, whose growing list of important victories has reached 10 All-breed Bests in Show, two Specialty Bests in Show and 43 Group 1sts, all owner-handled by J. Robert Jacobsen, Sing Lee Pekingese, Point Reyes Station, California. Bred by Mrs. Joan Mylecreest, Excelsior was one of America's Top Toys for 1985 and 1986. Pictured winning Best in Show at Ft. Bend K.C., April 1985.

8. Ch. Charles Raffles Jubilation Sing Lee, bred and owned by J. Robert Jacobsen, Point Reyes Station, California, is an all-breed Best in Show and multiple Specialty winner. Handled by Janet Allen to Best in Show for Mr. Jacobsen. Jubilation is by Ch. Sungarth Raffles Sing Lee by Ch. Dockleaf's Ming Cherry Sing Lee.

Overleaf: →

1. Belknap Bounteous was imported in 1985 from breeder Mrs. T.W. Horn. She is a granddaughter of the late Eng. Ch. Belknap Nero and the Top Producing sire Eng. Ch. Belknap Bravo. Tom and Kathy Masilla owners, New Orleans, Louisiana. Handler, Hiram Stewart.

2. Ch. Muhlin Madonna takes a Group placement at Greenville in 1985. Daughter of Ch. Belknap Little Nugget, this bitch is one of the current "stars" handled by Hiram Stewart for owners Kathy and Tom Masilla, New Orleans, Louisiana. She is a Specialty winner along with Group placements and other honors.

3. Ch. Vandor's Pandora, daughter of Group winning Ch. Ho-Toe of Fraser Manor. Bred by Dorothy Tyndall, Pandora produced two litters for owner Kathy Masilla before gaining her title with three majors. Santaverdi Pekingese, the Masillas, New Orleans, Louisiana.

4. Ch. Tomee Choo T'Sai Wen is an important little dog from the Santaverdi Pekingese owned by Tom and Kathy Masilla, New Orleans, Louisiana.

5. Ch. Bel-Mar Marina, dam of seven champions, foundation bitch at Sutton Place Kennels owned by Don Sutton and Steve Keating, Dallas, Texas. Marina is by Bennie of Troy ex Bel-Mar Bamboo.

6. Ch. Toimanor Elizabeth Anne is the newest champion at Toimanor Kennels. Owned by Audrey Drake, Janet Drake Oxford, and Vicki Martin Caliendo. By Ch. Charmin Jason of Toimanor ex Toimanor Lil Toi Dragon.

7. Ch. Su-Ke Lu of Sutton Place, by Ch. Wie Fu's Tiffany's Star Shine ex Ch. Bel-Mar Marina, homebred owned by Don Sutton and Steve Keating, Sutton Place Pekingese, Dallas, Texas.

8. Ch. Charmin Jason of Toimanor, America's Top Winning Pekingese for 1983 and 1984, Best in Show and Best in Specialty Show. Jason retired September 1984, six months after this photo was made. The Drake's Toimanor Kennels are at Fayetteville, Arkansas.

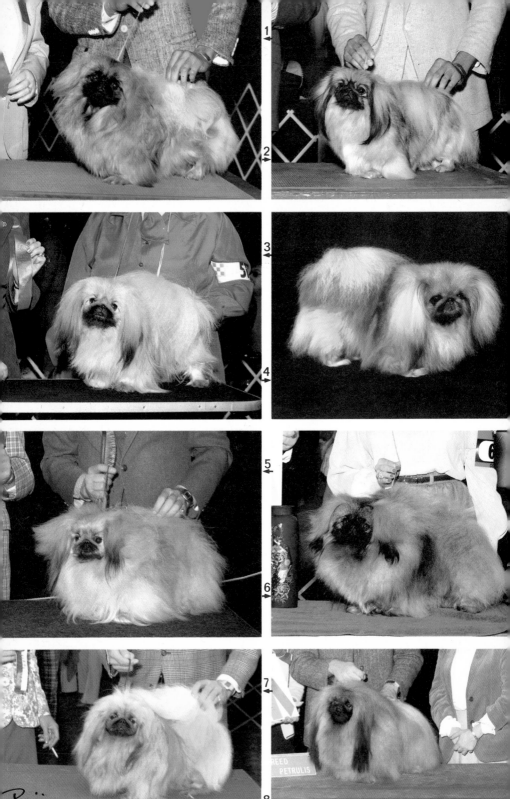

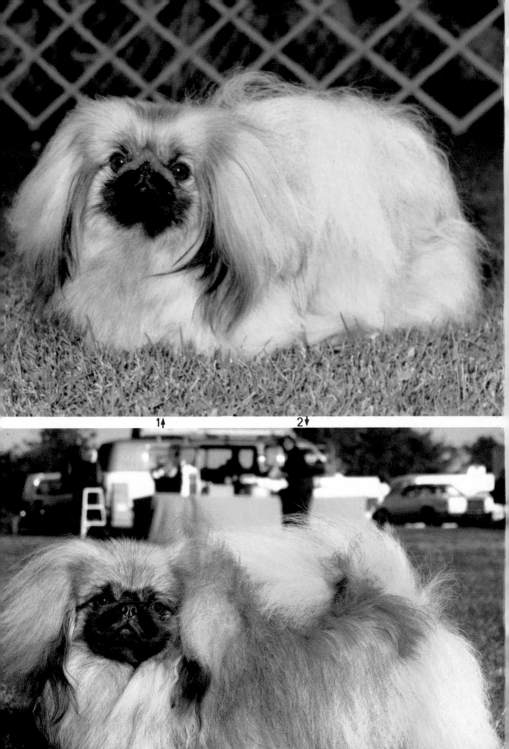

1↑ 2↓

← Overleaf:

1. Am. and Can. Ch. Lingling Gypsy Sue, Canadian Best in Show winner; Toy Group winner in the United States; and Challenge Certificate winner in Australia. Imported and owned by R. William Taylor, Montreal, Quebec, Canada.

2. Am. and Can. Ch. St. Aubrey Bumble Bee of Elsdon, bred by R. William Taylor. One of nine champion offspring of Can. Ch. St. Aubrey Honey Bee of Elsdon.

Overleaf: →

1. Ch. September Morn of Chambrae, bred, owned, and handled by Christine L. Hann, Racine, Wisconsin.

2. Ch. Claymore Dulcinea (*left*) with her son, age six months, who grew up to become Ch. Rosewood's Sea Dragon. Owned by Rosewood's Pekingese, Deborah Sprouse and William M. Sullivan, Warminster, Pennsylvania.

1↑ 2↓

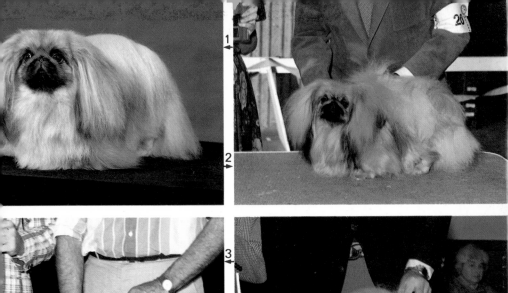

1

2

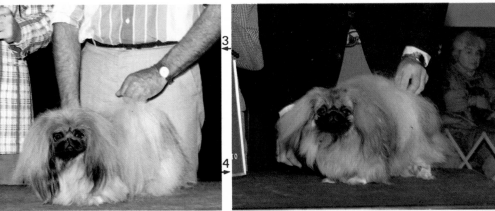

3

4

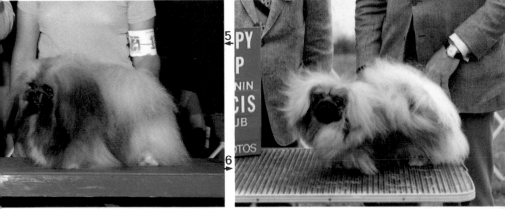

5

6

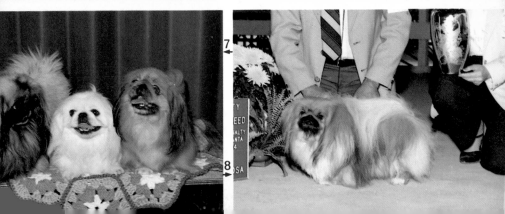

7

8

← Overleaf:

1. Am. and Can. Ch. St. Aubrey Dragonora of Elsdon, Top Winning Pekingese Bitch of all time in the United States. Bred by R. William Taylor, Montreal, Quebec, Canada. Dragonora was Best in Show at the Westminster
K.C. in 1982, one of only two Pekingese (and the only Pekingese bitch)
ever to have received this honor at America's most prestigious dog show.
Owned by Mrs. Ann Snelling, Ottawa, Canada. Handled throughout her
career in the United States by William Trainor.

2. Ch. St. Aubrey Romany of Elsdon, son of Am. and Can. Ch. Lingling Gypsy
Sue and sired by Can. Ch. St. Aubrey Dragonfly of Elsdon. Bred by Mr. R.
William Taylor, now owned by Miss Carol Hollands in Michigan, Romany is
pictured winning a Group. Handled by Mr. Nigel Aubrey Jones, Montreal.

3. Am. and Can. Ch. Gossip at St. Aubrey winning the Toy Group at Club
Canin de L'Estrie in August 1983 under judge Sandy Schwartz. Gossip
went on to take Best in Show that day owner-handled by R. William Taylor,
St. Aubrey-Elsdon, Montreal, Quebec, Canada.

4. Can. Ch. St. Aubrey Humming Bee of Elsdon, bred by R. William Taylor.
Campaigned by Mrs. Ann Snelling and later to become the property of Mrs.
Fortune Roberts, Bronxville, New York.

5. Am. and Can. Ch. St. Aubrey Yu Tong of Elsdon is owned by Frank Tingley, Charlotte, North Carolina, was bred by R. William Taylor, and was
handled by Eleanor Lamb at Central Florida in 1984.

6. Can. Ch. Tittle Tattle at St. Aubrey, daughter of Ch. St. Aubrey Dragonfly
of Elsdon and litter sister to American Ch. Gossip. Owner-handled by R.
William Taylor, Montreal, Quebec, she is winning a Canadian Puppy Toy
Group here.

7. This photo dates back to the days when the Western Pennsylvania K.A.,
during the 1970s, sponsored a series of mall exhibitions as a form of public
relations for their dog show. These three Peke participants are Aquarius,
Frosty Mist and Miss Nippy, all owned and shown by their owners, Tom
and Margie Harvey, Tom-Mar-A Pekingese, North Huntington, Pennsylvania.

8. Ch. Windmere's Blazing Dragon, Best of Breed, Pekingese Club of Georgia
Specialty, April 1984. Bred by Joy Thoms, "Blaze" is owned by Malcolm
Moore and Dr. Bowman, Merrimac Pekingese.

1. Ch. Win-Sox of Tom-Mar-A, by Ch. St. Aubrey's Micklee Twee Jin ex Tim-Mar-A's Miss Kiss of Kantu. This lovely bitch finished title at age 21 months in May 1981. Owned by Mr. and Mrs. T.V. Harvey, North Huntington, Pennsylvania.

2. *Left to right*: Ch. Japeke Shogun of Pickway, Mar-Pat Simon of Pickway, and Jai-Me of Pickway making a "clean sweep" of Peke awards on the day. The owner-handlers were Bessie Pickens, owner-founder of Pickway Kennels; and Steve and Judy Arnold, who have joined forces with her and who plan on continuing the Pickway lines when Mrs. Pickens, who is increasingly engrossed with her judging, decides to retire as a breeder. Pickway Pekingese are at Portland, Oregon.

3. Ch. Muhlin Magician of Wyn-D-Hill by Ch. Muhlin Boogaloo ex Ch. Belknap Cara, winning Best of Breed at Chenango Valley in 1982. Owner-handled by Mary McCracken, Jersey Shore, Pennsylvania.

4. Ch. Windemere's Well-Lee Fu Yong winning a Group 1st on his way to Best in Show, Victoria, British Columbia, Canada in 1974. Ranked No. 7 Pekingese in 1974. Joy Thoms, owner, Windemere Pekingese, Molalla, Oregon.

5. Ch. Wyn-D-Hill's Magician's Secret, by Ch. Muhlin Magician of Wyn-D-Hill ex Wyn-D-Hill's Magic Mist, bred and owned by Mary McCracken, Jersey Shore, Pennsylvania. Handled by Monica McCracken.

6. Ch. Windemere's Tzu-Lu Treasure, by Ch. Windemere's Stardust Fu Yong ex a daughter of the English import, Alderbourne Prince Tzu Lu. Handled by John Thoms, Rogue Valley K.C. 1984. Owned by Joy Thoms, Molalla, Oregon.

7. Ch. Knolland Dragonette winning the final points to the title at Santa Barbara 1985 under Finnish judge Rainer Voorinen. Edward B. Jenner breeder-owner; Luc Boileau handler.

8. At his last show for 1985, Ch. St. Aubrey Beeswing of Elsdon took one more step toward the 1985 record which made him the Top Winning Pekingese in the Nation that year. Here winning Best in Show at Skokie Valley under Mrs. Dorothy Welsh. Handled by Luc Boileau for owner Edward B. Jenner, Knolland Farm.

139

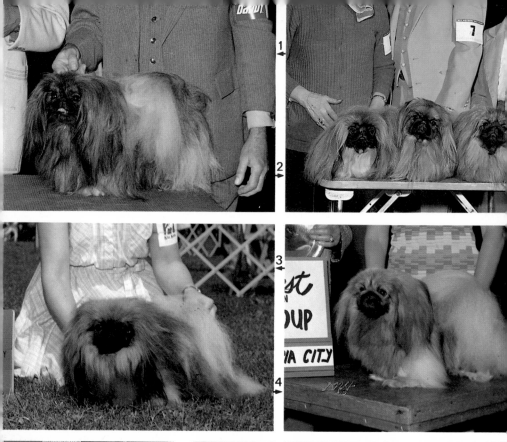

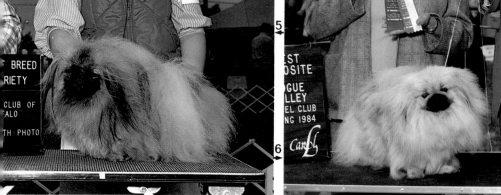
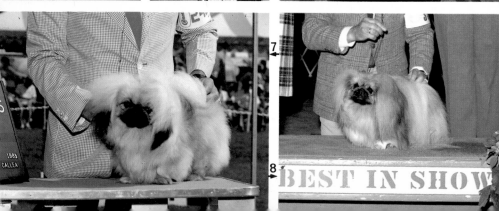

1↑ 2↓

← **Overleaf:**

1. Ch. Tiffany of Chambrae, bred, owned, and handled by Christine L. Hann, Chambrae Pekingese, Racine, Wisconsin.

2. Ch. Jomar Teddy Bear, sire of Ch. Jomar Sunni Bear, by Ch. Muhlin Mai O'Mai ex Ming Wah Woo. Owned by Jomar Pekingese, Margaret Zuber, West Monroe, Louisiana.

Overleaf: →

1. Ch. Toydom Modesty Permits, by Ch. Belknap El Dorado ex Toydom No Secrets, was Reserve in the Toy Group at Leeds Championship Show in 1985. Owned by Toydom Pekingese, Misses A. Summers and V. Williams, Purbright, Surrey. England.

2. Eng. Ch. Singlewell Wee Sedso at nine years. This famous dog has his name on very many important pedigrees of today. Sedso is a son of Honorable Mr. Twee of Kanghe ex Singlewell Sea Shell. Mrs. Pamela M. Edmond owner, N. Alton, Hants, England.

3. Eng. Ch. Singlewell Magic Charm, one of the progeny of Ch. Singlewell T'Sai Magic. Mrs. Pamela M. Edmond, owner, Singlewell Pekingese, Four Marks, Hants, England.

4. Eng. Ch. Singlewell Sensation, "off duty" from the show ring enjoying a bit of a game. Owned by Mrs. P.M. Edmond, Singlewell Pekingese, Four Marks, N. Alton, Hants, England.

5. Eng. Ch. Micklee Roc's Ru Ago, winner of 23 Challenge Certificates, 22 Bests of Breed, 11 Group wins, Best in Show Welsh K.C. All-Breed event, and England's Top Toy Dog for 1984 and 1985. this sire of Challenge Certificate winners in England and overseas is owned by Joyce and Jack Mitchell, Denholme, Bradford, England. Keith Lloyd photo.

143

1

2

3

4

5

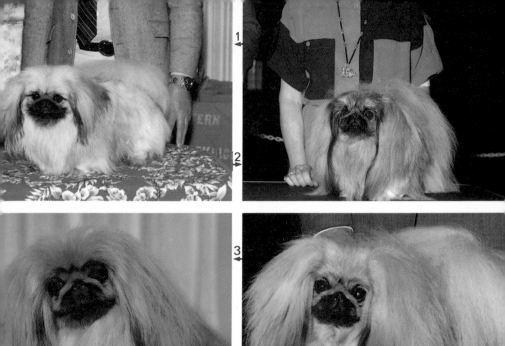

1

2

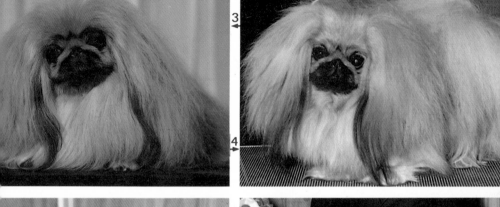

3

4

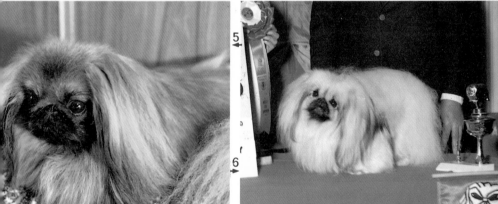

5

6

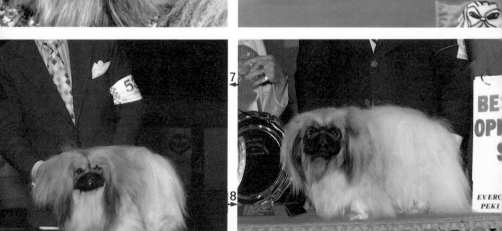

7

8

← Overleaf:

1. Can. and Am. Ch. Saimaifun's War Lord winning Best of Breed from the Open Class at the Western Canada Pekingese Specialty under English judge Mrs. L. Bull, Changte Pekingese, England. Bred, owned, and handled by Doug and Diane Kleinsorge, War Lord is by Ch. Bellerne's Yu-Benito (UK import) ex Glenferrar Crystal (UK import).

2. The owner's favorite dog show photo of Am. and Can. Ch. St. Aubrey Whispers of Elsdon, taken at Trumbull City K.C. in May 1985. Whispers is a Best in Show winner and a multi-breed and Group winner. Bred by R. William Taylor and Nigel Aubrey Jones. Mrs. Sidney Domina owner, Brockville, Ontario, Canada.

3. Headstudy of Am. and Can. Ch. St. Aubrey Tattler of Elsdon showing the quality that has helped to keep him in the winners circle. Owned by Sidney Domina, Brockville, Ontario, Canada.

4. Ch. St. Aubrey Queen Bee of Elsdon, bred and owned by R. William Taylor, St. Aubrey-Elsdon, Montreal, Quebec, Canada.

5. Cinnabar Yes-I-Can, by Ch. Mandragoza Bonfire ex Masterpeke Shady Lady, in December 1981. Owned by Cinnabar Pekingese, Pontypool, Ontario, Canada.

6. Can. and Am. Ch. Saimaifun Vi's Mighty Mite, bred/owned/handled by Doug and Diane Kleinsorge, Vancouver, British Columbia, here is winning Best in Specialty Show under judge Mrs. Antonia Horn, Belknap Pekingese, England.

7. Ch. St. Aubrey Ku Ting of Elsdon is owned by Mr. Nigel Aubrey Jones, St. Aubrey-Elsdon Pekingese, Montreal, Quebec, Canada.

8. Can. Am. Ch. Saimaifun's Gay Dina Mite in 1980 at the Evergreen State Pekingese Specialty, taking five points toward title with a Best of Winners and Best of Opposite Sex victory for breeders, owners and handlers Doug and Diane Kleinsorge, Vancouver, British Columbia, Canada.

146

Overleaf: →

1. Yamagee Pebbles, by Aust. Ch. Cholan Kei Wang ex Yamagee Rainbowe. Owned by Mrs. R.M. Cameron, Baulkhan Hills, NSW, Australia.

2. Aust. Ch. Jimgemajade Golda, by Ch. Tulyns Sosay Allofus ex Kandance Tai Tara. Owned by George and Alice Houghton, Kambah, ACT, Australia.

3. Aust. Ch. Jayville Jeraldo, by Ch. Jayville Gerard ex Jayville Janetta, winner of several "Class in Show" awards, and was a multiple Group winner for owners Albert and Heather Parton, Kylarkie Pekingese, Tamborine Mountain, Queensland, Australia.

4. Aust. Ch. Kylarkie Beau Derrick, owned by Albert and Heather Parton, Kylarkie Pekingese, Tamborine Mountain, Queensland, Australia.

5. Aust. Ch. Mayleet Wee Baron, by Aust. Ch. Kandence Wee Sedso ex Mayleet Duchess Davaar. Owned by George and Alice Houghton, Kambah, ACT, Australia.

6. Aust. Ch. Chindara Fancee Mee, bred, owned, and exhibited by Mrs. Denise King, Chindara Pekingese, Birkdale, Queensland, Australia.

7. Aust. Ch. Mahjong the Egan at 17 months age following a day of victory in the show ring. This famous Australian winner bred by Brian Wilson is owned by Caledonian Kennels, Mr. and Mrs. C. Lidden, Wagga Wagga, NSW, Australia.

8. Aust. Ch. Frawai Little Sir Jai is one of the outstanding Pekingese owned by Mrs. Frances Wickens, Emu Plains, NSW, Australia.

Sequel

← Overleaf:

1. Mrs. Walter M. Jeffords (breeder/owner/handler) here is winning Best of Breed at the Westminster K.C. in 1984 with her multi-Group and Best in Show "star" Ch. Randolph of Chinatown.

2. Am. and Can. Ch. St. Aubrey Whispers of Elsdon pictured winning her first Best in Show (in the rain) under judge Langdon Skarda in June 1985. Handled by J. Garrett Lambert for owner Sidney Domina, Brockville, Ontario, Canada. Sired by Ch. St. Aubrey Bees Wings of Elsdon ex Ch. St. Aubrey Gossip of Elsdon, both Best in Show winners, Whispers is carrying on in the family tradition.

3. This lovely puppy is Jomar Fleur De Lis, by Ch. Jomar Teddy Bear ex Jomar Kaiti Kan. Co-owned by Margaret Zuber, West Monroe, Louisiana and Kathleen G. Smith, Monroe, Louisiana.

Overleaf: ⟶

1. Ch. St. Aubrey Royal Star of Elsdon is the producer of five champions plus eight pointed on the way to finish. Has been a successful dog in specials and Toy Group competition as well as in quality offspring. Sakota (Sandy) Wheat owner, Mugiechun Pekingese, Phoenix, Arizona.

2. Littermates Am. and Can. Ch. Audrianne's Kissy Kristibel and Am. and Can. Ch. Audrianne's Kandy Kristibel are by Am. and Can. Ch. Audrianne's Kerr's Kristi Kopi ex Am. Ch. Claymore Jezebel. These two homebreds finished their titles with four majors each along the way. They make a beautifully matched brace, as our readers will note. Bred and owned by Miss Audrey A. Atherton, Audrianne Pekingese, Mentor, Ohio.

3. Ch. St. Aubrey Beeswing of Elsdon, Top Toy Dog in America for 1985, in two and a half years of showing has amassed 31 Bests in Show and 118 Group 1sts. Bred by R. William Taylor and Nigel Aubrey Jones, "Peter" has been handled throughout his career in the United States by Luc Boileau for Edward B. Jenner, Knolland Farm.

151

← Overleaf:

1. This pretty white bitch is Chi Lia Liu Tees of Katering who already has points from the 6–9 months class. She is a daughter of Popa's Ta Li Shih ex Crown Chantilly Snow Princess. Owned by Katering Pekingese, Gwenn Southmayd, Boring, Oregon.

2. Ch. Briarcourt's Royal Odyssey, by Ch. St. Aubrey Laparata Dragon ex Ch. St. Aubrey Phantasy of Elsdon. Bred, owned, and handled by Mrs. Joan Mylchreest, Yardley, Pennsylvania, to Best of Winners at the Summer Specialty of Pekingese Club of America in 1982.

3. Future Ch. Mama's Beauty O'Honeybear at age seven months. By Ch. Muhlin Most Royal ex Ch. Papa's Penny O'Honeybear. Owner-breeder Annette L. Borders, Abilene, Texas.

1. Ch. Dud-Lee's Khi-Lyn's Wind-Up-Toy finished at Southeastern Iowa in 1980. Sired by Ch. Dud-Lee's Khi-Lyn's Masterpiece ex Dud-Lee's Marla Lil Tim's Star. This is a seven pound miniature bitch, full sister to the noted multiple Group winner Ch. Dud-Lee's Ku-Lyn's Masterpiece. Bred, owned, and handled by Mrs. W.W. (Ruby) Dudley, Creston, Iowa.

2. Ch. Yan Kee Bernard was 17 times Best in Show, won 52 Toy Groups, and was a Pekingese Club of America winner during his show career. Owned by Mrs. Walter Jeffords and Mr. Michael Wolf with Mr. Wolf handling. Bred by David Arnold.

3. Fourwinds Lyra and Fourwinds Lyndon winning their first points at age six months, June 1984 at Paper Cities. Owned and handled by Mr. and Mrs. Robert M. Jackson, Seneca, Illinois.

← **Overleaf:**

1. Ch. Peris Command Performance; winner of three all-breed Bests in Show, 20 Group 1sts, and a Specialty Show Best of Breed. Bred and co-owned by Pat and Ed Saurman, co-owners with J. Robert Jacobsen, Point Reyes, California.

2. Ch. Hope's Koko Puff Dragon finished at nine months under judge Bill Taylor, January 1986. A Group-placer from the puppy class en route to title. Hope Hartenbach, owner, St. Louis, Missouri.

3. English Pekingese puppies, Sunsalve the Gay Gambler, (*left*) and By Agreement with Toydon, (*right*) are co-owned by Patricia and Charles Farley of Chu Lai and Elizabeth Whitford of Pleiku. They are approximately three months old.

Char-Min's Miss Amy Lou, Top Producing Bitch in the history of the breed (as of May 1986), with nine champions and five more pointed offspring. Owned by Elpha Sun Pekingese, Duane Doll and Joe McGinnis, Lakeland, Florida.

PANORA

Panora Pekingese in Irwin, Pennsylvania, are owned by Mrs. Ruthe Painter who is, without a doubt, one of the most dedicated Pekingese fanciers a breed possibly could have. Her enthusiasm includes not only the breeding and showing of Panora Pekes but many other aspects as well. (The actual handling is done by Elaine Rigden, but Mrs. Painter is very much involved and interested in everything to do with her own dogs and with the breed in general.) This interest has led her to become a talented and successful breeder, a writer on the breed, a collector of Pekingese art, a traveller who makes frequent trips to England in search of outstanding additions to her kennel, and the guiding spirit behind her local Pekingese Club whose *match* shows usually far exceed in size the Specialties of the National championship events in the breed.

Mrs. Painter has had a steady succession of leading winners representing her at the shows since the early 1970s. At that time it was Champion Oakmere The Baron, who recently died in his 16th year, a remarkably long life span for a Peke.

Bred by Olive Clay in England, sired by Champion Mr. Redcoat of Kanghe from Oakmere Kai-Ann, the Baron always did things with a flair. For example, he spent his last day in England, prior to leaving for his new home, winning three large classes at Crufts, one of five undefeated Pekingese.

His first American Best in Show was won during a raging thunder and lightning storm, which left him unconcerned and although several larger dogs in the ring were cringing, Baron could not have cared less. He became an American champion in 39 days, and then proceeded on a winning career which brought him to Top Pekingese in the Nation for 1975 and 1976.

Although not used at stud a great deal, Baron was still siring at age 12 years. His children and grandchildren have played their part in carrying on his greatness. The last of his daughters, and several granddaughters, are still doing so at Panora.

Baron was a television star as well as in the dog show ring. He made his final T.V. appearance at age 13 years.

Champion Beaupres Wonderview Prisca was a magnificent dog who, in addition to being a successful show campaigner, sired 16 champions. Among the latter were Champion The First Knighter of Panora, who in June 1976 was No. 2 Pekingese in the United States, Champion The Knight Robert of Panora; Champion

Ch. The Knight Robert of Panora, another son of Ch. Beupres Wonderview Prisca, winning Best of Breed at Pittsburgh in 1978. Handled by Mrs. Elaine Rigden for Mrs. Ruthe Painter, Panora Pekingese.

Prisca's Frankly Speaking, one of Mrs. Painter's particular favorites who is a Best in Show and multiple Toy Group winner; Champion Melissa's Josephine of Panora; and Champion The Earl of Elegance Pekingese. These are just a few of the wonderful Panora Pekes.

Champion Jonjo of Etive blazed a trail of glory for Mrs. Painter and the Panoras. Imported from England, this son of Champion Etive of Copplestone Pu Zin Julier made his American show debut at the Allegheny Pekingese Club Specialty under Jack R. Watts, where he romped off with a five-point major by taking Best of Winners, completing title in the next four shows, undefeated for four majors. On his fourth ring appearance here he took his first

Best in Show from the classes at the Kingsport Kennel Club, going on to add Toy Groups and all-breed Bests in Show at an amazing rate of speed.

Champion Wild Venture of Lotusgrange is yet another who has done well for Panora, both as the sire of champions and in the show ring.

At this time, something new has been added at Panora—an American-bred Pekingese from the West Coast who will be co-owned by Mrs. Painter and his breeder, Jean Thomas of Ai Kow fame. This dog is Champion Ai Kou Master Chimes, a name we predict you will be hearing frequently. As with all the Panora dogs, Master Chimes will be presented in the ring by Elaine Rigden.

PEACOCK

Peacock Pekingese are owned by Betty Claire Peacock of Dumas, Arkansas, and they were born of an idea in 1969, when Betty Claire and her husband, Tom, were enjoying a Saturday in San Francisco at the beautiful Golden Gate Kennel Club Dog Show. There they met Jean Thomas and saw her Ai Kou Pekingese, and it was love at first sight. Although Betty Claire had owned Pekingese continuously since early childhood, she had never seen any of such exquisite beauty as those she saw that day. Then and there, she resolved to own and show dogs of this quality.

In 1978, Tom Peacock's Air Force assignment put them close enough to retirement to settle down in his home town, making it possible for them to purchase Betty Claire's first show dog, Ai Kou Bell Boi, a double grandson of English Champion Ralsham's Hum-Dinger. Although he did not finish, Bell Boi was an excellent dog to learn with, being a real showman. He sired Betty Claire's first homebred champion, Peacock Pu-Ying Poppit, from Champion Peacock's Lady Keiko of Kade, and he has a pointed son as well.

Betty Claire finished her first Champion Ai Kou Myrddin Emrys, bred and co-owned by Jean Thomas, in 1982. From the puppy class, Merlin won a five-point major and a four-point major, going on to Best of Breed over specials.

Throughout this period, Betty Claire had been learning everything possible about grooming and handling Pekes, thanks to Lois Frank, who has been so helpful a friend to her in this regard. Because she especially delights in this aspect of the dog world, Betty

Ch. Peacock's Lady Keiko of Kade, owner-handled by Betty Claire Peacock, taking the points at Shreveport K.C. in 1982.

Claire was given the opportunity to handle and co-own Margaret Zuber's Jomar Pekes. Among those whose titles she put on have been Champion Jomar Ruffles and Flourishes, Best of Winners at the 1983 Texas Specialty Fall Show; Champion Darling Little Abra of Jomar, who was No. 7 Pekingese bitch in 1984; and Champion Jomar Sunni Bear, who has enjoyed a successful career as a special. Betty Claire also finished Champion Xanadu Ting Tong Tu O'Ir-Wyn, co-owned with Carol Simonton, bred by Margaret Zuber.

Although she breeds very few litters, Betty Claire has now four young homebred puppies for whom hopes are high, and another who is already pointed.

The current Peacock breeding program is based principally upon her Ai Kou stock, with some Jomar, and with two bitches out of Annette Borders' lovely and sound Honeybear dogs. Ai Kou Yu Sun, by Champion Ai Kou Sunni Dragon, is her leading stud, and is linebred on the English import, Champion Cherangani Bombadier. He was Best in Show at the 1986 Arizona Pekingese Specialty over specials, and at this time has both his majors.

Betty Claire's interest in Pekingese has led to her becoming Chief Ring Steward and Vice President of two all-breed dog clubs, a member of three Pekingese Clubs, and a columnist for the Pekingese magazine, *Orient Express*.

PEKE-A-TOI

Peke-A-Toi Pekingese are owned, in Smithfield, Pennsylvania, by Mrs. Evelyn Magun.

Mrs. Magun has a small kennel of finest bloodlines, and has owner-handled her dogs to many good wins. Among her Best of Breed winners are Champion Peke-A-Toi's Venture Domique and Champion Prisca's Rip Cord of Peke-A-Toi.

PICKWAY

The name "Pickway" was selected all the way back in 1959 by Mrs. Bessie V. Pickens of Portland, Oregon, with which to identify the Pekingese which she was then planning to breed, own, and show. Over the years, a great many outstanding dogs have been seen bearing this prefix, as Mrs. Pickens has met with very satisfactory success in the undertaking.

In the beginning it was difficult settling on a breeding program, as the original stock was from "Orchard Hill," and following Mrs. Quigley's death and the dispersal of her kennel, there was nowhere to go for future generations.

Bessie Pickens's first champion was in 1966, from the Orchard Hill bloodlines, and he completed his title by winning the Toy Group that day. He was Champion Sir Bugg-Zee of Pickway. At this same show (Whidby Island), his half sister was Winners Bitch and Best of Opposite Sex, going on to become Champion Gleymoors Pedlo of Pickway. Unfortunately, due to Mrs. Pickens' heavy work load during the late 1960s, neither was ever bred. Bugg-Zee's excellent type is very obvious (the author's first thought was "how proud Dorothy Quigley would be of him"), and Mrs. Pickens comments that he was one of the soundest Pekes she has ever owned or seen.

Bessie Pickens with her first champion, in 1966. Ch. Sir Bugg Zee of Pickway was of Orchard Hill breeding, and finished his title by winning the Toy Group at Whidby Island K.C. Owner-handled by Mrs. Pickens, Pickway Kennels.

It was love at first sight for Bessie Pickens when she saw a lovely young male owned by Thelma Zaccagnini, a "lovely, stubborn, six-and-a-half pound dog" named Wee Wee Tonni whom Thelma had bred and who was a grandson of Champion Beyli Shaman, thus going back to the admired Champion Caversham Ku Ku of Yam. Bessie gained co-ownership of this little fellow, who quickly attained championship, and won Best in Specialty Show from the classes the very first time she showed him. Despite his dislike of the show ring, Tonni was of such quality that he won under a great many judges, winding up with a notable collection of Groups and Specialties to his credit. A bitch named Mar-Pat Glory Be of Dan Lee, owned by Martha Bingham and Pat Miller, was bred to Tonni, she being descended from Champion Tiko of

Pekeboro and Champion Calartha Mandarin of Jehol. Mrs. Pickens was given her choice of the five male puppies, who grew up to become multi-Group and Best in Specialty Show winner Champion Mar-Pat Bobba of Pickway. He was the complete opposite of his sire in his super showmanship and love of dog shows. Of him, Bessie Pickens says, "Of all the Pekes I have had before or since, Bobba was my love."

Bobba produced four champions: Mar-Pat Bobbilee of Pickway (from Champion Mar-Pat Wings Violin), Champion Burke's Hi Cherub of Oaklane, and Champion Glen Eden Beyliof Pickway, along with the latter's litter sister, Champion Eve-Eden Bunnee of Wun Sum, the last-mentioned two from Lowlands Jina of Han-Bee, also descended from Champion Tiko of Pekeboro and Champion Calartha Mandarin of Jehol.

Bobbilee sired a lovely red bitch, bred by Evelyn Sommerfelt, which was later co-owned by Bessie Pickens. Never finishing her championship although pointed, this bitch was bred to a grandson of Champion Mar-Pat Pier Pipers Piccolo, producing the outstanding winning Champion Mar-Pat Dally of Pickway. This dog won more Groups and Bests in Specialty Shows than any of the other Pickway champions; yet that wished-for Best in Show always seemed to elude him although he was "runner up" on numerous occasions.

Dally is a dark red sable with the full black mask. Champion Eve-Eden Bunnee of Wun-sum was bred to him, and they produced, to quote Mrs. Pickens, "the most beautiful male of them all—the all-breed Best in Show and Best in Specialty Show winner, Champion Wun-Sum Ko-Lee of Pickway." What a heartbreak for this lovely dog to have been killed by a Malamute at a dog show when only two-and-a-half years old! One tragedy on top of another for Mrs. Pickens, as only a few months previously, Champion Beyli had suffocated on an airliner.

It took considerable effort, on the part of Bessie Pickens and friends, for her to get herself together again after these inestimable losses. But finally they did succeed, and she bred Dally to a daughter of Champion Beyli, Holly of Pickway, whom she co-owns with Marjory Nye White. The result was her current great winner Champion Japeke Shogun of Pickway, whose lovely litter sister, Champion Jo-Lu-Wee's Shansi of Pickway, is owned by Joan Arnold and co-owned by Bessie Pickens.

Next, a bitch was leased, Champion Pierrot's Pure Trash, from Neva Sloan. Bred to Dally, she produced Steve Arnold's Champion Jai-Me of Pickway; Champion Junie Moon of Pickway, co-owned by Mrs. Pickens; and Champion Pierrot's Jezebel of Bergum, owned by Elaine Bergum, for whom she has produced three champions. Junie Moon was bred to Shogun and had three lovely puppies.

During the late 1960s, Bessie Pickens met Joan Arnold at a Specialty Show. They immediately became close friends, deciding to combine their breeding programs. A few years later Joan's brother, Steve Arnold and his wife Judy, also joined in the breeding and showing of Pekes. Steve has been the "hand on the lead" with Shogun, taking him to many breed wins, Groups, and Group placements. Since Mrs. Pickens is doing more judging and has the entire Toy Group now, she does not feel comfortable herself competing in the Best of Breed and Toy Group ring as an exhibitor. Bessie Pickens must be very happy in the knowledge that Steve and Judy plan to carry on the Pickway kennel name when she does decide to retire.

Over the years, it has been Bessie Pickens' pleasure to finish her own dogs, preferably from the "Bred-by" class. Only one time has she used a professional handler, Dean Passe; he finished Champion Mar-Pat Dally of Pickway, lovingly known by him and his wife as Pieface.

RICHDEE

Richdee Pekingese are owned by Richard and Dee Creighton in Granby, Connecticut, where some truly handsome Pekingese reside.

Champion Richdee's Tien-Yin Lilbit is a grandson of Champion St. Aubrey Laparata Dragon (on his sire's side) and of Champion First Knighter of Panore (on his dam's side). Handled by Terence Childs, he has done some very nice winning for his owners; in just three-and-a-half months of showing, his Group placements and Bests of Breed added up to a praiseworthy total. He became, over that period, No. 8 Pekingese in the country.

The latest champion at Richdee is Mugiechun St. Aubrey Sajoewin, by Champion Mugie's St. Aubrey Dragonwind ex Champion St. Aubrey Maydrena of Elsdon. Bred by Sandra Wheat, "Sajoe" completed his title during March 1986 at the age of 16 months, having won Best of Breed on six occasions, twice over specials. The day after he finished at Elm City, he won a Group third.

These are two very special dogs who should be good producers for their owners as well as successful in the show ring. We wish them continued success. All of the Richdee Pekingese are handled by Terence Childs.

ROSEWOOD

Rosewood Pekingese, in Warminster, Pennsylvania, are owned by Deborah Sprouse and William M. Sullivan, the kennel having been founded in 1975 by Miss Sprouse when she acquired a pet bitch, whom she decided to show in obedience.

The bitch never finished her C.D., owing to her "hamming it up" and her love of pleasing the crowd with her games. A second pet bitch had also been acquired; she did complete her C.D., in three straight shows, including a High in Trial.

Seeing the beautiful dogs being shown in conformation, Debbie soon decided that she, too, wanted to breed that kind. A search was then underway for exactly the right bitch to begin showing, and to start a breeding program.

After much disappointment and several false starts, a truly lovely bitch was acquired from Mrs. Robert Ballinger. This was Claymore Dulcinea, who was shown and lacked just one major when she was temporarily retired to raise a litter. Bred to Chinese Sun Dragon of Appin, she produced Rosewood's first champion, the handsome Champion Rosewood's Sea Dragon. Two weeks after her son completed his title, Dulcinea did likewise.

Champion Claymore Dulcinea was specialed on a limited basis, and among her wins were Best of Opposite Sex to Best of Breed at Westminster Kennel Club twice, at eight and nine years of age! She has also been Best of Opposite Sex at the Pekingese Club of Central New Jersey and at the Allegheny Pekingese Club from the Veterans Class.

Rosewood's Black Eyed Susan, a Dulcinea daughter, was bred to Yu Darlin Jade Prince of Appin, also owned by Miss Sprouse, producing Rosewood Jade Dragon, now pointed, who was sold to William Sullivan. A strong friendship developed and a partnership was formed between Miss Sprouse and Mr. Sullivan, who had bred Basset Hounds and Shih Tzus prior to becoming interested in breeding and showing Pekes.

Ch. Rosewood's Sea Dragon taking Group placement at Dan Emmett K.C. 1984. Karen Schultz handling for owners, Deborah Sprouse and William Sullivan, Rosewood Kennels.

Quality is the byword in this kennel. All dogs are owner-handled in the classes to their titles, then specialed by either their owners or by Karen Schultz. Other champions owned by this kennel are Rosewoods Mystic Warrior, English import Kalafrana Fancy Man, and Lakshmi's Rosemary. On the way to their titles are Rosewood's Ivalace, Rosewood's Jade Dragon, and Fourwind's Jay's Gem.

SANTAVERDI

Santaverdi Pekingese, of New Orleans, Louisana, are owned by Tom and Kathy Masilla. This small kennel produces a few litters each year, the pedigrees based heavily on the Belknap, Bugatti, Copplestone, and Muhlin bloodlines.

Tom and Kathy Masilla's love of Pekingese began with their own courtship. Tom's mother, Mrs. Santa Masilla, had two Pekingese females, Sandy and Tamee, and for Kathy Verdi, it was love at first sight for the breed.

Shortly after their marriage, the Masillas purchased a puppy bitch from a breeder who proudly displayed her stock for Kathy.

That very moment Kathy was sure that she wanted to raise these magnificent little creatures herself.

However, it was not until several years later that the Masillas became interested in the exhibiting side of Pekingese ownership. Through local contacts, they were introduced to Vance and Dorothy Tyndall of Tacoma, Washington, and the handsome red bitch they purchased became Champion Vandor's Missi by Manni.

Other champions from the Tyndalls followed, based on the Bugatti-Copplestone bloodlines. Then, in 1980, the Masillas became involved with the black Pekes for whom they are so widely known today.

Through Jack R. Watts, a former longtime breeder and authority on Pekingese, they met Ron Young, whose Ron-Ju Pekingese are traced principally to the He'Lo and Orchard Hill strains. From Mr. Young they purchased a good black daughter of Champion Top Hat's Black Magic, named Magic's Mignon of Ron-Ju. This bitch gained her title in short order, but it was another daughter of Champion Top Hat's Black Magic, this one Magic's Solitaire of Ron-Ju, purchased a year later from Mr. Young, who became the true foundation bitch for the Masilla's breeding program once she had completed her title.

At about the same time, Mrs. Masilla developed a friendship with Patricia Mullendore (Muhlin Pekingese), and their shared love of the black Peke led to the black-on-black breedings of the Ron-Ju bitches to the stud dogs Champion Muhlin Black Magic and the renowned Champion Muhlin Boogaloo. Ch Black Magic and Champion Solitaire produced Champion Santaverdi Magic Image, a Best in Specialty winner on the way to his title, and litter brother Champion Santaverdi Double Whammy, who finished with multiple Group placements. Champion Boogaloo and Champion Solitaire produced Champion Santaverdi Moonlight Samba and Champion Santaverdi Shingaling.

Champion Mignon was bred only once, but in that litter, sired by Champion Boogaloo, was a puppy who became American and Canadian Champion Santaverdi Ming Th' Merciless. "Boogie," as he is known, has produced several pointed offspring currently being shown. At the same time, Solitaire's grandchildren are beginning to make their presence strongly felt as well.

The Masillas share a great interest in the parti-color Pekingese, and have finished two. They are Champion Shady Acres Sam-

Am. and Can. Ch. Tomee Choo T'Sai Wen, held by his handler, Hiram Stewart, is over 12 years old and one of the great favorites at Santaverdi Pekingese.

beau's Thunder, a black-and-white who finished with two Group placements; and homebred Champion Santaverdi the Jazzman, a red-and-white Bugatti linebred dog, who gained title when he was slightly over a year old.

Continued friendship with Patty Mullendore, and more recently with Diana Mehling, led to the inclusion of the Belknap strain as an outcross, the results of which have been splendid.

Currently in residence at Santaverdi are the multiple Best in Specialty winner Champion Muhlin Midas and the well-known winning bitch Champion Muhlin Madonna. Both are sired by the famous stud dog, Champion Belknap Little Nugget.

Recently, the Masillas imported a splendid red bitch from the Belknap Pekingese of Mrs. Antonia Horn in England. This is Belknap Bounteous, granddaughter to English Champion Belknap Nero and English Champion Belknap Bravo. Bounteous has quickly proven herself a success in the show ring, being halfway to her championship.

The Masillas claim that much of their success has been due to good friends, lots of hard work, and a dash of good luck. As a

172

breed columnist for three Pekingese magazines over the years, Mrs. Masilla thoroughly believes in sharing knowledge and being helpful to other breeders. At the same time, she and her husband also believe in reading and re-reading everything on the breed, their feeling being that one never stops learning. Which of her dogs are the most outstanding to Kathy Masilla? Champion Tomee Choo T'Sai Wen and Champion Muhlin Madonna.

SING LEE

Sing Lee Pekingese, at Point Reyes Station, California, are owned by J. Robert Jacobsen, who says of himself, "it seems like there has never been a time I didn't have a Pekingese as part of my family." Bob's brother owned a little red-and-white particolor when they were growing up; but "Snuffy" was *his* dog, and his affections were, quite naturally, directed more towards his own pet, a black Cocker Spaniel. Bob owned and exhibited a Welsh Terrier during the 1950s, but that proved to be a "disaster." It was in 1962 that Bob's serious interest in Pekingese was re-kindled after attending the Golden Gate Pekingese Specialty in San Francisco. It was there that he met Irene Ruschaupt and her fantastic Sing Lee Pekingese.

Bob Jacobsen exhibited his first Pekingese in 1965. His first two champions were Champion Turner's Sui Tong (the first champion son sired by Champion Ku Chin Tommi of Seng Kye) and his daughter Champion Tong's Chia San Sing Lee. They both produced many champions, and over the years their influence is still strong, mainly through the lines of Champion Bo-Jac's Tong Tuo of Soo Hoo (Bob's kennel name in those days was Bo-Jac).

In 1976, after Irene Ruschaupt passed away, Bob Jacobsen inherited the remaining "Sing Lees," including the kennel suffix. Another valuable thing he inherited was a tremendous amount of knowledge of the breed from a person who knew as much about Pekingese as anyone who ever lived. Two key dogs who played a major role in Bob's subsequent success were Champion Sunbeam Dockleaf, a Ku Ying of Jamestown son Irene had imported from England; and Bo-Lero Sing Lee, a beautiful red bitch who had injured her eye and could not be exhibited.

Dockleaf, immediately upon his arrival in America, won the Golden Gate Specialty from the classes, and had several other spectacular wins, until his show career was interrupted by Irene's

173

illness and subsequent death. His coat had gone downhill during Irene's illness, but after he came to live with Bob Jacobsen it took only six months until he was back in full bloom again. At the next San Francisco Specialty, which was dedicated to Irene's memory, Bob took "Doc" to a five-point major win from the Eastern breeder/judge Irene Franzoso. Within two months he had completed his title. He is the grandsire of the magnificent Champion Raffles Jubilation Sing Lee, an all-breed Best in Show winner as well as Best of Breed winner at the Pekingese Club of America March Specialty in 1984 over an entry of 133. He was handled to these wins by Janet Allen.

Bo-Lero was a beautiful red bitch who, had it not been for her eye injury, would surely have done well in the show ring. Her pedigree included *all* of the Sing Lees for 20 plus generations; she was doubled on Tommi, Sun-t, Shanling, and on Ku-Chello. Of course, she produced fabulously well with any of Bob's linebred Sing Lee dogs. Her daughter, Champion Tong Tuo's FlamBo Sing Lee, was the dam of Bob's record-breaking litter brothers, Champions California Gold Sing Lee and Blazers Beauregard Sing Lee, these two being the only all-breed Best in Show winning litter brothers in breed history. One of the most exciting days as an exhibitor for Bob Jacobsen was the one on which California Gold was awarded Best of Breed and Best Toy at Ventura under Iris de la Torre Bueno; he then went on to Best in Show in an entry of 3527 dogs under Edith Nash Hellerman.

The current star at Sing Lee is Champion Briarcourt's Excelsior, winner of 11 Bests in Show, two Specialty Bests in Show, and 43 Groups, whose numbers are increasing steadily.

For seven years previous to his application for a judging license, Bob Jacobsen was a handler of numerous Toys other than Pekes. He also has handled a dozen Chow Chows to their titles, eight of them home bred and one owned with Janet Allen. His first love remains Pekingese, but he admits to finding Chows another fascinating Oriental breed and adds, "believe it or not, I have learned even more about Pekingese from having had a close relationship with Chows." Bob has shown 60 champions to their titles, 42 of which were Pekingese. He has had six different Pekingese dogs win all-breed Bests in Show, 12 different Toy Group Pekes, one Group winning Peke bitch, and 12 Specialty Best in Show winners.

Ch. California Gold Sing Lee, All Breed Best in Show and multiple Specialty Best of Breed winner, with Janet Allen handling for owner J. Robert Jacobsen, Sing Lee Pekingese.

Ch. Lejervis Wise Man, English import bred by Mrs. L.A. Rolfe-Hazell, is by Eng. Ch. Jay Trump of Sunsalve ex Lejervis Kara. Owned by Don Sutton and Steve Keating, Sutton Place Pekingese.

SUTTON PLACE PEKINGESE

Sutton Place Pekingese are located in Dallas, Texas, at the home of their owners, Don Sutton and Steve Keating. The kennel started in June 1977, Bel-Mar Marina having been the first show quality Pekingese owned by them. Earlier than this, their first two Pekingese were white females and strictly pet quality.

Attending their first dog show, a Sanctioned B Match hosted by the Pekingese Club of Texas in June 1977, both Don and Steve quickly realized that you cannot start with pet quality.

Marina, bred by Mary Davis of Borger, Texas, was purchased in July 1977, and was two years old at the time. She had one point then, was totally out of coat, and had never been bred. In November 1977 she had her first litter, of which two puppies survived, growing up to become Champions Su-Ke Tu of Sutton Place and Tyne Lace of Sutton Place.

During 1978, Marina was coated up and shown until being bred again in September of that year. As had her first litter, this one required delivery by Caesarean section and produced only one surviving puppy, Little Lady of Sutton Place. Again Marina was coated up, and this time made her presence felt in the ring, com-

176

pleting her championship in April 1979, just 20 days prior to the arrival of her third litter, which this time she free-whelped, with four of the puppies surviving. They were to become known as Champion Koty-Kee of Sutton Place, (D. Doll and J. McGinnis), Champion Bush-EE Su of Sutton Place, Champion Honnee Comb of Sutton Place (Claire Eitman), and Ni-Ke-Tu of Sutton Place.

The old wives' tale, "once a section always a section," didn't hold true in Marina's case, as she later went on to whelp three more litters (a total of six litters), producing Champions Krystal of and Boo-Ku Bugatti of Sutton Place.

Sutton Place has owned 17 champions, who are as follows:

Champion Mr. Bugatti's Greywings Sun; Champion Bel-Mar Marina; Champion Su-Ke To of Sutton Place; Champion Tyne Lace of Sutton Place; Champion San-Tee of Sutton Place; Champion Bush-EE Su of Sutton Place; Champion Koty-Ke of Sutton Place; Champion Honne Comb of Sutton Place; Champion Shasta of Sutton Place; Champion Stygian Hue of Sutton Place; Champion Boo-Ku Bugatti of Sutton Place; Champion Krystal of Sutton Place; Champion Lejervis Wise Man; Champion Snuggy of Sutton Place; Champion China Doll O'Honeybear; Champion Summer Luv of Sutton Place; and Champion Tootsie of Sutton Place.

TOIMANOR

Toimanor Pekingese are owned by Audrey Drake and her daughter, Janet Drake-Oxford, who are situated in Fayetteville, Arkansas. The Drakes are an Air Force family, and their love of Pekingese developed when they were stationed in Audrey's native England.

While living in the lovely English town of Banbury, they attended an English dog show where they met Mrs. Hilda Garwood of Hydlewood Pekingese. From her they purchased their first Pekes, Koo Rudi of Hydlewood and Koo Ying of Hydlewood. With Mrs. Garwood's encouragement, they exhibited at the English shows. Soon afterward they purchased Tartar of Coughton and Oscar of Coughton from Lady Isabel Throckmorton. Tartar, together with an Oscar daughter, Sherida of Essdee, was shown quite successfully in England by Audrey.

When the Drakes returned to the United States in 1967, they brought back five English Pekes with them. Sherida of Essdee

177

gained her American championship in seven shows with five majors and one reserve to a major. Unfortunately, Oscar of Coughton, one of England's leading sires when brought over here, was tragically blinded at the hands of a veterinarian, by the misuse of a steroid in an injured eye shortly after his arrival here.

In 1969, the Drake family was again transferred to England, taking with them their five original Pekingese. However, the prospect of four years without dog shows was too depressing; so Champion Sherida of Essdee was exhibited there, doing some quite satisfactory winning.

When the family returned from Europe in 1970, they decided to make Fayetteville, Arkansas, their permanent home. Audrey and Janet changed their kennel prefix from Essdee to Toimanor, the identification they have used since that time.

Feeling the need for a younger stud dog, the Drakes next purchased Champion Windemere's Dragon Power, whose pedigree is loaded with important English Pekes. He is a Group winner, and has proven an outstanding sire. Next came Szu Nori's Velvet Peepers, who descends from the Jamestown dogs and the Sing Lees, including International Champion Ku Chin Tommi of Seng Kye.

In autumn 1981, it was decided to buy a new outcross puppy to combine the new bloodlines with the lines of their English bitches. The result of this was their purchase, from Mrs. Minnie Wisdom, of the puppy who was to grow up to be Best in Show and Specialty Best in Show-winning Champion Charmin Jason of Toimanor. Entered for his first show at age seven months, and due to the illness of Audrey and the pregnancy of Janet, a handler was selected for the new young star, the late Max Kerfoot. It was love at first sight between Max and Jason, the two forming a team who accounted for 16 Bests in Show, more than 100 Toy Group firsts, plus about 150 additional Group placements according to Audrey Drake's figures. Jason was America's No. 1 Pekingese in 1983 and 1984, and No. 2 Toy for 1984 as well. A show dog every inch of the way, in the hands of a most knowledgeable handler, they made a memorable combination. Jason was retired immediately from the show ring upon Max's death in September 1984. Now he is at home at Toimanor, loved and spoiled beyond belief, we are told.

Champion Windemere's Dragon Power and Champion Charmin Jason of Toimanor are having a tremendous imfluence on the new

178

The dog behind so many of the Tomainor Pekingese, Oscar of Coughton, was born in July 1963, bred by Miss Mould (Kanghe Pekingese). Oscar was a Junior Warrant winner in England, plus a Challenge Certificate and two Reserves. Unfortunately, the loss of an eye cut short his career in the United States. Nonetheless, he has proven his value many times over as a sire. Owned by Audrey Drake and Janet Drake Oxford.

puppies in this kennel. Jason's latest champions include Champion Toimanor Centre Stage and Champion Toimanor Quiet Riot.

Littermates Toimanor Jason of Dud-Lees, now owned by Ruby Dudley, and Toimanor Elizabeth Anne had a very good weekend at their first show. Both continued at a rapid pace, and Elizabeth Anne finished her title at nine months' age in seven shows with three of them majors. She was shown by her co-owner, Vicki Martin Caliendo.

Janet's four-year-old daughter, Sheilah-Anne, has inherited Audrey's and Janet's love of Pekingese and cannot wait to show dogs. It now looks like there will be a third generation carrying on Toimanor sometime in the future.

179

TOM-MAR-A

Tom-Mar-A Pekingese is a kennel of long duration, owned by Mr. and Mrs. T.V. Harvey of North Huntington, Pennsylvania.

Among the champions to be found here are Baron's Jai-Son of Tom-Mar-A, who, when he completed his title in August 1979, became the first American champion son of the famous Champion Oakmere The Baron. His dam was Bel-Mar's Hanky Panky.

There is also the lovely and successful Champion Win-Sox of Tom-Mar-A, son of Champion St. Aubrey's Micklee Twee Jin ex Tom-Mar-A's Miss Kiss of Kantu.

The Harveys, both of whom are active in the Western Pennsylvania Kennel Club, take much pleasure from the Pekes, and both are in the habit of doing the exhibiting themselves.

WINDEMERE

Windemere Pekingese, owned by Joy Thoms (Strickler) in Molalla, California, owe their beginning to a white male purchased by Joy at Bakersfield. Since childhood, Joy has had a very great admiration for white animals, her pets having included white horses and white cats, both of which she raised while growing up in Nebraska.

Upon graduation from college, the horses became difficult to transport from one teaching assignment to another, as were the dogs. Not until the birth of her first son did Joy purchase a Pekingese. And, as so frequently happens with the purchase of a pet, the next step was a bitch to breed.

Finally, after two false steps to establish a line of her own, a bitch from Eve Magun's kennel, Peke-A-Toi's Ah Mee's Lu-Tina, became the foundation of the Windemere line and produced the first Pekingese shown to the title "champion" by Joy, Champion Well-Lee Sing of Lost Park. He, along with two sons of Champion Fu Yong of Jamestown and a grandson of Champion Dan Lee Dragonseed, became the stud foundation dog at Windemere, stamping the look that is still recognizable today.

First of all a breeder and secondly an exhibitor, Joy campaigns champions very rarely, but she did enjoy specialing American and Canadian Champion Windemere's Well-Lee Fu Yong to No. 7 Pekingese in 1974. Among his winnings were an American Specialty Best in Show, many Group placements, and a Canadian Best in Show, all owner-handled. "E.J." remains one of her favorites.

180

Am. and Can. Ch. Windemere's Well Lee Fu Yong, Best of Breed, owner-handled by Joy Thoms (*left*). His grandson, Am. Ch. Windemere's Dandy Dragon, Best of Winners for a major with Kathi Commer (*center*). And Am. Ch. Han Bee's Moon Mist of Mar-Lu, Winners Bitch, handled by Gene Hahnlen (*right*). Photo courtesy of Joy Thoms.

The Windemere whites of today are descended from Hi Frosty's Kyu of Brown's Den, purchased as a puppy from longtime breeder-friend Cora Brown. Kyu was later sold to June Suhm in Oklahoma, but his descendants are still to be seen at Windemere. The whites make an attractive contrast to the other beautiful Pekes with black masks. One of the latest litters is sired by Champion Rodari The Dragon at Lon-Du, owned by Arlon Duit, and is out of a black Kyu granddaughter. June Suhm has already championed the black male in the litter, Windemere's Midnight Dragon, at 14 months, and he immediately won Group placements. The two show males are just now starting their show careers with the Thoms.

After many years of "going it alone," Joy had the good fortune to meet and marry John Thoms, and the past eight years have seen them attending shows together on the weekends. At first, John was only willing to help out to ringside, but it wasn't long before another pair of hands were needed inside the ring, and he was gently nudged into becoming a full fledged exhibitor.

The Windemere trademark has always been soundness, and never has this been sacrificed in 22 years of breeding. Glamor is great—the icing on the cake—but at Windemere, four good legs and sound bodies take precedence.

WYN-D-HILL

Wyn-D-Hill Pekingese, of Jersey Shore, Pennsylvania, resulted from a Christmas gift received by Mary Brewer McCracken in 1969—a Pekingese puppy sired by Champion St. Aubrey Argus of Wellplace. This puppy was destined to live only a few short months, but his charm and endearing personality laid the foundation of an interest in Pekingese which has continued to grow and thrive over a period of more than 22 years.

The half brother of this original Peke became the first owner-handled Group winner from Wyn-D-Hill. He was Champion Runkel's Top Secret. Another brother, Pat-tez Sir Camelot, lacked two points for his championship.

Marvel Runkel and Pat McCann became a strong guiding influence to Mary during those first years, and it was Marvel Runkel who sold her Champion Copplestone Pu-Zee-toi. At five years of

Ch. Ho Man Dee Wee Tina of Wyn-D-Hill off to a good start with a Group 1st in the Adult Division at Mid-Susquehanna Valley Match Show. Handled by co-owner Mary McCracken. Bred by Ken Rotella (co-owner) and Marlene Rotella.

age, this fine dog became a champion by winning a five-point major at Western Pennsylvania Kennel Association.

During the 1970s, Wyn-D-Hill was located in Central Pennsylvania. Some of its greatest accomplishments stem from one small dog, Champion Muhlin Magician of Wyn-D-Hill, who weighed less than eight pounds. Magician sired five champions and himself became a multi-Group and Best in Specialty Show winner. He was sired by Champion Muhlin Boogaloo ex Champion Belknap Care. His half sister, Champion Wyn-D-Hill's Magic Trick, finished with three five-point majors, though she hated dog shows.

Magic Trick's litter sister, Wyn-D-Hill's Black Queen, finished her title at ten months and received all her majors by going Best of Winners and was once Best of Breed over a special. Shown as a specials bitch, she always caught the judge's eye. As a producer, she became the dam of Wyn-D-Hill's Black Ty, who is now owned by Steve and Debora Trout of Rochester, New York. Ty was judged Best in Sweepstakes at the Pekingese Club of America Winter Specialty in 1986.

Mary was co-founder of the Allegheny Pekingese Club, Inc., with Richard Cullen of Cheltenham Pekingese, and she became that organization's first President.

In June 1985, Mary McCracken traveled to the Peoples' Republic of China, where she purchased trophies to be offered at the Allegheny Pekingese Club's Specialty Shows.

Mary's very special interest is in breeding parti-color Pekingese. While working towards a Ph.D. at Penn State University, she became interested in color genetics, and one of Wyn-D-Hill's most famous parti-colors is Champion Ir-Wyn's Parti-Patch of Wyn-D-Hill, one of the few black and white parti-colored champions bitches of record.

Monica, Mary's daughter, has frequently been seen in the Pekingese ring since six years of age, helping to show the Pekes. She finished her first champion, Ho Man Dee Wee Tina of Wyn-D-Hill, when she was only beginning Junior Showmanship at age ten. Monica could also be seen at the obedience ring with her tiny Peke. She was instrumental in helping to finish Champion Wyn-D-Hill's Magician's Secret, Champion Wyn-D-Hill's Mighty Dragon, and Champion Wyn-D-Hill's Dragon's Puff. She has also been noted in the Group ring with the imported Champion Heathghyll's Aluetta and Chop Hoi Carousel.

Am. and Can. Ch. St. Aubrey Sha Sha of Elsdon, bred and owned by Nigel Aubrey Jones and R. William Taylor, St. Aubrey-Elsdon, Montreal, Quebec, Canada.

Chapter 4

Pekingese in Canada

There has been Pekingese interest in Canada since the 1920s. One of the breeders of that period was Mrs. A.R. Caruso, who began with the breed in 1928; her kennel was based on an English importation and several who came later, all generally carrying bloodlines of the English "Chinatowns." Chinatown was also the dominant strain behind Mrs. Winifred King's dogs, as she, too, imported her first brood matron from there, breeding many "Kingways" of note.

Archie Semple had a large, highly successful Pekingese kennel of many fine winners during that period. Champion Chipps of Chinatown was imported from the Weils in England, becoming the sire of numerous Canadian-bred champions.

A very famous Canadian breeder who started around the 1930s–1940s was Mrs. Gladys Creasey. Her kennel began with stock from the United States with a British background. Mrs. Creasey's first dogs were on the Cha Ming San Fu line from California, sired by Champion King San Fu of Wu-Kee ex Champion Cha Ming Wee Tykee II; the Cha Ming and Wu Kee dogs were noted for producing top quality stock. Mrs. Creasey also had an Ashcroft outcross through the descendants of Champions Monarque and Regent of Ashcroft. Obviously, she was doing things right, as her dogs were starred with successful winners, at both Canadian and United States dog shows.

185

Mrs. Hilda M. Brint came to the United States for her foundation stock: Hill Ridge consisting of Orchard Hill (Mrs. Quigley); Whitworth (Mrs. Herbert L. Mapes); Toytown (Judith Connell); and Ashcroft (Mrs. Martel). A little dog, Champion Romeo Tu of Orchard Hill, sired handsome winners for her, combining the blood of Tri-International Champion Pierrot of Hartlebury, Champion Sutherland Avenue Han Shih, and others from Mrs. Quigley's great imported dogs.

Mrs. Germaine Mattice, with her Wu San Kennels, joined the Canadian Pekingese world in the 1940s. This lady visited John B. Royce's Dah Lyn Kennels in Massachusetts for her founding stock. Her foundation bitches had Champion Nanling Noel and Champion Kai Lung of Remenham behind them, as well as lines from several additional noted kennels.

Am. and Can. St. Aubrey Tattler of Elsdon was bred by R. William Taylor and is owned by Sidney Domina, Brockville, Ontario. Successfully campaigned in both countries, he is pictured taking a Group 2nd, owner-handled, at Thousand Islands Kennel Club in 1985.

Mrs. David H. Mabon and her Sanpans were in the limelight of the early 1960s, especially with Champion Chop Chop of Elmore, who was the winner of her first all-breed Best in Show in 1965. Sadly, an untimely death cut short Chop Chop's career soon after this event. In 1968, Mrs. Mabon imported an outstanding dog from W. Hindlay Taylor's Kyratown Kennels in England, Champion Puz Althea of Kyratown. To him she bred her bitch Champion Sanpan Penelope from which came Mrs. Mabon's second Best in Show winner, Champion Sanpan Perry Puz Kin.

Michael Hill is a gentleman whose dogs have had successful impact on the Canadian Pekingese world. The Pekewind Kennels at Harrow, Ontario, are owned by Veronica Reich and Veronica Walton.

CINNABAR

Cinnabar Pekingese are owned by Mrs. Dee Dee Jones in Pontypool, Ontario, a lady who has always had dogs and has owned Pekingese her entire adult life. They are her first love in the canine world. Cinnabar was established in 1974. Unfortunately, it has not been possible for Mrs. Jones to do much showing of her dogs thus far owing to business commitments; but she and her husband, Walter, intend to change that in the near future. This kennel is entirely linebred back to Fu Yong of Jamestown and Cherangani Chips, with a dash of "Orchard Hill" and "Laparata" thrown in.

LIMIER HILL

Limier Hill is a very fmous kennel identification in Canadian and American dog show circles. In the past, it has been specifically for the identification of the superb winning and producing Bloodhounds owned by Sidney Domina of Brockville, Ontario. But starting in 1983, a new look was taken on as Sidney fulfilled a long time dream with the purchase, after waiting severals years for "just the right one," of a Pekingese, Whispers of St. Aubrey, from her good friends Nigel Aubrey Jones and R. William Taylor. Then came the second Peke, also from Nigel and Bill, American and Canadian Champion St. Aubrey Tattler of Elsdon.

Mrs. Domina got off to a good start with the Pekes. Whispers, fawn with a black mask, started her show career with a Group placement as a puppy under Edna Joel; winning Best in Sweepstakes at the Colony Pekingese Specialty; Winners Bitch and Best

Puppy at the Pekin Palace Dog Club Specialty in Toronto; Best in Specialty Match, Colony Pekingese Club; and Best Bitch in Show at the Greater Pittsburgh Pekingese Club Specialty Match in an entry of 200.

With maturity, Whispers really started to add up points, which included those for Winners Bitch at Westminster under Ed Jenner, and on various occasions took Best of Breed.

For two months during 1985, Whispers was specialed by L. Garrett Lambert to multiple Best in Show wins, becoming No. 2 Pekingese in Canada for that year. In addition, she was in the Top Twenty in the United States.

Next it was Tattler's turn. He became a Group winner from the classes and had numerous other placements, all owner-handled. His earliest victories included Best in Sweepstakes at a Colony Pekingese Show, along with Best in the Puppy Classes; some Best Puppy in Group awards, then on to the point winning until he soon had his title in both countries.

R. William Taylor bred both of these Pekes. Whispers is by American and Canadian Champion St. Aubrey Bees Wing of Elsdon (American and Canadian Champion St. Aubrey Laparata Dragon–Canadian Champion St. Aubrey Honey Bee of Elsdon) from Canadian Champion Gossip of St. Aubrey (Canadian Champion St. Aubrey Dragonfly of Elsdon–Canadian Champion Gin Lu of Tseng Liz). Tattler is by American and Canadian Champion Laparata Celestial Prince (Champion Laparata Celestial Star–Champion Laparata Precious Madame) ex Canadian Champion Tittle Tattle at St. Aubrey (Canadian Champion St. Aubrey Dragonfly of Elsdon–Canadian Champion Gin-Lu of Tseng-Liz).

Sidney and Joe Domina are getting settled in their new home in Stuart, Florida, having sold their incomparably beautiful house, right at the water's edge in Brockville, which has been their home for quite some years. They are not entirely deserting Brockville, however, and Sidney plans, as soon as the new house in Florida is settled, to return to look for a summer cottage, to be used over the hot weather months, in Brockville or the immediate area. We are quite sure that when all these matters are in place, Sidney will be producing an occasional litter of Limier Hill Pekes, based on her excellent St. Aubrey stock, and we have confidence that she will do so with the same high level of success she attained with her Bloodhounds.

SAIMAIFUN PEKINGESE

Saimaifun Pekingese of North Vancouver, British Columbia, came into existence following the Christmas 1969 gift of a male Pekingese by Doug Kleinsorge to his wife Diane. A visit to a local dog show followed soon thereafter, and upon meeting some of the local exhibitors at this show, they decided that they would establish a kennel based on their English bloodlines.

In 1974, Diane visited England and brought home a seven-month-old bitch, Glenferrar Crystal, a daughter of English Champion Etive Master Chimes. The following summer they were offered a three-year-old son of English Champion Yu-Yang of Jamestown, namely Champion Bellerne's Yu-Benito. From the union of Crystal and Benito came their first top show dog, American and Canadian Champion Saimaifun Vi's Mighty Mite, who won Best of Winners at Specialty Shows in Seattle, Portland, and San Francisco in the United States, as well as winning Best in Show at two Specialties and many Group firsts prior to retirement. Mighty Mite became one of the top USA Pekingese stud dogs during the early 1980s, according to the *American Kennel Gazette/Pure-Bred Dogs*, and he produced numerous AKC and Canadian champions.

Diane and Doug visited England again in 1976, with a desire to find another outstanding bitch to complement their existing bloodlines. At the Bellerne Kennels they were entranced by the beautiful Bellerne's Gay Pippin, who incorporated the same lines as Benito on her dam's side and brought in English Champion Samotha Gay Lad of Beaupres as her sire. The Kleinsorges succeeding in persuading her breeder, Mrs. Beryl Blackmore, to allow her to emigrate to Canada, where she was immediately launched on her show career, becoming an easy champion, winning breed and Group placements over specials, and following up with Best of Winners and Best of Opposite Sex at Specialties in Canada, Washington, and Oregon prior to retirement to matronly duties.

Pippin, when bred to Yu-Benito, produced American and Canadian Champion Saimaifun's Silhouette, who became dam of five champions in her own right. Bred to Mighty Mite, she produced American Champion Saimaifun's Mighty Macho, and American Champion Saimaifun's Mighty Presh's, all in the same litter. This breeding was so successful that it was later repeated, producing Champion Saimaifun's Gay DinaMite, who began her show career by winning Best Puppy in Sweeps her first time out (at the Central California Pekingese Specialty when just over six months old). She continued her winning ways by taking Best of Winners and Best of Opposite Sex at Specialties in Portland and Seattle. Her exciting show career was cut short by her death, during a Caesarean section, giving birth to her only litter. There were two pups born and hand-raised, one male and one female.

The male grew up to become the Kleinsorges's famous top winning all-breed Best in Show dog, American-Canadian Champion Saimaifun's Hot Shot. At four-and-a-half years, he won countless Groups, an all-breed Best in Show, and four Specialty Bests in Show all down the Pacific Coast: Vancouver, Seattle, Portland, and San Francisco. One of the Kleinsorges's most treasured possessions is the Pekingese Club of England's Year Book for 1982, where some kind words of praise of Hot Shot appear, written by R. William Taylor.

The litter sister, Champion Saimaifun's Cover Girl, was bred back to her grandfather, Mighty Mite, producing Champion Saimaifun Fair N Square (Timmy), who at three years of age was sire of three Canadian champions, one American champion, and two American-Canadian champions, with many other youngsters entered in the show ring.

A breeding into the Josto line has also had its successes, producing Champion Saimaifun's Copper Trinket, dam of American and

Ch. Saimaifun's Cover Girl taking Best of Opposite Sex under judge Mrs. Rosemary McKnight. Bred, owned, and handled by Diane and Doug Kleinsorge.

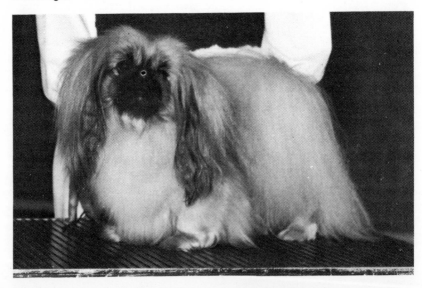

Mrs. May Robertshaw with Am. and Can. Ch. Saimaifun Vi's Mighty Mite; his daughter Am. and Can. Ch. Saimaifun Gay Dinamite; and his half sister Saimaifun Sparkle Plenty. Three generations of Saimaifun breeding owned by Diane and Doug Kleinsorge. Mrs. Robertshaw is owner of Lotusgrange Pekingese, one of Great Britain's foremost Pekingese kennels.

Canadian Champion Sparkle Saimaifun Tu; and Champion Saimaifun Square Shooter, both highly successful young winners.

Doug and Diane Kleinsorge have continued to linebreed whenever possible. With only ten dogs generally in their kennel, they find it necessary to carefully weigh the pros and cons of each planned breeding before it actually takes place, and they introduce new blood only after careful consideration of the possible effect on their future breeding program.

Despite holding the line on the number of breedings as they do, never with more than one or two litters annually, during the past ten years this kennel has produced and shown 23 champions, ten of which carry titles in two countries. There are also a good number of Saimaifun dogs now on their way to success in both the States and Canada.

The kennel name, Saimaifun is pronounced "Symyfun," and is derived from the translation of their own Dutch name, meaning "Little Sorrows" or "Little Worries."

Mr. Kleinsorge has been the President of the Western Canada Pekingese Club for 11 of its 13 years. Each Specialty hosted by this Club has been judged by a leading breeder-judge either from Canada, the United States, or England. Himself a judge, Mr. Kleinsorge has judged several English matches over the years, and he judged the Birmingham Open Pekingese Show in 1980.

191

ST. AUBREY–ELSDON

St. Aubrey-Elsdon Pekingese, owned by Nigel Aubrey Jones and R. William Taylor at Montreal, Quebec, is probably the most widely known Pekingese kennel anywhere in the world.

Long before they had actually met one another, Nigel and Bill were pen pals, sending letters back and forth across the Atlantic, which must have made lively reading considering the interest of both in this breed. Those were the days when Bill lived in Canada and Nigel was still at home in his native Wales.

Bill Taylor then made a visit to England, at which time it was decided that Nigel should return to Canada with him, and that they should breed and show Pekingese there. This was a fateful decision for the future of the Pekingese breed, we might add, as we think over the number of superb Pekingese carrying the St. Aubrey-Elsdon banner, and the heights to which these dogs have carried the breed. Bill Taylor's kennel name had been Elsdon; Nigel's had been St. Aubrey's.

Early importations from England to St. Aubrey-Elsdon include that great Caversham dog, English Champion Caversham Ko Ko of Shanruss, who came to them following a highly successful career in England. His arrival was followed by a Group win in Canada and one in the United States, and then came the Summer Specialty Show of the Pekingese Club of America in conjunction with Westchester in 1956. That was the day the ball really started to

Can. Ch. St. Aubrey Mugie Chun Maybell winning Best Puppy in Group in 1985. A future "star" from all appearances. Owned by R. William Taylor, St. Aubrey-Elsdon.

roll, as Ko Ko first won the Specialty, from the Open Class to Best of Breed, which is in itself an exciting achievement. He then took first in the Toy Group and finally Best in Show all-breeds. I have frequently heard Bill Taylor refer to this as the most memorable dog show day of his life, as this was the occasion on which St. Aubrey-Elsdon gained a Best in Show in the United States for the very first time! This was also the most prestigious and largest American Dog Show at which a Pekingese had won Best in Show at that date, although others had done so at smaller events; but this was a *huge* show for the mid-1950s, adding frosting to the cake of everyone's joy. It is sad that this magnificent little dog, who was sold almost immediately to Mrs. Saunders L. Meade of Seafren Poodles, had the misfortune to perish in a kennel fire before there had been any great opportunity to use him at stud.

The next British import to St. Aubrey-Elsdon from Caversham was the dog who broke all records for the breed, and made himself unforgettable to us all—English Champion Chik T'sun of Caversham, who arrived the year following Ko Ko. With Nigel and Bill at the helm, he made Dog of the Year in Canada, after which he was sold to Charles Venable in Georgia, for whom he was campaigned by the late Clara Alford, to 121 all-breed Bests in Show, a record not broken until 1980.

During the period from 1955 through 1967, Nigel and Bill imported a steady procession of fantastic Pekingese—contributing inestimably to the quality of the breed—such dogs as Champion Calartha Mandarin of Jehol (who sired more than 20 champions); Champion Rikki of Calartha; and Champion St. Aubrey Seminole of Wanstrow who, along with Champion St. Aubrey Mario of Elsdon, was sold to Mrs. Vera Crofton, a very busy fancier at her California kennel in those days. Another was English, American and Canadian Champion Goofus Bugatti, the beauty of whose pictures in an English magazine of the time fairly drove the Fancy wild—everyone wanted him badly!

At this same time, Nigel and Bill were breeding memorable Pekingese at the kennels in Montreal as well. Especially notable among them was American and Canadian Champion St. Aubrey Tinkabelle of Elsdon, a Mandarin daughter who was also a Chik T'sun granddaughter. Tinkabelle won Best of Breed at the Summer Specialty of the Pekingese Club of America, and was Best Bitch there three times consecutively, remaining unchallenged as leading Pekingese bitch winner in the States until 1980, when another exquisite St. Aubrey-Elsdon bitch came along and reached new heights—Mrs. Snelling's Champion St. Aubrey Dragonora of Elsdon.

In 1969, Bill Taylor decided that he would like to have, if not a rest, at least a change of scene, and set off with Nigel for England, where they remained for seven years. The kennel was disbanded in Montreal, with Mrs. Gilma Moss purchasing many of the dogs for her Ho Dynasty Kennels in New Jersey, where they made valued additions to her Orchard Hill and other imported stock.

Goofus Bugatti returned, with Nigel and Bill, to his homeland when they made that trip, having left there in a blaze of glory in 1944, after winning Best of Breed at Crufts. His return was equally auspicious, for as a six-year-old (following the six-month quarantine period dogs arriving in Great Britain must endure), he re-entered the toughest show competition and took Best in Specialty Show at the huge Championship event of the Pekingese Club.

While in England during this period, in the spring of 1968, English Champion St. Aubrey Carnival Music of Eastfield was keeping Nigel and Bill in the winners circle and, by the end of that year, had gained five challenge certificates which included becoming a champion and was, as well, the leading Challenge Certificate winning Pekingese for that period.

Champion St. Aubrey Fairy Ku of Craigfoss made 1969 her year, starting out, as a puppy, by promptly gaining her title, and during the remainder of the year she gained a higher total of Challenge Certificates than any other Pekingese. Thus St. Aubrey-Elsdon became the top Challenge Certificate-winning Pekingese Kennel. Fairy Ku held her own through 1970 as well, bringing her total number of Challenge Certificates to a total of 17, in addition to being Top Winning Pekingese bitch of the year. Then came another notable English Champion bitch during the same year, St. Aubrey Pekehuis Honey Dew.

A ten-week-old puppy, who was to become English Champion St. Aubrey Pekehuis Petula, was purchased and owned briefly by Nigel and Bill a bit later on. Although she was maturing more than satisfactorily, business commitments during the same period led to the realization that they would not be able to do justice to her show career, and so she was sold back to her breeder, Mrs. I.

194

Partridge. Not only did she become a champion, but she was to win a grand total of 36 Challenge Certificates, thus becoming the leading Pekingese Challenge Bitch in the history of the breed in Great Britain.

When Nigel and Bill decided to return to Canada, they were anxious to resume breeding activities and re-open St. Aubrey-Elsdon there. For foundtion stock at this point, they had the choice of rounding up descendants of their original dogs, especially Mandarin and Chik T'sun descendants, or starting fresh with new lines altogether. They agreed upon the latter course, bringing back several bitches of top English lines who appeared to have exceptional potential to form the nucleus of a new breeding kennel. Within six years the kennel seemed stronger than ever, which was contributed to inestimably by the fabulous influence of a memorable young sire, American and Canadian Champion St. Aubrey Laparata Dragon.

To say that Dragon admirably fulfilled his early potential would be an understatement; his success has been far beyond the anticipation of even his greatest admirers, as the more than 100 champions he has sired far and away exceed the number titled by *any* other Pekingese stud dog. His progeny include numerous Best in Show winners; a still greater number of multiple Group winners; Specialty Show winners; and dogs with notable records under the Ratings Systems.

We feel certain that Dragon will add many more champions to his list. He was sold by Nigel and Bill to Ed Jenner at Knolland Farm Kennels, for whom he had a brilliant show career. But it is as a sire that Dragon has had his principal impact on Pekingese. Fortunately, he has been appreciated from the very beginning, with breeders from far and wide using him on their finest bitches, and the quality of his offspring speaks for itself.

On a judging trip to Australia, three lovely Pekingese bitches were discovered and brought back for the St. Aubrey-Elsdon breeding program. One of these included the Australian-bred American and Canadian Champion Lingling Gypsy Sue, a challenge certificate winner at the famed Melbourne Royal Dog Show as a puppy. These bitches have worked well with Dragon and the other St. Aubrey-Elsdon studs, with more champions for Bill and Nigel as the result.

Only two Pekingese have ever won Best in Show at Westminster

195

Am. and Can. Ch. St. Aubrey Debonair of Elsdon taking Best in Show at the 1965 United Kennel Club in Montreal under judge Percy Roberts. Debonair was a multiple Best in Show winner in both the United States and Canada. Owned by Vera F. Crofton, Nigel Aubrey Jones (handling) and R. William Taylor.

Kennel Club. Their names are Champion Chik T'sun of Caversham, in 1960; and Champion St. Aubrey Dragonora of Elsdon, in 1982. Nigel and Bill are responsible for both dogs—in Chik T'sun's case as the ones who brought him to America; in Dragonora's as her breeders. Chik T'sun was purchased from Nigel and Bill by the Charles Venables in Georgia.

America's Top Winning Toy Dog in the United States for 1985, winner of the Ken-L-Biskit Award for this accomplishment, was Champion St. Aubreys Beesknees of Elsdon, bred by Nigel and Bill, now owned by Mr. Jenner; he is a son of Dragon.

Breeding of fabulous Pekingese continues at St. Aubrey-Elsdon and, despite the fact that both Nigel and Bill travel extensively on their judging assignments, this will remain the case. A move to a new, and a bit smaller, location, which will also be in the Montreal area, has been made. Once settled, however, we are sure that there will be more Peke litters coming along, and more great young dogs in the St. Aubrey-Elsdon tradition.

196

Chapter 5

Pekingese Around the World

PEKINGESE IN AUSTRALIA

For some years now, as judges have gone back and forth between the United States and Australia, I have been hearing glowing accounts of the quality and beauty of the Australian-bred Pekingese. Thus I felt it of utmost importance that this book include a good representation, and I am proud of the response my request for photos and kennel information brought forth. I am sure that you will find the following kennel histories interesting, and the pictures of the dogs truly excellent.

Australian breeders are doing a good job on many fronts. But I must say that from what I have seen, heard, and read, the Pekingese people deserve perhaps an extra bit of credit. The breed has been established there for a considerable length of time, and it has obviously prospered.

Various people have asked me what is meant by the Australian designation "Royal" in referring to some of the larger Australian events. Albert and Heather Parton give us the answer: the "Royals" are the most prestigious shows, which are held in the capital cities and bigger cities. Exhibitors bring their dogs from near and

197

far to compete at these "Royals," where overseas judges usually officiate. The structure of a "Royal" differs from that of a Championship Show in that fewer awards are presented. There is a Group winner, then Best of Opposite Sex to Group Winner. There is a Puppy in Group winner and a Best Opposite Sex. The winners of these awards then compete for the "in Show" awards. The cream of Australia's dogs compete for these honors.

Caledonian

The Caledonian Pekingese, in Wagga Wagga, New South Wales, are owned by Mr. and Mrs. C. Lidden who, over a period of 30 years as breeders (in a country where long spaces of time frequently pass between dogs shows), have proudly owned 18 Pekingese champions.

They consider their best dog to have been Champion Mahjong The Egan who, despite not having been shown until ten months old (the Australians start many of their dogs as entrants in the "Baby Puppy" class at three months' age), had completed his title at age 13 months. Among outstanding show successes for Egan was the May 1981 event of the Pekingese Club of New South Wales, which had brought Mrs. Betty Shoemaker from the United States to serve as judge. There were 184 Pekingese in competition, and Egan went through to the supreme honor of Best Dog in Show for the Junior Class (under 18 months). At that time, he was 17 months old and had earned 300 championship points. Mrs. Shoemaker is quoted as having told the Liddens that "The Egan would be a Top Peke in any country."

Brian Wilson, owner of the Mahjong Pekingese at Victoria, was the breeder of The Egan. The latter is the result of an aunt and nephew mating, his sire being Champion Mahjong the Pretender (by Champion Copplestone Contender, UK import, ex Mahjong Catrena), his dam being Champion Mahjong Lee Kwan, sister to Catrena, as both are daughters of Champion Mahjong Clark Gable of Coughton. The Egan is now retired with 1300 championship points.

Another outstanding Pekingese belonging to the Liddens is Champion Mahjong Nanette, born January 1983, sired by Champion Yamagee Keis Son from Champion Mahjong Nicola. She, too, was bred by Brian Wilson. One of her outstanding accomplishments has been winning Challenge Bitch at the Melbourne Royal in 1985.

The Australian Best in Show Winner, Ch. Chindara Empress Say Yu, daughter of Ch. Burndale Fameschon ex Ch. Chindara Lola Sed So, is owned by Noel and Denise King, Chindara Pekingese.

Chindara

Chindara Pekingese are owned by Noel and Denise King of Birkdale, Queensland, who acquired their first of the breed as a pet from a friend in 1969. She was a very tiny girl, too small to accomplish anything particular in either the show ring or for breeding.

The Kings' first show dog was bought, for only $50, at the Joewil Kennels. This was a marvelous bargain, as he was Champion Joewil Jon Romeo, who numbered among his wins three Bests in Show, twice was Best of Breed at the Brisbane Royal, and had many "in Group" awards as well—all accomplished while his owners were still very new in the breed. Next came the sound and beautiful bitch, Champion Chindara Nannette, a daughter of Champion Joewil Prince Kulo from Joewil Samantha.

For their next purchases, the Kings turned to Linbourne Pekingese, owned by Mrs. G. Pateman (who, in 1985, celebrated 50 years of breeding Pekes). Linbourne bloodlines are the principle ones on which Chindara was established, occasionally outcrossing but then breeding immediately back into Linbourne to strengthen type. The foundation bitch for the Kings was Champion Lady Lola, by Samsuma Ku Ku Gable ex Linbourne The Princess.

Of Lady Lola, the Kings say, "she gave us everything we could ask: beautiful bitches, and in turn, her daughters did likewise." Both of the Kennel's best producing bitches were Lady Lola daughters, namely Champion Chindara Lola Sedso, who was by Champion Singlewell Wot Say Yu (UK import); and Chindara Society Cindy, by Champion Linbourne Li Cheng. Cindy is a beautiful bitch like her mother, but is unshown, owing to an eye injury. She surely made a major contribution to the breed, however, when she produced the multi-Best in Show daughter Champion Chindara Society Rose, who to date is Australia's Top Winning Pekingese Bitch. Rose, says her owners, "has it all: a beautiful head, fabulous body, is totally sound, and has loads of stunning apricot coat." She was sired by Champion Borndale Famechon, who was by Champion Copplestone Contender. Her show victories include Best in Specialty Show at both the Pekingese Club of New South Wales and the Pekingese Club of Victoria; and Challenge Bitch at the Sydney Royal, although she is still at the start of her career, which deferred to her three litters of puppies, whelped prior to her embarkment in the show ring.

Australian Champion Linbourne Li Cheng (Champion Markel Sun Yeng–San Toi Mei Li) was bred by Mrs. G. Pateman. He has been the winner of 21 Bests in Show; Best Exhibit in Toy Group, Sydney Royal, under Mr. H. Glover; winner of two Pekingese Specialty Shows; Best Exhibit in Group at the 1979 Sydney Spring Fair Dog Show, repeated in 1980 under Mr. C. Aldercrutz of Sweden; Best in Show at the North of the Harbour Winter Classic; and other awards too numerous to list. Suffice to say that he was Top Pekingese in Sydney, New South Wales, for six years.

Australian Champion Chindara Fancy Pants, owned by Mrs. P. LeBrun in Sydney, was Top Winning Peke male for the past five years. He was Challenge Dog, Pekingese Club of Sydney, for two years; Challenge Dog Sydney Royal, Best in Group, Spring Fair; and Best Exhibit in Group, Sydney Royal.

Australian Champion Chin Fancee Mee, by Champion Linbourne Li Ching ex Chindara Lola Sed So, is the winner of many Best in Toy Group and Best in Show awards.

Australian Champion Burndale Famechon is the winner of eight all-breed Bests in Show, and was Best Exhibit in Toy Group, Sydney Royal and Best of Breed, Brisbane Royal. Famechon is the sire of Queensland's sensational winning bitches, Australian Champion Chindara Empress Say Yu and Society Rose.

The Kings look forward to breeding Pekingese for years to come.

Aust. Ch. Linbourne Li Cheng, the famous winner and sire who is so important a factor behind Noel and Denise King's Chindara Pekingese.

Frawai

Frawai Pekingese in Emu Plains, New South Wales, were started around 1960 by Mrs. Frances Wickens when, as a Christmas gift for her mother, she purchased a Peke puppy which she had to care for over several weeks prior to the holiday. In those short weeks, Mrs. Wickens was converted into a lifetime fancier of the breed, to the point that she has never since been without one; and she admits, as I had begun to suspect, that her mother did *not* receive the puppy as a gift that year!

From the moment she had Ming, Mrs. Wickens' love for Pekingese flourished, and the numbers in her Pekingese family expanded. She bred her very first litter in 1961, when she was a young newlywed. She comments, "I shudder to think of it now, but I was at the beach when the four beautiful puppies were born. I had been told that it would take 63 days, and this was only the 58th. It was very hot, so my husband and I went sunning."

Aust. Ch. Frawai Roseita, by Aust. Ch. Windermere Ching-Se Ling ex Frawai Kalo Kalo, Challenge Bitch Royal Easter Show 1976. Also a Best in Show winner. Mrs. F. Wickens, owner.

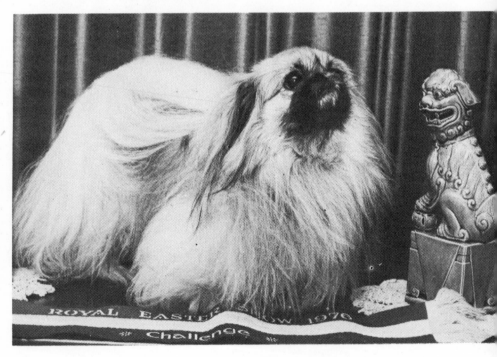

Aust. Ch. Frawai Puzin Dominator. A Best in Show winner. Best Toy at the RASKC Spring Fair 1983. Owned by Mrs. F. Wickens. Photo by T. Dorizas.

Ming had a beautiful little black female in her litter, which Mrs. Wickens was longing to keep; but being a novice, she took the advice of an old hand with the breed, who advised her to "get rid of the black as soon as possible, as you don't want a black near your kennel." Since then, she has learned better, and will always make it a point to have a black in her breeding program for coat texture and pigmentation.

The Pekingese still continue to be a source of true pleasure to Mrs. Wickens, and they are doing well for her, too, in show competition. Her foster daughter, Marie Patten, now does the handling. This young lady also has a very strong devotion to Pekingese, and one day will carry on the Frawai prefix.

Among the most exciting of the show dogs presently in the Frawai Kennels is Australian Champion Frawai Apollo Creed, born in August 1983, owned by Marie Patten and bred by Mrs. Wickens. He is a multi-Best in Show winner, and his achievements include Best in Show at the Pekingese Championship Show in 1985, in addition to many other exciting awards to his credit.

Jimgemajade

Jimgemajade Kennels are owned by George and Alice Houghton, at Kambah, ACT. The Houghtons had their first dogs while in England. These were Pugs, and it was not until they arrived in Australia in 1964 that they acquired their first Pekingese (living at that time in South Australia). Two years later they relocated in New South Wales, where they obtained a beautiful Pekingese dog named Lankari Camalot. Camalot was descended from UK import Ping Gable of Coughton.

Since that time, after moving into the ACT in the mid-1970s, the Houghtons' kennel has gradually increased; they now have 22 dogs. Their daughter is also into Pekingese, under the kennel prefix of "Starpeke."

Among the noted Pekingese owned by the Houghtons, one finds Australian Champion Tulyns Sosay Allogus, born July 1979, bred by D.B.B. Horan, sired by Australian Champion Kandence Wee Sedso from Kandence Snow White, who came to the Houghtons at the age of one year. He has won eight Bests in Toy Groups, numerous Bests in Show, and many times Best of Breed. Sosay's daughter, Jimgemajade Samantha, lives in Tucson, Arizona, with her owner, Mrs. Judy Nickerson.

Australian Champion Shindand Imagem was born October 1979, her breeder I.M. McLean. She is a fawn brindle by Huanme Cheong Eboi ex Kunium Blossom. "Pipper" got her championship the hard way: a bad experience with a bee sting had made her a bit temperamental in the ring. She did, however, in her showing time, gain a good number of Bests of Breed, Best Open, Best Australian Bred, and Best Intermediate in groups at shows. Shindand Imagem comes down from English and US champions and imports, such as Australian Champion Ralshams Imagem (UK import) and Australian Champion Ku-Tuo of Montressor (UK import).

Australian Champion Venesse Shouling, February 1979, was obtained by the Houghtons as a brood matron, but after her first litter of two pups, she put on so much body, coat and condition that it was decided there would be no harm in showing her. She gained her Australian championship, and was then retired from the ring to live, as she now does, in the lap of luxury. She is by Kandence Black Zulu from Hagentown Babie Jane.

Kandence Tai Tara, May 1981, is a cream daughter of Kandence

Aust. Ch. Tulyns Sosay Allofus, by Aust. Ch. Kandance Wee Sedso ex Kandance Snow White. Owned by George and Alice Houghton.

Mr. Bojangles ex Kandence Chippa Tara. Although she never did much in the show ring, she is an exceptional brood bitch, thus highly valued by her owners.

Australian Champion Mayfleet Wee Baron, December 1983, is by Australian Champion Kendence Wee Sedso ex Mayleet Wee Baron, thus is a half- brother to Sosay. The dam's sire was Australian Champion Burndale Famechon, and his grandsire was Australian Champion Copplestone Contender (UK import).

Baron has numerous Bests of Breed to his credit, and various "in show" and "in Group" awards, including third place in the Canberra Royal Show during the Canberra Kennel Association's Guineas final for all breeds of dogs for 1986. There were 28 dogs shown in the final.

Australian Champion Jimgemajade Golda, April 1983, is a light cream daughter of Australian Champion Tulyns Sosay Allofus ex Kandence Tai Tara, thus a full sister to Samantha, now living in the USA. She has won numerous show awards, the most exciting of which was Best Intermediate Bitch and Reserve Challenge Pekingese Bitch at the 1986 Sydney Royal Easter Show. From there, she took Challenge Bitch, Best of Breed, and Best Australian-bred in Toy Group at the Canberra All-Breeds Kennel Club Show two days later.

Several young dogs for whom hopes are high as we write include Jimgemajade Susie Wong, born September 1984; Jimgemajade Mr. Chimes, May 1985; and Jimgemajade Little Gem, born 1986, a tiny sleeve.

205

Aust. Ch. Shantzi Superman, by Aust. Ch. Linbourne Just Me ex Shantzi Mei Kuei. Owned by Kotlepeb Pekingese.

Kotlepeb

Kotlepeb Pekingese are owned by Mrs. R.M. Cameron and are located in Baulkham Hills, New South Wales.

Mrs. Cameron's top male Pekingese, Shantzi Superman, was bred in Mulgoa, a suburb of Sydney, by Mrs. Lesze, a well-known breeder of more than 18 years. Superman likes showing, and has been very successful in the ring.

The lovely bitch, Yamagee Pebbles, also comes from good breeding, from the well-established kennels of Mrs. Richardson in Western Australia. Pebbles also does well in show competition, and has 84 points, although she was shown only eight times due to maternal duties.

Mrs. Cameron is a new breeder, having been showing for only a few years, but she thoroughly enjoys it and takes great pleasure from her dogs.

206

Kylarkie

Kylarkie Pekingese at Tamborine Mountain, Queensland, are the result of a little Pekingese having been given, as a gift, from Albert Parton to his wife, Heather, on their first wedding anniversary. This was a gift with far-reaching results when one stops to consider the enjoyment both Partons have had with the breed, and the success with which their dogs have met. The year of this event was 1974, and that puppy, who had been bought purely as a pet, remained so during her life with the Partons.

Meanwhile, however, they had been attending a few dog shows, which had increased their enthusiasm for the breed and made them want a dog with which they could win. They then saw an advertisement of a 15-month-old dog for sale, which they went to see and promptly purchased. He was owned by Patricia Smith, Ormalu Kennels in Brisbane, who encouraged the Partons in every way, from selling them a good dog to teaching them how to groom and show it! This dog was Champion Ashbourne Ku Rixson, by Champion Dominion Ku Ricky from Tuo Choo Lisa Jane.

The Partons took "Nicky" to his Australian title, and had the fun of starting their exhibiting career with some good wins. He was a multiple Group winner, had many Class in Show awards, and even took a Reserve Best in Show. After all that, the Partons were thoroughly hooked on being show dog folks!

Next they went to Melbourne, where they became friends with Jill Davis (Jayville) and Brian Wilson (Mahjong), both well-known in the breed. From Jill Davis they purchased a nine-week-old male puppy who grew up to become Champion Jayville's Jeraldo, by Champion Jayville's Gerard from Jayville Jenetta. This dog won several Class In Show awards and became a multiple Group winner.

Then a bitch was selected from Brian Wilson, Marok Mandy Toy Lou, which was made an Australian Champion and was then started on their breeding program. She carried Mahjong lines, and the Partons bred her to Hansu Timothy Gable, a dog from Western Australia who also carrying the Mahjong strain behind him.

Mandy Toy Lou produced two beautiful bitches from her first litter, one of which was sold, the other kept. The latter was named Kylarkie Camilla, and she, too, made her presence felt in the show ring, as she gained her championship and many other honors.

Best in Show, Gold Coast Canine Club, was won by Aust. Ch. Ormalu William Gable. This is only one of the goodly number of prestigious awards gained by this handsome dog. Owned by Albert and Heather Parton.

After that, Camilla was mated to Champion Yamages Kies Son, bred in Western Australia, owned by Brian Wilson, and dominated by Mahjong lines. From this breeding, Champion Kylarkie Beau Derek was whelped in 1982. Beau Derek's wins included the Brisbane Royal in 1984; the Toy Group at the Toowoomba Royal that same year, and in 1985 she won a Best in Show. Her litter sister was sold to a South Australian fancier, going on to gain her Australian championship. Camilla was then mated to Champion Mahjong The Pretender, whom the Pattons own, a sire who has produced many champion dogs and bitches in Australia and overseas.

From this mating, a male parti-color, which the Partons kept, the future Champion Kylarkie Parti-Crasha, was born November 1983. During his short career, Parti-Crasha won 11 Puppy in Show awards. Along with 18 other puppies of different breeds, which included the entire state of Queensland, he was asked to compete in the "Pal Puppy of the Year" competition, sponsored by the makers of Pal Dog Food.

208

Kylarkie Parti-Crasha gained his Australian championship title at the age of ten months by winning four consecutive Groups, each having 25 points. In so doing, he competed against older dogs of all breeds in the Toy Group plus dogs and bitches who were already Australian championship titleholders—no easy feat for a dog not yet out of the puppy classes. He also won Reserve in Show and Opposite Sex in Show at the New South Wales Pekingese Specialty, climaxing his first year by winning Puppy in Group under Peter Thomson in 1984.

In addition, there is Champion Ormalu William Gable, by Champion Hansu Timothy Gable from Ashbourne Genevieve. William Gable's wins, too, are notable and memorable. He also made his presence felt as a sire, and among his progeny is the lovely bitch Champion Ying Tang New Year's Eve.

Liam

Liam Pekingese in Warner's Bay, New South Wales, are owned by Mrs. Nuree MacKay who, in 1958, acquired a lovely chun red Pekingese from Mrs. Kelp, bred down from "Changte" kennels.

Aust. Ch. Barramba Kymel at seven months. By N.Z. Ch. Toydom Enchanted of Singlewell (U.K. import) ex Saigon Ai Jen, bred by Mrs. D. Wilson, Palmerston North, New Zealand. Kymela completed championship by age 14 months. Owned by Nuree MacKay.

Right then she was sold on the breed, on learning more about it, and on raising and showing these dogs.

In the early years of breeding, Mrs. MacKay was mostly concerned with producing type and soundness, and for the first ten years concentrated on bloodlines representing the English imports with good show records. Deciding on the "Joewil" kennels for breeding stock and advice, she gradually bred a kennel of 36 Pekingese, from which she has had to cut down since the early 1980s, due to local regulations, now limiting her stock to 15 in number.

Mrs. MacKay has introduced the Copplestone line, Steer and Forster's Burndale Kennel, and Mrs. D. Wilson's New Zealand line from her Singlewell imports.

Interested in linebreeding, and in dogs with soundness and good temperament, Mrs. MacKay is really enjoying the breeding of some Best in Show winners—which, as she notes, is the "ultimate goal of most breeders."

Aust. Ch. Choonan Wei Jemi, born November 1976, by Ch. Augusta Superman (U.K. import) ex Choonan Gia Gia. Owned by Mrs. M. and Miss N. Cowpan.

Velvart

Velvart had been selected, and approved, as the kennel name by which Mrs. M and Miss M. Cowpar would identify their Pekingese in South Penrith, New South Wales, back in 1964.

The first dog for them came from Tientsin Kennels. Their first champion was Australian Champion Regalen Kee Mark Lee in 1974, who carried the bloodlines of Shalwyn, Dreamland, and Yentui Kennels. Since that time, this kennel has made up a total of seven champions and needs just nine more points to make an eighth.

Australian Champion Wei Jemi was born November 1976. A multiple In Show and Group winner, including Best in Show at the Pekingese Club of New South Wales, he has proven himself equally well as a sire, with champions and Best in Show winners. Wei Jemi carried the bloodlines from England of Copplestone, Pendarvis, and Ralshams; from Australia of Holviet, Kandence, and Solitaire.

Velvart Banjo was born June 1983, by Champion Choonan Wei Jemi ex Pingyang Ku Donnah. This lovely Peke is also a Group winner. Velvart Ribbons, from the same litter as Banjo, has been a winner at the Royal Easter Show and has Group success on the list of credits.

Australian Champion Velvart Christmas Eve was born on Christmas Eve 1983, by Australian Champion Mysticleigh Sambo ex Pingyang Ku-Donnah. A multiple Group and also In-Show winner, she was recently the top winner at the Pekingese Club of New South Wales. Her breeding carries the bloodlines of Toydom, Maykel, Copplestone, Loofoo, Shalwyn, and Frawai Kennels.

PEKINGESE IN SOME EUROPEAN COUNTRIES

Pekes have long enjoyed popularity on the continent, and over the years, France, Spain, Monaco, and many other countries have had splendid representatives of the breed. We are especially happy to have this Norwegian information, and perhaps it will break the ice for the future!

The successful Scandinavian kennel of Boni Sorenson based in Oslo, Norway, started in 1977 when she imported, from the Toydom Kennels in England, Toydom Aphrodisia, a son of Sungarth Kanga of Toydom, who quickly gained his title in his new home.

A successful breeder and exhibitor of Great Danes, Boni

211

International and Nordic Ch. Pendenrah Robin, by Sungarth Kanga of Toydom ex Pendenrah Some Charmer, is the Top Winning Toy Dog in Scandinavia for 1985 and 1986. Owned by Miss Borghild Sorgensen in Norway.

quickly built up an equally successful kennel of Pekingese, campaigning another son of Kanga to become the Top Winning Dog All Breeds in Norway in 1982, International Champion Sunsalve Come Play With Me at Toydom.

During the years she has been active in the breed, Boni Sorenson has certainly made her mark, having in that period of time bred eight champions, and having actually made up 15. Many of these went on to become Group and Best in Show winners. A most recent champion at Hotpoints is International Champion Pendenrah Robin, also a Kanga son. At the moment, it appears that he is going to follow in Come Play With Me's pawprints as a record holder, for at this time he is in the lead in his country for top honors.

Chapter 6

The Pekingese Standard

It is in the immortal words of the Dowager Empress Tzu Hsi, last great ruler of the ancient Chinese Empire, that we find the words which have obviously served as the foundation for the standards of our Pekingese breed throughout these many years. For who could possibly be more qualified than this Empress, who so dearly loved the breed, who devoted time and thought and attention to them, and who bred selectively, remembering each dog and its ancestors for several generations. The Empress had great knowledge concerning these dogs: read her words, read the present standards, and think about their meaning. You will then realize how very little change has occurred in what is now considered correct in a Pekingese and in what the Empress Tzu Hsi sought in her dogs.

In describing the forebears of the modern Pekingese, the Empress Tzu Hsi said: "Let the Lion Dog be small; let it wear the swelling cape of dignity around its neck; let it display the billowing standard of pomp above its back.

"Let its face be black; let its forefront be shaggy; let its forehead be straight and low, like unto the brow of an Imperial harmony boxer. Let its eyes be large and luminous; let its ears be set like the sails of a war junk; let its nose be like that of the monkey god of the Hindus. Let its forelegs be bent, so that it shall not desire to wander far, or leave the Imperial Palace.

"Let its body be shaped like that of a hunting lion spying for its prey. Let its feet be tufted with plentiful hair that its footfall may be soundless; and for its standard of pomp, let it rival the

213

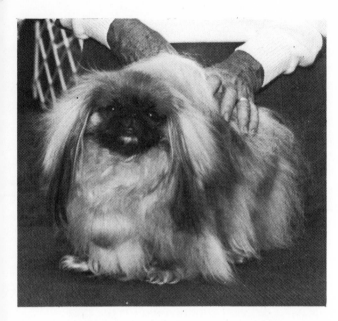

Ch. Changkim
Moongold owned by
Mrs. Walter M. Jeffords
here is taking Best of
Opposite Sex and
Southern Maryland K.C.
in 1982.

whisk of the Tibetan Yak, which is flourished to protect the Imperial litter from the attacks of flying insects.

"Let it be lively, that it may afford entertainment by its gambols; let it be timid that it may not involve itself in dangers; let it be domestic in its habits that it may live in amity with the other beasts, fishes or birds that find protection at the Imperial Palace.

"And for its color, let it be that of the lion—a golden sable to be carried in the sleeve of a yellow robe, or the color of a red bear, or a black or a white bear, or striped like a dragon, so that there may be dogs appropriate to every costume in the Imperial wardrobe. Let it venerate its ancestors and deposit offerings in the canine cemetery of the Forbidden City on each new moon. Let it comport itself with dignity; let it learn to bite the foreign devils instantly.

"Let it be dainty in its food that it shall be known for an Imperial dog by its fastidiousness. Sharks' fins, curlew livers, and the breasts of quails, on these it may be fed; and for drink, give it the tea that is brewed from the spring buds of the shrub that groweth in the province of Hankow, or the milk of the antelope that pasture in the Imperial parks.

"Thus it shall preserve its integrity and self-respect; and for the day of sickness let it be anointed with the clarified fat of the leg

214

of a sacred leopard, and give it to drink a throstle's eggshell full of the juice of the custard apple in which has been dissolved three pinches of shredded rhinoceros horn, and apply to it piebald leeches. So shall it remain—but if it die, remember thou too art mortal!"

The author finds the words of the Empress quite stirring—on reading them, one realizes how very true to the original type our Pekingese have remained.

AKC STANDARD

● **Expression**—Must suggest the Chinese origin of the Pekingese in its quaintness and individuality, resemblance to the lion in directions and independence and should imply courage, boldness, self-esteem and combativeness rather than prettiness, daintiness or delicacy.

● **Skull**—Massive, broad, wide and flat between the ears (not dome-shaped), wide between the eyes. *Nose*–Black, broad, very short and flat. *Eyes*–Large, dark, prominent, round, lustrous. *Stop*–Deep. *Ears*–Heart-shaped, not set too high, leather never long enough to come below the muzzle, nor carried erect, but rather drooping, long feather. *Muzzle*–Wrinkled, very short and broad, not overshot nor pointed. Strong, broad underjaw, teeth not to show.

● **Shape of Body**—Heavy in front, well-sprung ribs, broad chest, falling away lighter behind, lionlike. Back level. Not too long in body; allowance made for longer body in bitch. *Legs*–Short forelegs, bones of forearm bowed, firm at shoulder; hindlegs lighter but firm and well shaped. *Feet*–Flat, toes turned out, not round, should stand well up on feet, not on ankles.

● **Action**—Fearless, free and strong, with slight roll.

● **Coat, Feather, And Condition**—Long, with thick undercoat, straight and flat, not curly nor wavy, rather coarse, but soft; feather on thighs, legs, tail and toes long and profuse. *Mane*–Profuse, extending beyond the shoulder blades, forming ruff or frill around the neck.

● **Color**—All colors are allowable. Red, fawn, black, black and tan, sable, brindle, white and parti-color well defined; black masks and spectacles around the eyes, with lines to ears are desirable. *Definition of a Parti-Color Pekingese.* The coloring of a parti-color Pekingese must be broken on the body. No large portion of any one color should exist. White should be shown on the saddle. A dog of any solid color with white feet and chest is not a particolor.

• *Tail*—Set high; lying well over back to either side; long, profuse, straight feather.

• *Size*—Being a toy dog, medium size preferred, providing type and points are not sacrificed; extreme limit 14 pounds.

SCALE OF POINTS

Expression	5	Shape of Body	15
Skull	10	Legs and Feet	15
Nose	5	Coat, Feather, Condition.	15
Eyes	5	Tail	5
Stop	5	Action	10
Ears	5		
Muzzle	5	**Total**	100

Faults—Protruding tongue; badly blemished eye; overshot, wry mouth.

Disqualifications—Weight–over 14 pounds. Dudley nose.

Approved April 10, 1956.

COMMENTS ON THE BRITISH STANDARD FOR PEKINGESE

Basically the Standard for evaluating Pekingese in Great Britain is describing the same dog as in America, although somewhat more specifically. The latter principally in the area of action, where Gait is listed as "Slow, dignified, rolling gait in front" and continues that the action should be "close behind," and that "absolute soundness essential." We like this reference that a Pekingese should be "slow" in movement as it is the author's feeling that too many exhibitors rush their Pekes around American show rings far too fast for a judge to make accurate evaluation of whether the dog actually rolls correctly or not. Also we like the reference that rear action should be close.

The British Standard is specific, too, about the neck, which is an important feature of the breed yet ignored in the American Standard. The British Standard states "NECK Very short and thick." We feel that this statement is important since many judges seem unaware of it. A Pekingese with a long neck is atypical; yet in America people, including some who judge it, are of the opinion that a Pekingese neck should be long!

The size requirements in Great Britain are smaller than here, they state that dogs should not exceed 11 pounds; and bitches not exceed 12 pounds. In America 14 pounds is stated as the extreme limit in both sexes.

There are no breed disqualifications in the British Pekingese Standard.

CORRECT TYPE AND SHOW QUALITY

One will recognize, upon reading and comparing the Empress Tzu Hsi's words with those of the American Standard, that basically the Pekingese of today is little changed from the Pekingese as the Empress knew the breed. Refined, improved in some ways, perhaps more glamorous; but there it is, now as then, the need for the same characteristics as in the royal dogs.

As one who has been judging Pekingese for more than 50 years, mine has been a somewhat unique opportunity to observe the changes and the progress which breeders have brought about in Pekingese. Although basically the same dog, our Pekingese of today stand as an ovation and a tribute to those knowledgeable and dedicated breeders who have, intelligently and with patience, brought Pekingese to their present heights of beauty and excellence. It has not been easy, I am sure; for, as one feature has improved, another has required improvement. The breeders have arisen to each challenge as it has appeared, and I cannot help but feel that the Pekingese of today is at its highest point of the past five decades. No longer are the good dogs isolated delights—they are the norm. The biggest problem about judging the breed has become making a choice between the many exquisite dogs in competition rather than, as at various times over the years, deciding which of the numerous undesirables is the least so.

Looking back to the early dog shows I attended, and the Pekes I owned, during the late 1920s–early 1930s, two of the most striking improvements over the years have been in heads and in coat. The early Pekes would have been considered poor in head from the late 1930s onward. Most of the early heads were massive; but they were also "nosey," showing a length which would horrify Pekingese connoisseurs of present times should they run across one today. In addition, the gorgeous "finish of face," provided by our

217

now taken for granted unbroken wrinkle, had not yet been developed.

Breeders really worked on Pekingese heads in order to bring them to the present. Shorter faces; better nose placement; more width; correct underjaw (neither the Bulldog look nor the chinless one we once saw so frequently); all became fixed features of the breed, perfected by careful, intelligent breeding.

The breeders of the 1930s and the 1940s were working on coat and fringes as well as on heads, with the longer, more luxuriant, body coats and fringes—which, again, we casually take for granted today—becoming more so by the month.

The only problem was that while the heads and coats were taking precedence in breeders' thoughts, strange things were happening to correct legs and bodies. Many Pekingese were becoming long; this led to a rush of preference for the too short. And unsound (i.e. out at shoulder) forequarters were being confused in the minds of judges with correct forelegs which remained, as they should, firm and well-knit at the shoulders. It is these "out at shoulder" Pekes who fail to carry their topline correctly level, as the back becomes, of necessity, low at the withers.

Of course, these two faults were promptly reflected in other ways. The too-long Pekes had a lanky, "shelly" appearance that was undesirable; for, although the standard does make an allowance for a bit more length in bitches than in dogs (for easier carriage and delivery of puppies), the spring of rib must be noticeable and the dog, or bitch, who is long must not be *excessively* so. The breeders recognized this fact and started breeding for shorter backs, which wound up going to the *other* extreme, as Pekes began being referred to as "cobby." Heaven forbid! First of all, this is atypical, as who has ever seen a "cobby" lion? Secondly, it is absolutely impossible for an *overly* short-backed dog to move with the correct roll, as this movement is created by a combination of width of chest, shortness of forelegs with correct shoulder placement, and sufficient length of body to enable the dog to roll. A dog who is excessively short in body may look cute, compact, and trappy, but the action accompanying this excessive shortness is more a hop than a roll, jerky rather than smooth. Incidentally, to really show off a correctly moving Pekingese, the dog should not be *rushed* around the ring; rather, he should be moved at his *natural* speed in order to display his unique "roll" to advantage.

218

Over the years, in judging, I have met with all sorts of hind-quarters on Pekingese; I am happy to say that, with increasing frequency lately, I have noted a vast improvement in that area. How it ever came about that so many Pekingese hindlegs were shaped rather like distorted corkscrews, I shall never know! But they were, and I could never forget the distress this fact brought me on frequent occasions. The Pekingese hindleg should be firm, well muscled, with a well-let-down stifle-hock assemblage. When handled in judging, it should have definite shape and substance.

I have judged Pekes who were double jointed at the hock; who have been completely without angulation; who have been cow-hocked; and who have been the opposite to that—bandy-legged. I have judged Pekes whose hindquarters have seemed utterly without musculation, with so little substance, and feeling almost pitiful to the touch. I would say that this has been the "forgotten area" of the Pekingese. I am glad to say that, whether accidentally or on purpose, Peke hindquarters are improving to the extent that one is now finding far more normally-formed hindlegs than has been the case at many periods.

On countless occasions I have heard Pekingese referred to as being one of the most difficult of all breeds to judge. This is a debatable question, as it is no harder to learn to understand what makes a Pekingese correct than any other breed. But they are a unique breed, and as such, it is impossible to group them under the manner in which you regard some half dozen other breeds, and to try to judge them from that perspective. If you are going to judge Pekingese in the ring (or for your own information), you will have to give time to the study of that individual breed, as just "general dog knowledge" will not suffice for you.

With almost half the points of perfection placing emphasis on the head, it is obvious that the Peke is a "head breed!" In evaluating a member of this breed, the head must be large and massive—to the touch as well as to the eye. It is important that the head be handled and examined carefully as you go over the dog, as there are many grooming tricks which can camouflage faults. The head must be big and bony, with the topskull broad and absolutely flat to the touch from ear to ear. An experienced groomer can create this effect, and a tight lead pulled closely around the neck can sometimes help to create an illusion of flatness; so use your hands as well as your eyes. At the same time, very heavily coated dogs

Ch. Midtown of Chinatown, by Ch. Changkim Madison Avenue ex Ch. Parti Girl of Chinatown, winning Best of Breed at Maryland K.C. in 1985. Handled by Hernan Martinez for breeder-owner Mrs. Walter M. Jeffords, New York.

may carry an unusually thick head of hair on the topskull which can create an illusion of roundness; bear this in mind, too, in going over the dog.

To correctly examine a Pekingese head, smooth the hair on top of the skull; then, placing your hands behind the dog's ears (finger tips level with the skull), work the ears gently forward and down. A correct skull will appear flat.

The Pekingese face, studied from the front, is broad and short with nose leather set directly between well-spaced eyes, the entire face having a "wide open" look about it. Pinched or crowded features are ugly and atypical in a Pekingese. The forehead should be low, the stop deep, and the muzzle well-padded, being of equal breadth, or nearly so, with the forehead. The correct face must give the appearance of massive squareness, being *slightly* shorter from the top to bottom (skull to underjaw) than it is wide. The popular term nowadays is the "envelope" face, but one forgets that there are envelopes and envelopes—numerous sizes and shapes of them!

Twenty years ago the tendency was toward heads whose height

220

exceeded the width. Later, the other extreme became desirable with heads wide but so shallow that they appeared anything but massive—they made the dog seem poorly balanced. More recently, I am happy to say, the tendency has been moving away from extremes—the massive head, just slightly wider than square in appearance, is now in style, as it should be.

Broad, short, and level lips should neatly circle the Pekingese underjaw on top and sides, never underhanging or overhanging to cause a look of "lippiness." Weak, receding underjaws are ugly and are considered by many, including the author, to be a serious fault. The teeth of the Pekingese should *not* be level. When they are, one often finds the jaw undershot, which ruins the aggressive Pekingese expression. The upper row should meet just behind the lower row of teeth for a perfect effect when the mouth is closed. There is no penalty for missing teeth, and since the correctness of the mouth, or lack of it, is clearly visible as one looks at the closed mouth, Pekingese authorities feel that so long as the closed mouth, lips, and jaws appear correct, it should be assumed that they are; and no manual examination of them should be made by the judge.

Short-faced dogs, especially Pekes, hotly resent having their mouths opened; provoking a Peke in this manner is senseless, unless, of course, there is some evidence of wryness or other deformity which the judge feels must be investigated. But if all appears normal, trust your eye and forget about digging further.

In profile, the Pekingese face must be absolutely flat and tipped slightly back from underjaw to topskull. The bone structure of the face is not only flat but upturned, providing the deep stop required by the Standard, which is easily discernible behind the nose leather when the skin of the forehead is pulled gently back— the deeper the stop the better.

Correct roundness and darkness of eye are tremendously important, as is eye placement. Ears should be set at the corners of the skull and heavily fringed. The nose leather should be black and broad with well open nostrils. Pinched nostrils, which make for difficult breathing, are a health hazard and should not be encouraged.

As in the days of the Empress Tzu Hsi, many colors of Pekingese are popular. The author's feeling is that the diversity of color is one of the Peke's charms, making breeding more interesting.

Ch. St. Aubrey Beeswing of Elsdon winning Best of Breed at the A.K.C. Centennial Specialties in November 1984. Luc Boileau handled as always, for owner Edward B. Jenner, Knolland Farm.

Chapter 7

The Purchase of Your Pekingese

Careful consideration should be given to what breed of dog you wish to own prior to your purchase of one. If several breeds are attractive to you, and you are undecided as to which you prefer, learn all you can about the characteristics of each before making your decision. As you do so, you are thus preparing yourself to make an intelligent choice; and this is very important when buying a dog who will be, with reasonable luck, a member of your household for at least a dozen years or more. Obviously, since you are reading this book, you have decided on the breed—so now all that remains is to make a good choice.

It is never wise to just rush out and buy the first cute puppy who catches your eye. Whether you wish a dog to show, one with whom to compete in obedience, or one as a family dog purely for his (or her) companionship, the more time and thought you invest as you plan the purchase, the more likely you are to meet with complete satisfaction. The background and early care behind your pet will reflect in the dog's future health and temperament. Even if you are planning the purchase purely as a pet, with no thoughts

223

of showing or breeding in the dog's or puppy's future, it is essential that, if the dog is to enjoy a trouble-free future, you assure yourself of a healthy, properly raised puppy or adult from sturdy, well-bred stock.

Throughout the pages of this book you will find the names and locations of many well-known and well-established kennels in various areas. Another source of information is the American Kennel Club (51 Madison Avenue, New York, New York 10010), from whom you can obtain a list of recognized breeders in the vicinity of your home. If you plan to have your dog campaigned by a professional handler, by all means let the handler help you locate and select a good dog. Through their numerous clients, handlers have access to a variety of interesting show prospects; and the usual arrangement is that the handler re-sells the dog to you for what his cost has been, with the agreement that the dog be campaigned for you by him throughout the dog's career. It is most strongly recommended that prospective purchasers follow these suggestions, as you thus will be better able to locate and select a satisfactory puppy or dog.

Your first step in searching for your puppy is to make appointments at kennels specializing in your breed, where you can visit and inspect the dogs, both those available for sale and the kennel's basic breeding stock. You are looking for an active, sturdy puppy with bright eyes and intelligent expression and who is friendly and alert; avoid puppies who are hyperactive, dull, or listless. The coat should be clean and thick, with no sign of parasites. The premises on which he was raised should look (and smell) clean and be tidy, making it obvious that the puppies and their surroundings are in capable hands. Should the kennels featuring the breed you intend to own be sparse in your area or not have what you consider attractive, do not hesitate to contact others at a distance and purchase from them if they seem better able to supply a puppy or dog who will please you—*so long as it is a recognized breeding kennel of that breed.* Shipping dogs is a regular practice nowadays, with comparatively few problems when one considers the number of dogs shipped each year. A reputable, well-known breeder wants the customer to be satisfied; thus, he will represent the puppy fairly. Should you not be pleased with the puppy upon arrival, a breeder, such as described, will almost certainly permit its return. A conscientious breeder takes real interest and concern in the wel-

224

fare of the dogs he or she causes to be brought into the world. Such a breeder also is proud of a reputation for integrity. Thus on two counts, for the sake of the dog's future and the breeder's reputation, to such a person a *satisfied* customer takes precedence over a sale at any cost.

If your puppy is to be a pet or "family dog," the earlier the age at which it joins your household the better. Puppies are weaned and ready to start out on their own, under the care of a sensible new owner, at about six weeks old; and if you take a young one, it is often easier to train it to the routine of your household and to your requirements of it than is the case with an older dog which, even though still technically a puppy, may have already started habits you will find difficult to change. The younger puppy is usually less costly, too, as it stands to reason the breeder will not have as much expense invested in it. Obviously, a puppy that has been raised to five or six months old represents more in care and cash expenditure on the breeder's part than one sold earlier; therefore he should be, and generally is, priced accordingly.

There is an enormous amount of truth in the statement that "bargain" puppies seldom turn out to be that. A "cheap" puppy, raised purely for sale and profit, can and often does lead to great heartbreak, including problems and veterinarian's bills which can add up to many times the initial cost of a properly reared dog. On the other hand, just because a puppy is expensive does not assure one that is healthy and well reared. There have been numerous cases where unscrupulous dealers have sold, for several hundred dollars, puppies that were sickly, in poor condition, and such poor specimens that the breed of which they were supposedly members was barely recognizable. So one cannot always judge a puppy by price alone. Common sense must guide a prospective purchaser, plus the selection of a *reliable*, well-recommended dealer whom you know to have well-satisfied customers or, best of all, a specialized breeder. You will probably find the fairest pricing at the kennel of a breeder. Such a person, experienced with the breed in general and with his or her own stock in particular, through extensive association with these dogs, has watched enough of them mature to have obviously learned to assess quite accurately each puppy's potential—something impossible where such background is non-existent.

One more word on the subject of pets. Bitches make a fine

choice for this purpose as they are usually quieter and more gentle than the males, easier to house train, more affectionate, and less inclined to roam. If you do select a bitch and have no intention of breeding or showing her, by all means have her spayed, for your sake and for hers. The advantages to the owner of a spayed bitch include avoiding the nuisance of "in season" periods which normally occur twice yearly—with the accompanying eager canine swains haunting your premises in an effort to get close to your female—plus the unavoidable messiness and spotting of furniture and rugs at this time, which can be annoying if she is a household companion in the habit of sharing your sofa or bed. As for the spayed bitch, she benefits as she grows older because this simple operation almost entirely eliminates the possibility of breast cancer ever occurring. It is recommended that all bitches eventually be spayed—even those used for show or breeding when their careers have ended—in order that they may enjoy a happier, healthier old age. Please take note, however, that a bitch who has been spayed (or an altered dog) *cannot be shown at American Kennel Club dog shows once this operation has been performed.* Be certain that you are *not* interested in showing her before taking this step.

Also, in selecting a pet, never underestimate the advantages of an older dog, perhaps a retired show dog or a bitch no longer needed for breeding, who may be available and quite reasonably priced by a breeder anxious to place such a dog in a loving home. These dogs are settled and can be a delight to own, as they make wonderful companions, especially in a household of adults where raising a puppy can sometimes be a trial.

Everything that has been said about careful selection of your pet puppy and its place of purchase applies, but with many further considerations, when you plan to buy a show dog or foundation stock for a future breeding program. Now is the time for an in-depth study of the breed, starting with every word and every illustration in this book and all others you can find written on the subject. The Standard of the breed has now become your guide, and you must learn not only the words but also how to interpret them and how to apply them to actual dogs before you are ready to make an intelligent selection of a show dog.

If you are thinking in terms of a dog to show, obviously you must have learned about dog shows and must be in the habit of attending them. This is fine, but now your activity in this direc-

Ch. Quilkin the Stringman winning one of his three Pekingese Club of America Specialty Shows, this time under Mrs. Bessie Pickens in 1976. This famous dog was owned by Mrs. Walter M. Jeffords and Mr. Michael Wolf, handled by the latter. The winner of 11 all-breed Bests in Show.

tion should be increased, with your attending every single dog show within a reasonable distance from your home. Much can be learned about a breed at ringside at these events. Talk with the breeders who are exhibiting. Study the dogs they are showing. Watch the judging with concentration, noting each decision made, and attempt to follow the reasoning by which the judge has reached it. Note carefully the attributes of the dogs who win and, for your later use, the manner in which each is presented. Close your ears to the ringside know-it-alls, usually novice owners of a dog or two and very new to the Fancy, who have only derogatory remarks to make about all that is taking place unless they happen to win. This is the type of exhibitor who "comes and goes" through the Fancy and whose interest is usually of very short duration, owing to lack of knowledge and dissatisfaction caused by the failure to recognize the need to learn. You, as a fancier whom we hope will last and enjoy our sport over many future years, should develop independent thinking at this stage; you should learn to draw your own conclusions about the merits, or lack of them, seen before you in the ring and, thus, sharpen your own judgement in preparation for choosing wisely and well.

Note carefully which breeders campaign winning dogs—not just an occasional isolated good one, but consistent, homebred winners. It is from one of these people that you should select your own future "star."

If you are located in an area where dog shows take place only occasionally or where there are long travel distances involved, you will need to find another testing ground for your ability to select a worthy show dog. Possibly, there are some representative kennels raising this breed within a reasonable distance. If so, by all means ask permission of the owners to visit the kennels and do so when permission is granted. You may not necessarily buy then and there, as they may not have available what you are seeking that very day, but you will be able to see the type of dog being raised there and to discuss the dogs with the breeder. Every time you do this, you add to your knowledge. Should one of these kennels have dogs which especially appeal to you, perhaps you could reserve a show-prospect puppy from a coming litter. This is frequently done, and it is often worth waiting for a puppy, unless you have seen a dog with which you truly are greatly impressed and which is immediately available.

The purchase of a puppy has already been discussed. Obviously this same approach applies in a far greater degree when the purchase involved is a future show dog. The only place from which to purchase a show prospect is a breeder who raises show-type stock; otherwise, you are almost certainly doomed to disappointment as the puppy matures. Show and breeding kennels obviously cannot keep all of their fine young stock. An active breeder-exhibitor is, therefore, happy to place promising youngsters in the hands of people also interested in showing and winning with them, doing so at a fair price according to the quality and prospects of the dog involved. Here again, if no kennel in your immediate area has what you are seeking, do not hesitate to contact top breeders in other areas and to buy at long distance. Ask for pictures, pedigrees, and a complete description. Heed the breeder's advice and recommendations, after truthfully telling exactly what your expectations are for the dog you purchase. Do you want something with which to win just a few ribbons now and then? Do you want a dog who can complete his championship? Are you thinking of the real "big time" (i.e., seriously campaigning with Best of Breed, Group wins, and possibly even Best in Show as your eventual goal)? Consider it all carefully in advance; then honestly discuss your plans with the breeder. You will be better satisfied with the results if you do this, as the breeder is then in the best position to help you choose the dog who is most likely to come through for you. A breeder selling a show dog is just as anxious as the buyer for the dog to succeed, and the breeder will represent the dog to you with truth and honesty. Also, this type of breeder does not lose interest the moment the sale has been made but, when necessary, will be right there to assist you with beneficial advice and suggestions based on years of experience.

As you make inquiries of at least several kennels, keep in mind that show-prospect puppies are less expensive than mature show dogs, the latter often costing close to four figures, and sometimes more. The reason for this is that, with a puppy, there is always an element of chance, the possibility of it's developing unexpected faults as it matures or failing to develop the excellence and quality that earlier had seemed probable. There definitely is a risk factor in buying a show-prospect puppy. Sometimes all goes well, but occasionally the swan becomes an ugly duckling. Reflect on this as you consider available puppies and young adults. It just might be a good idea to go with a more mature, though more costly, dog if one you like is available.

When you buy a mature show dog, "what you see is what you get," and it is not likely to change beyond coat and condition, which are dependent on your care. Also advantageous for a novice owner is the fact that a mature dog of show quality almost certainly will have received show-ring training and probably match-show experience, which will make your earliest handling ventures much easier.

Frequently it is possible to purchase a beautiful dog who has completed championship but who, owing to similarity in bloodlines, is not needed for the breeder's future program. Here you have the opportunity of owning a champion, usually in the two-to-five-year-old range, which you can enjoy campaigning as a special (for Best of Breed competition) and which will be a settled, handsome dog for you and your family to enjoy with pride.

If you are planning foundation for a future kennel, concentrate on acquiring one or two really superior bitches. These need not be top show-quality, but they should represent your breed's finest producing bloodlines from a strain noted for producing quality, generation after generation. A proven matron who is already the dam of show-type puppies is, of course, the ideal selection; but these are usually difficult to obtain, no one being anxious to part with so valuable an asset. You just might strike it lucky, though, in which case you are off to a flying start. If you cannot find such a matron available, select a young bitch of finest background from top-producing lines who is herself of decent type, free of obvious faults, and of good quality.

Great attention should be paid to the pedigree of the bitch from whom you intend to breed. If not already known to you, try to see the sire and dam. It is generally agreed that someone starting with a breed should concentrate on a fine collection of topflight bitches and raise a few litters from these before considering keeping one's own stud dog. The practice of buying a stud and then breeding everything you own or acquire to that dog does not always work out well. It is better to take advantage of the many noted sires who are available to be used at stud, who represent all of the leading strains, and, in each case, to carefully select the one who in type and pedigree seems most compatible to each of your bitches, at least for your first several litters.

230

To summarize, if you want a "family dog" as a companion, it is best to buy it young and raise it according to the habits of your household. If you are buying a show dog, the more mature it is, the more certain you can be of its future beauty. If you are buying foundation stock for a kennel, then bitches are better, but they must be from the finest *producing* bloodlines.

When you buy a pure-bred dog that you are told is eligible for registration with the American Kennel Club, you are entitled to receive from the seller an application form which will enable you to register your dog. If the seller cannot give you the application form, you should demand and receive an identification of your dog, consisting of the name of the breed, the registered names and numbers of the sire and dam, the name of the breeder, and your dog's date of birth. If the litter of which your dog is a part is already recorded with the American Kennel Club, then the litter number is sufficient identification.

Do not be misled by promises of papers at some later date. Demand a registration application form or proper identification as described above. If neither is supplied, do not buy the dog. So warns the American Kennel Club, and this is especially important in the purchase of show or breeding stock.

ON OWNING A PEKINGESE

For people who actually prefer large breeds to a small dog, but are unable to accommodate the former, owing to lack of space, a Pekingese is the ideal solution. For in this small, furry bundle one finds all the heart, determination, energy, and personality of a giant among canines. The size of a Pekingese, believe me, is misleading. This is no lap dog no dog, to be coddled and babied, no dog to consider as merely a household ornament. He is 100% *dog*, and you will find him a delight once you have become closely acquainted with a member of the breed.

No dog is more companionable. No dog is more sensible. No dog is more completely free of the annoying habits which turn people off from some of the other Toy breeds.

It is unfortunate that Pekingese have been done grave injustice by people who obviously have had no association with the breed, which gives them a handicap to be lived down. They are *definitely* not "snappy," nor are they useless little creatures which are only capable of being carried around or held in one's lap and petted.

231

On the first of these two counts, I have never known a Pekingese to exhibit any sign of snappiness, and it is a puzzle to me how any such suspicion ever started. Dogs of almost *any* breed will bite when under stress—Pekes are no exception. Basically, however, they are dogs of sensible, even disposition who would only consider biting if teased, tormented, or hurt. Your chances of being bitten by a Pekingese are extremely remote unless one of these circumstances exists.

Pekingese are not the "satin cushion dogs" cartoonists were once fond of depicting. On the contrary, they dislike hugging, kissing, and other such indignities, even from someone they love. They are tremendously dignified dogs, who can actually be snobs in keeping with their background; you will note a pained facial expression and a struggle to get free at the earliest opportunity if they are subject to any sort of "babying." Those who know the breed delight in this aloofness, and they respect it in their own dogs.

You may never have thought of him in this capacity, but you could not have a more efficient watchdog than a Pekingese. He may lack the size and strength needed to tear a prowler apart, but he can and does make it very clear when someone who should not be on, or near, your premises is around. His low, warning growl is impressive, followed by furious barking, which cannot possibly fail to give warning to someone interested in working undetected. In addition, he does not make an easy target for the prowler to silence, being small, quick, and very handy at slipping under or behind furniture or other objects when he wants to be elusive. It is far easier to silence a big dog than a small one for just this very reason—Pekingese are more difficult to get at. Another bonus: Pekes are seldom so interested in food as to rush over and gobble "bait" from anyone's extended hand as are other, less aloof, breeds. And as Pekes are not given to senseless yapping, as are some dogs of other breeds, the "alarm" can be taken by the owner as a true and meaningful warning which should be investigated.

Pekingese are not in the least destructive, being in no way inclined to tear, dig, or scratch at household furnishings. They are almost catlike in their cleanliness, thus easy and reliable to housetrain. After all, did not their ancestors live in the Imperial Palace?

Pekingese are not delicate but hardy dogs and with decent care should live 12 to 15 years of age. They are fond of children and

Lejervis Casinoes Rose, English import bred by Mrs. L.A. Rolfe-Hazell. Sire, Eng. Ch. Rosayleen Casino Royale. Dam, Lejervis Christmas Cracker. This is a young "star" at Sutton Place Kennels, Don Sutton and Steve Keating.

enjoy their company. They should not, however, be handled roughly or urged into overly strenuous games as they are, after all, small dogs and can be hurt.

Pekingese like to be introduced to, rather than be overpowered by, new friends. Do not rush over and grab a Peke, as he will consider that a signal for him to get our of your reach. Let him make the advances, come over to you on his own, sniff the back of your hand, and generally become acquainted. This way he will be your friend for life.

One does not give orders to a Pekingese—one makes requests. A bullied Peke can out-stubborn any mule. However, he likes to please you and will make every effort to do just that, so long as he is following your *wish* rather than your command.

Laugh at a Peke and he will sulk for hours. Mutual respect is the key to this relationship, and you will find your Pekingese earning yours many times over.

The intelligence of a Pekingese is often amazing. Note how well members of the breed have fared in obedience. And think of the example you have seen when they have almost read your thoughts.

233

Joan Mylchreest shares a happy moment with Ch. Mahjong Mavina Gable, the dam of David Fitzpatrick's Ch. Coral Gable. Briarcourt Pekingese, Yardley, Pennsylvania.

Chapter 8

The Care of Your Pekingese Puppy

The moment you decide to be the new owner of a puppy is not one second too soon to start planning for the puppy's arrival in your home. Both the new family member and you will find the transition period easier if your home is geared in advance of the arrival.

The first things to be prepared are a bed for the puppy and a place where you can pen him up for rest periods. Every dog should have a crate of its own from the very beginning, so that he will come to know and love it as his special place where he is safe and happy. It is an ideal arrangement, for when you want him to be free, the crate stays open. At other times you can securely latch it and know that the pup is safely out of mischief. If you travel with him, his crate comes along in the car; and, of course, in traveling by plane there is no alternative but to have a carrier for the dog. If you show your dog, you will want him upon occasion to be in a crate a good deal of the day. So from every consideration, a crate is a very sensible and sound investment in your puppy's future safety and happiness and for your own peace of mind.

235

The crates most desirable are the wooden ones with removable side panels, which are ideal for cold weather (with the panels in place to keep out drafts) and in hot weather (with the panels removed to allow better air circulation). Wire crates are all right in the summer, but they give no protection from cold or drafts. Aluminum crates, due to the manner in which the metal reflects surrounding temperatures, are not recommended. If it is cold, so is the metal of the crate; if it is hot, the crate becomes burning hot.

When you choose the puppy's crate, be certain that it is roomy enough not to become outgrown. The crate should have sufficient height so the dog can stand up in it as a mature dog and sufficient area so that he can stretch out full length when relaxed. When the puppy is young, first give him shredded newspaper as a bed; the papers can be replaced with a mat or turkish towels when the dog is older. Carpet remnants are great for the bottom of the crate, as they are inexpensive and in case of accidents can be quite easily replaced. As the dog matures and is past the chewing age, a pillow or blanket in the crate is an appreciated comfort.

Sharing importance with the crate is a safe area in which the puppy can exercise and play. If you are an apartment dweller, a baby's playpen works out well for a young dog; for an older puppy use a portable exercise pen which you can use later when travelling with your dog or for dog shows. If you have a yard, an area where he can be outside in safety should be fenced in prior to the dog's arrival at your home. This area does not need to be huge, but it does need to be made safe and secure. If you are in a suburban area where there are close neighbors, stockade fencing works out best, as then the neighbors are less aware of the dog and the dog cannot see and bark at everything passing by. If you are out in the country where no problems with neighbors are likely to occur, then regular chain-link fencing is fine. For added precaution in both cases, use a row of concrete blocks or railroad ties inside against the entire bottom of the fence; this precludes or at least considerably lessens the chances of your dog digging his way out.

Be advised that if yours is a single dog, it is very unlikely that it will get sufficient exercise just sitting in the fenced area, which is what most of them do when they are there alone. Two or more dogs will play and move themselves around, but one by itself does little more than make a leisurely tour once around the area to check things over and then lie down. You must include a daily

236

walk or two in your plans if your puppy is to be rugged and well. Exercise is extremely important to a puppy's muscular development and to keep a mature dog fit and trim. So make sure that those exercise periods, or walks, a game of ball, and other such activities, are part of your daily program as a dog owner.

If your fenced area has an outside gate, provide a padlock and key and a strong fastening for it, and use them, so that the gate cannot be opened by others and the dog taken or turned free. The ultimate convenience in this regard is, of course, a door (unused for other purposes) from the house around which the fenced area can be enclosed, so that all you have to do is open the door and out into his area he goes. This arrangement is safest of all, as then you need not be using a gate, and it is easier in bad weather since then you can send the dog out without taking him and becoming soaked yourself at the same time. This is not always possible to manage, but if your house is arranged so that you could do it this way, you would never regret it due to the convenience and added safety thus provided. Fencing in the entire yard, with gates to be opened and closed whenever a caller, deliveryman, postman, or some other person comes on your property, really is not safe at all because people not used to gates are frequently careless about closing and latching them *securely*. Many heartbreaking incidents have been brought about by someone carelessly half closing a gate (which the owner had thought to be firmly latched) and the dog wandering out. For greatest security a fenced *area* definitely takes precedence over a fenced *yard*.

The puppy will need a collar (one that fits now, not one to be grown into) and a lead from the moment you bring him home. Both should be an appropriate weight and type for his size. Also needed are a feeding dish and a water dish, both made preferably of unbreakable material. Your pet supply shop should have an interesting assortment of these and other accessories from which you can choose. Then you will need grooming tools of the type the breeder recommends and some toys. Equally satisfactory is Nylabone®, a nylon bone that does not chip or splinter and that "frizzles" as the puppy chews, providing healthful gum massage. Avoid plastics and any sort of rubber toys, *particularly those with squeakers* which the puppy may remove and swallow. If you want a ball for the puppy to use when playing with him, select one of very hard construction made for this purpose and do not leave it

A safe chew toy for your Pekingese, or any dog breed, will be a Gumabone Pooch Pacifier®. Flexible and yet durable, this chew toy and exerciser will outlast a rubber or vinyl toy. Its hambone scent is especially attractive to both puppy and grown dogs, too. However, for hard chewing a regular Nylabone® therapeutic device is recommended.

alone with him because he may chew off and swallow bits of the rubber. Take the ball with you when the game is over. This also applies to some of those "tug of war" type rubber toys which are fun when used with the two of you for that purpose but again should *not* be left behind for the dog to work on with his teeth. Bits of swallowed rubber, squeakers, and other such foreign articles can wreak great havoc in the intestinal tract—do all you can to guard against them.

Too many changes all at once can be difficult for a puppy. For at least the first few days he is with you, keep him on the food and feeding schedule to which he is accustomed. Find out ahead of time from the breeder what he feeds his puppies, how frequently, and at what times of the day. Also find out what, if any, food supplements the breeder has been using and recommends.

Then be prepared by getting in a supply of the same food so that you will have it there when you bring the puppy home. Once the puppy is accustomed to his new surroundings, then you can switch the type of food and schedule to fit your convenience, but for the first several days do it as the puppy expects.

Your selection of a veterinarian should also be attended to before the puppy comes home, because you should stop at the vet's office for the puppy to be checked over as soon as you leave the breeder's premises. If the breeder is from your area, ask him for recommendations. Ask you dog-owning friends for their opinions of the local veterinarians, and see what their experiences with those available have been. Choose someone whom several of your friends recommend highly, then contact him about your puppy, perhaps making an appointment to stop in at his office. If the premises are clean, modern, and well equipped, and if you like the veterinarian, make an appointment to bring the puppy in on the day of purchase. Be sure to obtain the puppy's health record from the breeder, including information on such things as shots and worming that the puppy has had.

JOINING THE FAMILY

Remember that, exciting and happy an occasion as it is for you, the puppy's move from his place of birth to your home can be, for him, a traumatic experience. His mother and littermates will

Ch. Briarcourt's Excelsior is one of America's Top Toys for 1985–1986, a multiple all-breed Best in Show, and a Specialty and Toy Group winner. Bred by Mrs. Joan Mylchreest. Owned and handled by J. Robert Jacobsen, Pt. Reyes Station, California.

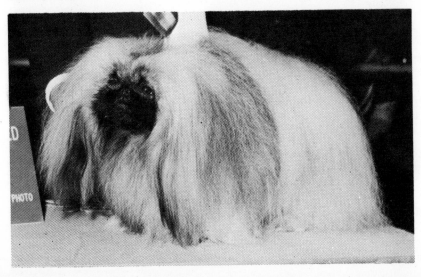

be missed. He quite likely will be awed or frightened by the change of surroundings. The person on whom he depended will be gone. Everything should be planned to make his arrival at your home pleasant—to give him confidence and to help him realize that yours is a pretty nice place to be after all.

Never bring a puppy home on a holiday. There is just too much going on with people and gifts and excitement. If he is in honor of an "occasion," work it out so that his arrival will be a few days earlier, or perhaps even better, a few days later than the "occasion." Then your home will be back to its normal routine and the puppy can enjoy your undivided attention. Try not to bring the puppy home in the evening. Early morning is the ideal time, as then he has the opportunity of getting acquainted and the initial strangeness should wear off before bedtime. You will find it a more peaceful night that way. Allow the puppy to investigate as he likes, under your watchful eye. If you already have a pet in the household, keep a careful watch that the relationship between the two gets off to a friendly start or you may quickly find yourself with a lasting problem. Much of the future attitude of each toward the other will depend on what takes place that first day, so keep your mind on what they are doing and let your other activities

Mi Gems Ting Lee of Lyt-ton, the first bitch, and the foundation bitch, at Mrs. Lamb's Mi Gems Kennels in West Palm Beach, Florida.

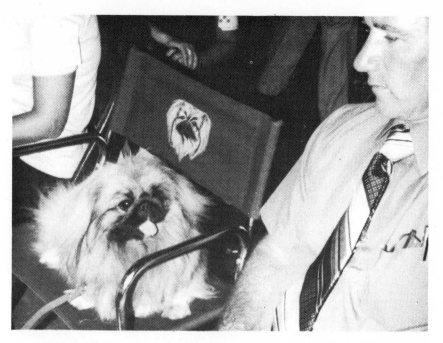

Ja Mie See Me Tu, U.D., waiting in his chair for his turn in the Utility Class. Mi Gems Pekingese, Jim and Eleanor Lamb, West Palm Beach, Florida.

slide for the moment. Be careful not to let your older pet become jealous by paying more attention to the puppy than to him, as that will start a bad situation immediately.

If you have a child, here again it is important that the relationship start out well. Before the puppy is brought home, you should have a talk with the youngster. He must clearly understand that puppies are fragile and can easily be injured; therefore, they should not be teased, hurt, mauled, or overly rough-housed. A puppy is not an inanimate toy; it is a living thing with a right to be loved and handled respectfully, treatment which will reflect in the dog's attitude toward your child as both mature together. Never permit your children's playmates to mishandle the puppy, tormenting the puppy until it turns on the children in self-defense. Children often do not realize how rough is too rough. You, as a responsible adult, are obligated to assure that your puppy's relationship with children is a pleasant one.

Do not start out by spoiling your puppy. A puppy is usually pretty smart and can be quite demanding. What you had considered to be "just for tonight" may be accepted by the puppy as

241

"for keeps." Be firm with him, strike a routine, and stick to it. The puppy will learn more quickly this way, and everyone will be happier as a result. A radio playing softly or a dim night light are often comforting to a puppy as it gets accustomed to new surroundings and should be provided in preference to bringing the puppy to bed with you—unless, of course, you intend him to share the bed as a permanent arrangement.

SOCIALIZING AND TRAINING

Socialization and training of your puppy should start the very day of his arrival in your home. Never address him without calling him by name. A short, simple name is the easiest to teach as it catches the dog's attention quickly; avoid elaborate call names. Always address the dog by the same name, not a whole series of pet names; the latter will only confuse the puppy.

Use his name clearly, and call the puppy over to you when you see him awake and wandering about. When he comes, make a big fuss over him for being such a good dog. He thus will quickly associate the sound of his name with coming to you and a pleasant happening.

Several hours after the puppy's arrival is not too soon to start accustoming him to the feel of a light collar. He may hardly notice it; or he may struggle, roll over, and try to rub it off his neck with his paws. Divert his attention when this occurs by offering a tasty snack or a toy (starting a game with him) or by petting him. Before long he will have accepted the strange feeling around his neck and no longer appear aware of it. Next comes the lead. Attach it and then immediately take the puppy outside or otherwise try to divert his attention with things to see and sniff. He may struggle against the lead at first, biting at it and trying to free himself. Do not pull him with it at this point; just hold the end loosely and try to follow him if he starts off in any direction. Normally his attention will soon turn to investigating his surroundings if he is outside or you have taken him into an unfamiliar room in your house; curiosity will take over and he will become interested in sniffing around the surroundings. Follow him with the lead slackly held until he seems to have completely forgotten about it; then try with gentle urging to get him to follow you. Don't be rough or jerk at him; just tug gently on the lead in short quick motions (steady pulling can become a battle of wills), repeating his name or trying to get him to follow your hand which is holding a bite of food or an interesting toy. If you have an older lead-trained dog, then it should be a cinch to get the puppy to follow along after *him*. In any event the average puppy learns quite quickly and will soon be trotting along nicely on the lead. Once that point has been reached, the next step is to teach him to follow on your left side, or heel. This will not likely be accomplished all in one day; it should be done with short training periods over the course of several days until you are satisfied with the result.

During the course of house training your puppy, you will need to take him out frequently and at regular intervals: first thing in the morning directly from the crate, immediately after meals, after the puppy has been napping, or when you notice that the puppy is looking for a spot. Choose more or less the same place to take the puppy each time so that a pattern will be established. If he does not go immediately, do not return him to the house as he will probably relieve himself the moment he is inside. Stay out with him until he has finished; then be lavish with your praise for his good behavior. If you catch the puppy having an accident indoors, grab him firmly and rush him outside, sharply saying "No!" as you pick him up. If you do not see the accident occur, there is little point in doing anything except cleaning it up, as once it has happened and been forgotten, the puppy will most likely not even realize why you are scolding him.

If you live in a big city or are away many hours at a time, having a dog that is trained to go on paper has some very definite advantages. To do this, one proceeds pretty much the same way as taking the puppy outdoors, except now you place the puppy on the newspaper at the proper time. The paper should always be kept in the same spot. An easy way to paper train a puppy if you have a playpen for it or an exercise pen is to line the area with newspapers; then gradually, every day or so, remove a section of newspaper until you are down to just one or two. The puppy acquires the habit of using the paper; and as the prepared area grows smaller, in the majority of cases the dog will continue to use whatever paper is still available. It is pleasant, if the dog is alone for an excessive length of time, to be able to feel that if he needs it the paper is there and will be used.

The puppy should form the habit of spending a certain amount of time in his crate, even when you are home. Sometimes the puppy will do this voluntarily, but if not, he should be taught to do so, which is accomplished by leading the puppy over by his collar, gently pushing him inside, and saying firmly, "Down" or "Stay." Whatever expression you use to give a command, stick to the very same one each time for each act. Repetition is the big thing in training—and so is association with what the dog is expected to do. When you mean "Sit," always say exactly that. "Stay" should mean *only* that the dog should remain where he receives the command. "Down" means something else again. Do not confuse the dog by shuffling the commands, as this will create training problems for you.

As soon as he had had his immunization shots, take your puppy with you whenever and wherever possible. There is nothing that will build a self-confident, stable dog like socialization, and it is extremely important that you plan and give the time and energy necessary for this, whether your dog is to be a show dog or a pleasant, well-adjusted family member. Take your puppy in the car so that he will learn to enjoy riding and not become carsick, as dogs may do if they are infrequent travelers. Take him anywhere you are going where you are certain he will be welcome: visiting friends and relatives (if they do not have housepets who may resent the visit), busy shopping centers (keeping him always on lead), or just walking around the streets of your town. If someone admires him (as always seems to happen when one is out with puppies), encourage the stranger to pet and talk with him. Socialization of this type brings out the best in your puppy and helps him to grow up with a friendly outlook, liking the world and its inhabitants. The worst thing that can be done to a puppy's personality is to shelter him. By always keeping him at home away from things and people unfamiliar to him, you may be creating a personality problem for the mature dog that will be a cross for you to bear later on.

FEEDING YOUR DOG

Time was when providing nourishing food for dogs involved a far more complicated procedure than people now feel is necessary. The old school of thought was that the daily ration must consist of fresh beef, vegetables, cereal, egg yolks, and cottage cheese as basics with such additions as brewer's yeast and vitamin tablets on a daily basis.

During recent years, however, many minds have changed regarding this procedure. Eggs, cottage cheese, and supplements to the diet are still given, but the basic method of feeding dogs has changed; and the change has been, in the opinion of many authorities, definitely for the better. The school of thought now is that you are doing your dogs a favor when you feed them some of the fine commercially prepared dog foods in preference to your own home-cooked concoctions.

The reason behind this new outlook is easily understandable. The dog food industry has grown to be a major one, participated in by some of the best known and most respected names in America. These trusted firms, it is agreed, turn out excellent products, so people are feeding their dog food preparations with confidence and the dogs are thriving, living longer, happier, and healthier lives than ever before. What more could one want?

There are at least half a dozen absolutely top-grade dry foods to be mixed with broth or water and served to your dog according to directions. There are all sorts of canned meats, and there are several kinds of "convenience foods," those in a packet which you open and dump out into the dog's dish. It is just that simple. The convenience foods are neat and easy to use when you are away from home, but generally speaking a dry food mixed with hot water (or soup) and meat is preferred. It is the opinion of many that the canned meat, with its added fortifiers, is more beneficial to the dogs than the fresh meat. However, the two can be alternated or, if you prefer and your dog does well on it, by all means use fresh ground beef. A dog enjoys changes in the meat part of his diet, which is easy with the canned food since all sorts of beef are available (chunk, ground, stewed, and so on), plus lamb, chicken, and even such concoctions as liver and egg, plain liver flavor, and a blend of five meats.

There is also prepared food geared to every age bracket of your dog's life, from puppyhood on through old age, with special additions or modifications to make it particularly nourishing and beneficial. Previous generations never had it so good where the canine dinner is concerned, because these commercially prepared foods are tasty and geared to meeting the dog's gastronomic approval.

Additionally, contents and nutrients are clearly listed on the labels, as are careful instructions for feeding just the right amount for the size, weight, and age of each dog.

With these foods the addition of extra vitamins is not necessary, but if you prefer there are several kinds of those, too, that serve as taste treats as well as being beneficial. Your pet supplier has a full array of them.

Of course there is no reason not to cook up something for your dog if you would feel happier doing so. But it seems unnecessary when such truly satisfactory rations are available with so much less trouble and expense.

How often you feed your dog is a matter of how it works out best for you. Many owners prefer to do it once a day. It is generally agreed that two meals, each of smaller quantity, are better for the digestion and more satisfying to the dog, particularly if yours is a household member who stands around and watches preparations for the family meals. Do not overfeed. This is the shortest route to all sorts of problems. Follow directions and note carefully

Am. and Can. Ch. Gossip At St. Aubrey owned by R. William Taylor, Montreal, Quebec, Canada.

Eng. Ch. Jay Trump at Sunsalve, the "star" of Sunsalve Kennels, belongs to Mr. Terry Nethercott, Hayes, Middlesex, England.

how your dog is looking. If your dog is overweight, cut back the quantity of food a bit. If the dog looks thin, then increase the amount. Each dog is an individual and the food intake should be adjusted to his requirements to keep him feeling and looking trim and in top condition.

From the time puppies are fully weaned until they are about twelve weeks old, they should be fed four times daily. From three months to six months of age, three meals should suffice. At six months of age the puppies can be fed two meals, and the twice daily feedings can be continued until the puppies are close to one year old, at which time feeding can be changed to once daily if desired. If you do feed just once a day, do so by early afternoon at the latest and give the dog a snack, a biscuit or two, at bedtime.

Remember that plenty of fresh water should always be available to your puppy or dog for drinking. This is' of utmost importance to his health.

247

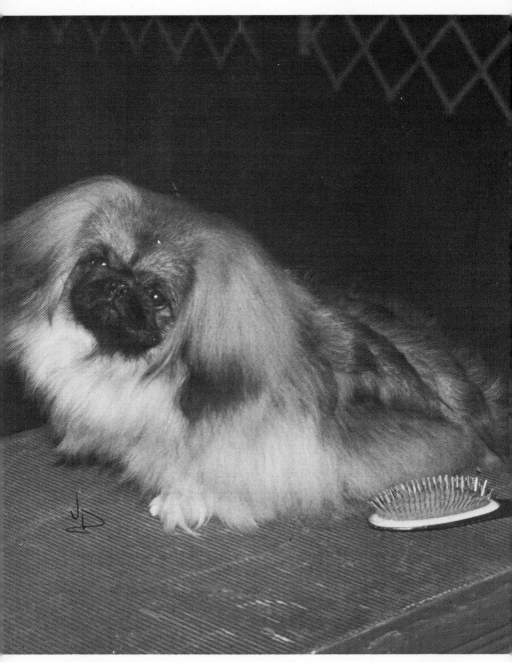

This gorgeously headed puppy, a point winner at an early age from the puppy classes, grew up to become Ch. Jomar Ruffles and Flourishes. Owned by Margaret Zuber of West Monroe, Louisiana.

Chapter 9

Grooming Your Pekingese

The Pekingese coat is one of his most glamorous features, truly his crowning glory. In the show Pekingese, one must learn to achieve perfection, or near perfection, as the success with which your show dog meets is considerably dependent on the amount, quality and condition of this coat. The care of the coat, thus, is important under any circumstances for, obviously, you want your pet to look handsome and well-groomed, too.

Technically speaking, the Pekingese has two coats; the undercoat which consists of short, soft, slightly "crimpy" fur; and the outer coat, which is long, straight, and feels harsh to the touch. In texture, there must be no "woolliness" about it; nor must it be silky or wavy. Typically, there should be a long, straight, heavy ruff of stand-off hair (reminiscent of the lion-like appearance), with the hair shorter over the hips and waist to accentuate the tapering lion-shaped body.

Fringes are long and plentiful. Pekingese exhibitors set quite a value on length and quantity of ear fringes, with some of them reaching amazing lengths. Without question, heavy ear fringes, which are usually softer in texture than the rest of the coat and frequently set off by long, black strands of hair, give a squareness

Ch. St. Aubrey Bees Knees of Elsdon is the full younger brother to Ch. St. Aubrey Beeswing of Elsdon, also owned by Edward Jenner. Carol Hollands is handling him to Best in Show at Grey-Bruce K.C. in 1985.

to the Pekingese head and add glamor to general appearance.

Breeches are another area where length and quantity are an asset, for if they are of the proper length, they do a fine job at helping to conceal poor hindleg assemblage and action. As for the tail, it must carry a long, thick plume. The most luxuriant tails often reach clear over the top of the head, with a side spread which entirely covers the back.

Long cuffs on the forelegs complete the picture. Feathering on the feet themselves should be watched and not permitted to overgrow, as toe fringes of excessive length can be an impediment to the dog, causing him to trip or otherwise move badly in gaiting.

For grooming your Pekingese, you will need a pure bristle brush; the bristles must be long and fairly stiff to get right down to the roots of the hair. Teach your Pekingese to be groomed on a table. (If your dog is to be shown, he will need a rubber-topped grooming table to take to the dog shows as well as for use at home, so the investment is a sensible one.) He should be brushed carefully with long strokes from the skin out, separating the hair into sections as you work. With the dog on his side, carefully brush stomach and underparts, paying particular attention to the places where mats may form, such as armpits, between hindlegs, etc. If a mat is forming, try to separate the hairs gently with your fingers and/or a comb without loss of hair. A larger mat can sometimes be cut into with scissors and then separated. If possible, however, do not cut mats off, as this will leave a hole in the coat that may take awhile to fill in properly. Brush carefully behind the ears, another area where mats form quickly. Remember that the best of all cures for mats is to not let them form in the first place!

In all brushing, be careful that you are working right from skin to tip, a small section at a time. As with our own hair, this will promote stimulation which conditions the coat.

Fringes should be carefully combed (with a steel comb) rather than brushed, as you are less likely to pull out any of the hairs this way.

The Pekingese coat, which is to have a stand-off appearance, should be brushed *against* the direction in which it naturally lies rather than with it, which causes the coat to look flat. As a finishing touch, smooth the coat lightly with your brush or a slicker brush where necessary.

It is better to avoid bathing your Pekingese, as doing so softens the coat texture. You will keep him equally clean and good smelling, and the possessor of a considerably more suitable coat texture than the dog who is plopped into the bath on the slightest provocation, by following this procedure several times a week. Dampen a wash cloth with a good coat preparation (you will find preparations for this purpose at your pet supplier's) and, with the dog on the grooming table, rub him all over thoroughly, then brush him dry.

This routine should keep your Pekingese's coat at its best. When you see shedding starting, make every effort to get the old

251

coat out quickly, as the new one will then come in much faster. Do this by thoroughly brushing the dog, working against the grain of the hair, each day until you stop getting noticeable amounts in your brush.

In preparation for the show ring, some extra touches must be added to the basic grooming for the day of the show. Always arrive early to allow yourself time in which to do a job of which you will be proud. Settle your dog on a turkish towel covering the top of his grooming table, then spray him with water or your favorite coat dressing (here again, there are many good ones at the pet supply shop or the concession stands on the show grounds), which you have selected by doing a bit of advance experimenting at home. Brush the dampened coat briskly, arranging the coat as it should look when you enter the ring.

To enhance the appearance of your Peke's head, first consider the topskull, on which the hair should be brushed flat. If the topskull is not absolutely level, you can help make it appear to be: flatten the slightly damp hair in the center of the skull, and at the

Aust. Ch. Liam Wohsing Karltu, by Aust. Ch. Joewil Count Karl ex Toniki Karmen, at age three years. A multiple Best in Show winner, bred and owned by Nuree MacKay, Warner's Bay, N.S.W., Australia.

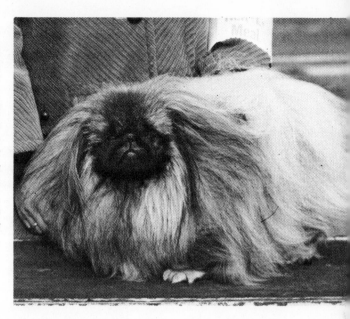

The author's favorite picture of the multi-Best in Show and multi-Group winning Ch. Coughton Sungable of Perryacre, an English import who made Pekingese history during the 1960s for owners Elaine Rigden and Amanda West. Handled throughout his American show career by Elaine Rigden.

same time work the hair forward so that the total effect becomes level. If your dog is very heavily coated, a bit of artistry in thinning out the thickest center section of the topskull should do the trick. Rubbing the hair forward with damp fingers can also add a broadened appearance to the cheeks and muzzle.

Talcum powder helps to give the coat a stand-off look, and is valuable for use on breeches, tail, and ear fringes. It should be rubbed in with your fingers, then brushed out carefully with no remaining traces to make the judge feel obliged to call it "foreign substance" (not permitted in the coat of any dog in the show ring).

Just before judging time, check, and dry with cotton, any dampness on the dog's face, especially around eyes or wrinkles. These areas, especially on well-wrinkled faces, need to be watched for accumulated dampness, which should be carefully dried out *immediately* to avoid a sore or smelly condition developing. Should this occur, your veterinarian will advise a healing ointment or other medication which can be safely used close to the eye. *Never neglect any developing problems of this kind*, as doing so can lead to a chronic condition and a Peke with the appearance of a moth-eaten face, and additionally, can cause scratching and rubbing which may result in an injured eye.

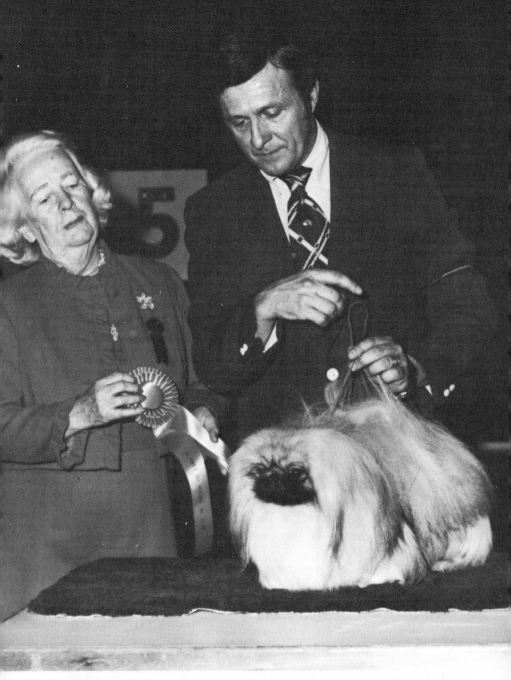

The great Ch. St. Aubrey Laparata Dragon of Elsdon with one of his many devoted admirers, the late Mary Lou Roberts who all her life loved Pekes and learned about them from her aunt and uncle, Johanna and Herbert Mapes of Whitworth Pekingese. Handling Dragon is Luc Boileau, for owner Edward B. Jenner. Schley photo.

Chapter 10

The Making of a Show Dog

If you have decided to become a show dog exhibitor, you have accepted a very real and very exciting challenge. The groundwork has been accomplished with the selection of your future show prospect. If you have purchased a puppy, it is assumed that you have gone through all the proper preliminaries concerning good care, which should be the same if the puppy is a pet or future show dog, with a few added precautions for the latter.

GENERAL CONSIDERATIONS

Remember the importance of keeping your future winner in trim, top condition. Since you want him neither too fat nor too thin, his appetite for his proper diet should be guarded, and children and guests should not be permitted to constantly feed him "goodies." The best treat of all is a small wad of raw ground beef or a packaged dog treat. To be avoided are ice cream, cake, cookies, potato chips, and other fattening items which will cause the dog to put on weight and may additionally spoil his appetite for the proper, nourishing, well-balanced diet so essential to good health and condition.

The importance of temperament and showmanship cannot pos-

255

sibly be overestimated. They have put many a mediocre dog across, while lack of them can ruin the career of an otherwise outstanding specimen. From the day your dog joins your family, socialize him. Keep him accustomed to being with people and to being handled by people. Encourage your friends and relatives to "go over" him as the judges will in the ring so this will not seem a strange and upsetting experience. Practice showing his "bite" (the manner in which his teeth meet) quickly and deftly. It is quite simple to slip the lips apart with your fingers, and the puppy should be willing to accept this from you or the judge without struggle.

Some judges prefer that the exhibitors display the dog's bite and other mouth features themselves. These are the considerate ones, who do not wish to chance the spreading of possible infection from dog to dog with their hands on each one's mouth—a courtesy particularly appreciated in these days of virus epidemics. But the old-fashioned judges still persist in doing it themselves, so the dog should be ready for either possibility.

Take your future show dog with you in the car, thus accustoming him to riding so that he will not become carsick on the day of a dog show. He should associate pleasure and attention with going in the car, van, or motor home. Take him where it is crowded: downtown, to the shops, everywhere you go that dogs are permitted. Make the expeditions fun for him by frequent petting and words of praise; do not just ignore him as you go about your errands.

Do not overly shelter your future show dog. Instinctively you may want to keep him at home where he is safe from germs or danger. This can be foolish on two counts. The first reason is that a puppy kept away from other dogs builds up no natural immunity against all the things with which he will come in contact at dog shows, so it is wiser to keep him up-to-date on all protective shots and then let him become accustomed to being among dogs and dog owners. Also, a dog who is never among strange people, in strange places, or among strange dogs may grow up with a shyness or timidity of spirit that will cause you real problems as his show career draws near.

Keep your show prospect's coat in immaculate condition with frequent grooming and daily brushing. When bathing is necessary, use a mild dog shampoo or whatever the breeder of your puppy may suggest. Several of the brand-name products do an ex-

Fourwinds Lypton at his first show, nine months old, Pekingese Club of Texas March 1986. Winning the 9 to 12 months Puppy Dog Class, Dallas Pekingese Club Sweepstakes, under judge Mrs. Kay Jeffords. Lypton was sired by Ch. Pendenrah Lysander of Sunsalve ex Fourwinds Cassie Bell. Bred, owned and handled by Ruby Dudley, Creston, Iowa.

Cinnabar Fu-Man-Chu is of Rodari parentage and is one of the lovely Pekingese to be found at Cinnabar Kennels owned by Dee Dee Jones at Pontypool, Ontario, Canada.

cellent job. Be sure to rinse thoroughly so as not to risk skin irritation by traces of soap left behind, and protect against soap entering the eyes by a drop of castor oil in each before you lather up. Use warm water (be sure it is not uncomfortably hot or chillingly cold) and a good spray. Make certain you allow your dog to dry thoroughly in a warm, draft-free area (or outdoors, if it is warm and sunny) so that he doesn't catch cold. Then proceed to groom him to perfection.

A show dog's teeth must be kept clean and free of tartar. Hard dog biscuits can help toward this, but if tartar accumulates, see that it is removed promptly by your veterinarian. Bones for chewing are not suitable for show dogs as they tend to damage and wear down the tooth enamel.

Assuming that you will be handling the dog yourself, or even if he will be professionally handled, a few moments each day of dog show routine is important. Practice setting him up as you have seen the exhibitors do at the shows you've attended, and teach him to hold this position once you have him stacked to your satisfaction. Make the learning period pleasant by being firm but lavish in your praise when he responds correctly. Teach him to gait at your side at a moderate rate on a loose lead. When you have mastered the basic essentials at home, then hunt out and join a training class for future work. Training classes are sponsored by show-giving clubs in many areas, and their popularity is steadily increasing. If you have no other way of locating one, perhaps your veterinarian would know of one through some of his other clients; but if you are sufficiently aware of the dog show world to want a show dog, you will probably be personally acquainted with other people who will share information of this type with you.

Accustom your show dog to being in a crate (which you should be doing with a pet dog as well). He should relax in his crate at the shows "between times" for his own well being and safety.

MATCH SHOWS

Your show dog's initial experience in the ring should be in match show competition. This type of event is intended as a learning experience for both the dog and the exhibitor. You will not feel embarrassed or out of place no matter how poorly your puppy may behave or how inept your attempts at handling may be, as you will find others there with the same type of problems. The

The lovely bitch, Ch. Christy Lee of Citadel owned by Gretchen Niessner and Ch. Jan G's O.K. Happy Silver owned by Jan Haddox. Both sired by Ch. Wild Venture of Lotusgrange ex Lori of Citadel (dam of three homebred champions). Photo courtesy of Mrs. Ruthe Painter.

important thing is that you get the puppy out and into a show ring where the two of you can practice together and learn the ropes.

Only on rare occasions is it necessary to make match show entries in advance, and even those with a pre-entry policy will usually accept entries at the door as well. Thus you need not plan several weeks ahead, as is the case with point shows, but can go when the mood strikes you. Also there is a vast difference in the cost, as match show entries only cost a few dollars while entry fees for the point shows may be over ten dollars, an amount none of us needs to waste until we have some idea of how the puppy will behave or how much more pre-show training is needed.

Match shows are frequently judged by professional handlers who, in addition to making the awards, are happy to help new exhibitors with comments and advice on their puppies and their presentation of them. Avail yourself of all these opportunities before heading out to the sophisticated world of the point shows.

POINT SHOWS

As previously mentioned, entries for American Kennel Club point shows must be made in advance. This must be done on an official entry blank of the show-giving club. The entry must then be filed either personally or by mail with the show superintendent or the show secretary (if the event is being run by the club mem-

Eng. Ch. Toydom a Touch of Class, by Toydom Trump Card ex Toydom Purdy, was Best of Breed at Crufts in 1982. Owned by Toydom Pekingese, Misses A. Summers and V. Williams, Pirbright, Surrey, England.

Ch. Mike Mar's China Dragon, at the height of his show career, winning Best in Show at the Maryland Kennel Club for owners Mrs. Alan Robson and Mr. Michael Wolf, the latter handling.

bers alone and a superintendent has not been hired, this information will appear on the premium list) in time to reach its destination prior to the published closing date or filling of the quota. These entries must be made carefully, must be signed by the owner of the dog or the owner's agent (your professional handler), and must be accompanied by the entry fee; otherwise they will not be accepted. Remember that it is not when the entry leaves your hands that counts, but the date of arrival at its destination. If you are relying on the mails, which are not always dependable, get the entry off well before the deadline to avoid disappointment.

A dog must be entered at a dog show in the name of the actual owner at the time of the entry closing date of that specific show. If a registered dog has been acquired by a new owner, it must be entered in the name of the new owner in any show for which entries close after the date of acquirement, regardless of whether the new owner has or has not actually received the registration certificate indicating that the dog is recorded in his name. State on the

261

entry form whether or not transfer application has been mailed to the American Kennel Club, and it goes without saying that the latter should be attended to promptly when you purchase a registered dog.

In filling out your entry blank, type, print, or write clearly, paying particular attention to the spelling of names, correct registration numbers, and so on. Also, if there is more than one variety in your breed, be sure to indicate into which category your dog is being entered.

The **Puppy Class** is for dogs or bitches who are six months of age and under twelve months and who are not champions. The age of a dog shall be calculated up to and inclusive of the first day of a show. For example, the first day a dog whelped on January 1st is eligible to compete in a Puppy Class at a show is July 1st of the same year; and he may continue to compete in Puppy Classes up to and including a show on December 31 of the same year, but he is *not* eligible to compete in a Puppy Class at a show held on or after January 1 of the following year.

The Puppy Class is the first one in which you should enter your puppy. In it a certain allowance will be made for the fact that they *are* puppies, thus an immature dog or one displaying less than perfect showmanship will be less severely penalized than, for instance, would be the case in Open. It is also quite likely that others in the class will be suffering from these problems, too. When you enter a puppy, be sure to check the classification with care, as some shows divide their Puppy Class into a 6-9 months old section and a 9-12 months old section.

The **Novice Class** is for dogs six months of age and over, whelped in the United States or Canada, who *prior to the official closing date for entries* have *not* won three first prizes in the Novice Class, any first prize at all in the Bred-by-Exhibitor, American-bred, or Open Classes, or one or more points toward championship. The provisions for this class are confusing to many people, which is probably the reason exhibitors do not enter in it more frequently. A dog may win any number of first prizes in the Puppy Class and still retain his eligibility for Novice. He may place second, third, or fourth not only in Novice on an unlimited number of occasions, but also in Bred-by-Exhibitor, American-bred and Open and still remain eligible for Novice. But he may no longer be shown in Novice when he has won three blue ribbons

262

in that class, when he has won even one blue ribbon in either Bred-by-Exhibitor, American-bred, or Open, or when he has won a single championship point.

In determining whether or not a dog is eligible for the Novice Class, keep in mind the fact that previous wins are calculated according to the official published date for closing of entries, not by the date on which you may actually have made the entry. So if in the interim, between the time you made the entry and the official closing date, your dog makes a win causing him to become ineligible for Novice, change your class *immediately* to another for which he will be eligible, preferably either Bred-by-Exhibitor or American-bred. To do this, you must contact the show's superintendent or secretary, at first by telephone to save time and then in writing to confirm it. The Novice Class always seems to have the fewest entries of any class, and therefore it is a splendid "practice ground" for you and your young dog while you are getting the "feel" of being in the ring.

Bred-by-Exhibitor Class is for dogs whelped in the United States or, if individually registered in the American Kennel Club Stud Book, for dogs whelped in Canada who are six months of age or older, are not champions, and are owned wholly or in part by the person or by the spouse of the person who was the breeder or one of the breeders of record. Dogs entered in this class must be handled in the class by an owner or by a member of the immediate family of the owner. Members of an immediate family for this purpose are husband, wife, father, mother, son, daughter, brother, or sister. This is the class which is really the "breeders' showcase," and the one which breeders should enter with particular pride to show off their achievements.

The **American-bred Class** is for all dogs excepting champions, six months of age or older, who were whelped in the United States by reason of a mating which took place in the United States.

The **Open Class** is for any dog six months of age or older (this is the only restriction for this class). Dogs with championship points compete in it, dogs who are already champions are eligible to do so, dogs who are imported can be entered, and, of course, American-bred dogs compete in it. This class is, for some strange reason, the favorite of exhibitors who are "out to win." They rush to enter their pointed dogs in it, under the false impression that by doing so they assure themselves of greater attention from the judges. This really is not so, and some people feel that to enter in one of the less competitive classes, with a better chance of winning it and thus earning a second opportunity of gaining the judge's approval by returning to the ring in the Winners Class, can often be a more effective strategy.

One does not enter the **Winners Class.** One earns the right to compete in it by winning first prize in Puppy, Novice, Bred-by-Exhibitor, American-bred, or Open. No dog who has been defeated on the same day in one of these classes is eligible to compete for Winners, and every dog who has been a blue-ribbon winner in one of them and not defeated in another, should he have been entered in more than one class (as occasionally happens), *must* do so. Following the selection of the Winners Dog or the Winners Bitch, the dog or bitch receiving that award leaves the ring. Then the dog or bitch who placed second in that class, unless previously beaten by another dog or bitch in another class at the same show, re-enters the ring to compete against the remaining first-prize winners for Reserve. The latter award indicates that the dog or bitch selected for it is standing "in reserve" should the one who received Winners be disqualified or declared ineligible through any technicality when the awards are checked at the American Kennel Club. In that case, the one who placed Reserve is moved up to Winners, at the same time receiving the appropriate championship points.

Winners Dog and Winners Bitch are the awards which carry points toward championship with them. The points are based on the number of dogs or bitches actually in competition, and the points are scaled one through five, the latter being the greatest number available to any one dog or bitch at any one show. Three-, four-, or five-point wins are considered majors. In order to become a champion, a dog or bitch must have won two majors under two different judges, plus at least one point from a third judge, and the additional points necessary to bring the total to fifteen. When your dog has gained fifteen points as described above, a championship certificate will be issued to you, and your dog's name will be published in the champions of record list in the *Pure-Bred Dogs/American Kennel Gazette,* the official publication of the American Kennel Club.

The scale of championship points for each breed is worked out by the American Kennel Club and reviewed annually, at which time the number required in competition may be either changed (raised or lowered) or remain the same. The scale of championship points for all breeds is published annually in the May issue of the *Gazette*, and the current ratings for each breed within that area are published in every show catalog.

When a dog or bitch is adjudged Best of Winners, its championship points are, for that show, compiled on the basis of which sex had the greater number of points. If there are two points in dogs and four in bitches and the dog goes Best of Winners, then *both* the dog and the bitch are awarded an equal number of points, in this case four. Should the Winners Dog or the Winners Bitch go on to win Best of Breed or Best of Variety, additional points are accorded for the additional dogs and bitches defeated by so doing, provided, of course, that there were entries specifically for Best of Breed competition or Specials, as these specific entries are generally called.

If your dog or bitch takes Best of Opposite Sex after going Winners, points are credited according to the number of the same sex defeated in both the regular classes and Specials competition. If Best of Winners is also won, then whatever additional points for each of these awards are available will be credited. Many a one- or two-point win has grown into a major in this manner.

Moving further along, should your dog win its **Variety Group** from the classes (in other words, if it has taken either Winners Dog or Winners Bitch), you then receive points based on the greatest number of points awarded to any member of any breed included within that Group during that show's competition. Should the day's winning also include Best in Show, the same rule of thumb applies, and your dog or bitch receives the highest number of points awarded to any other dog of any breed at that event.

Best of Breed competition consists of the Winners Dog and the Winners Bitch, who automatically compete on the strength of those awards, in addition to whatever dogs and bitches have been entered specifically for this class for which champions of record are eligible. Since July 1980, dogs who, according to their owner's records, have completed the requirements for a championship after the closing of entries for the show (but whose championships are unconfirmed) may be transferred from one of the regular classes to the Best of Breed competition, provided this transfer is made by the show superintendent or show secretary *prior to the* *start of any judging at the show.*

This has proved an extremely popular new rule, as under it a dog can finish on Saturday and then be transferred and compete as a Special on Sunday. It must be emphasized that *the change must be made prior to the start of any part of the day's judging, not for just your individual breed.*

In the United States, Best of Breed winners are entitled to compete in the Variety Group which includes them. This is not mandatory; it is a privilege which exhibitors value. (In Canada, Best of Breed winners *must* compete in the Variety Group or they lose any points already won.) The dogs winning *first* in each of the seven Variety Groups *must* compete for Best in Show. Missing the opportunity of taking your dog in for competition in its Group is foolish, as it is there where the general public is most likely to notice your breed and become interested in learning about it.

Non-regular classes are sometimes included at the all-breed shows, and they are almost invariably included at Specialty shows. These include Stud Dog Class and Brood Bitch Class, which are judged on the basis of the quality of the two offspring accompanying the sire or dam. The quality of the latter two is beside the

Etive's Black Prince, owned by Rockhill Kennels, Louis and Marta Vieillard, winning a Best of Breed. Judged at this occasion by the author.

Six-month-old Ch. Fraser Manor Pixie going Winners Bitch, Best of Winners and Best of Opposite Sex for her first time in the ring. Owned by Robin and Bobbie Fraser, Fraser-Manor Pekingese, Seattle, Washington.

point and should not be considered by the judge; it is the youngsters who count, and the quality of *both* are to be averaged to decide which sire or dam is the best and most consistent producer. Then there is the Brace Class (which, at all-breed shows, moves up to Best Brace in each Variety Group and then Best Brace in Show) which is judged on the similarity and evenness of appearance of the two brace members. In other words, the two dogs should look like identical twins in size, color, and conformation and should move together almost as a single dog, one person handling with precision and ease. The same applies to the Team Class competition, except that four dogs are involved and, if necessary, two handlers.

The Veterans Class is for the older dog, the minimum age of whom is seven years. This class is judged on the quality of the dogs, as the winner competes in Best of Breed competition and has, on a respectable number of occasions, been known to take that top award. So the point is *not* to pick out the oldest dog, as some judges seem to believe, but the best specimen of the breed, exactly as in the regular classes.

Then there are Sweepstakes and Futurity Stakes sponsored by

many Specialty clubs, sometimes as part of their regular Specialty shows and sometimes as separate events on an entirely different occasion. The difference between the two stakes is that Sweepstakes entries usually include dogs from six to eighteen months of age with entries made at the same time as the others for the show, while for a Futurity the entries are bitches nominated when bred and the individual puppies entered at or shortly following their birth.

JUNIOR SHOWMANSHIP COMPETITION

If there is a youngster in your family between the ages of ten and sixteen, there is no better or more rewarding hobby than becoming an active participant in Junior Showmanship. This is a marvelous activity for young people. It teaches responsibility, good sportsmanship, the fun of competition where one's own skills are the deciding factor of success, proper care of a pet, and how to socialize with other young folks. Any youngster may experience the thrill of emerging from the ring a winner and the satisfaction of a good job well done.

Entry in Junior Showmanship Classes is open to any boy or girl who is at least ten years old and under seventeen years old on the day of the show. The Novice Junior Showmanship Class is open to youngsters who have not already won, at the time the entries close, three firsts in this class. Youngsters who have won three firsts in Novice may compete in the Open Junior Showmanship Class. Any junior handler who wins his third first-place award in Novice may participate in the Open Class at the same show, provided that the Open Class has at least one other junior handler entered and competing in it that day. The Novice and Open Classes may be divided into Junior and Senior Classes. Youngsters between the ages of ten and twelve, inclusively, are eligible for the Junior division; and youngsters between thirteen and seventeen, inclusively, are eligible for the Senior division.

Any of the foregoing classes may be separated into individual classes for boys and for girls. If such a division is made, it must be so indicated on the premium list. The premium list also indicates the prize for Best Junior Handler, if such a prize is being offered at the show. Any youngster who wins a first in any of the regular classes may enter the competition for this prize, provided the youngster has been undefeated in any other Junior Showmanship Class at that show.

Junior Showmanship Classes, unlike regular conformation classes in which the quality of the dog is judged, are judged solely on the skill and ability of the junior handling the dog. Which dog is best is not the point—it is which youngster does the best job with the dog that is under consideration. Eligibility requirements for the dog being shown in Junior Showmanship, and other detailed information, can be found in *Regulations for Junior Showmanship*, available from the American Kennel Club.

A junior who has a dog that he or she can enter in both Junior Showmanship and conformation classes has twice the opportunity for success and twice the opportunity to get into the ring and work with the dog, a combination which can lead to not only awards for expert handling, but also, if the dog is of sufficient quality, for making a conformation champion.

PRE-SHOW PREPARATIONS

Preparation of the items you will need as a dog show exhibitor should not be left until the last moment. They should be planned and arranged several days in advance of the show in order for you to remain calm and relaxed as the countdown starts.

The importance of the crate has already been mentioned and should already be part of your equipment. Of equal importance is the grooming table, which very likely you have also already acquired for use at home. You should take it along with you to the shows, as your dog will need last minute touches before entering the ring. Should you have not yet made this purchase, folding tables with rubber tops are made specifically for this purpose and can be purchased at most dog shows, where concession booths with marvelous assortments of "doggy" necessities are to be found, or at your pet supplier. You will also need a sturdy tack box (also available at the dog show concessions) in which to carry your grooming tools and equipment. The latter should include: brushes; combs; scissors; nail clippers; whatever you use for last minute clean-up jobs; cotton swabs; first-aid equipment; and anything you are in the habit of using on the dog, including a leash or two of the type you prefer, some well-cooked and dried-out liver or any of the small packaged "dog treats" for use as bait in the ring, an atomizer in case you wish to dampen your dog's coat when you are preparing him for the ring, and so on. A large turkish towel to spread under the dog on the grooming table is also useful.

Take a large thermos or cooler of ice, the biggest one you can accommodate in your vehicle, for use by "man and beast." Take a jug of water (there are lightweight, inexpensive ones available at all sporting goods shops) and a water dish. If you plan to feed the dog at the show, or if you and the dog will be away from home more than one day, bring food for him from home so that he will have the type to which he is accustomed.

You may or may not have an exercise pen. While the shows do provide areas for exercise of the dogs, these are among the most likely places to have your dog come in contact with any illnesses which may be going around, and having a pen of your own for your dog's use is excellent protection. Such a pen comes in handy while you're travelling; since it is roomier than a crate, it becomes a comfortable place for your dog to relax and move around in, especially when you're at motels or rest stops. These pens are available at the show concession stands and come in a variety of heights and sizes. A set of "pooper scoopers" should also be part of your equipment, along with a package of plastic bags for cleaning up after your dog.

Bring along folding chairs for the members of your party, unless all of you are fond of standing, as these are almost never provided by the clubs. Have your name stamped on the chairs so that there will be no doubt as to whom the chairs belong. Bring whatever you and your family enjoy for drinks or snacks in a picnic basket or cooler, as show food, in general, is expensive and usually not great. You should always have a pair of boots, a raincoat, and a rain hat with you (they should remain permanently in your vehicle if you plan to attend shows regularly), as well as a sweater, a warm coat, and a change of shoes. A smock or big cover-up apron will assure that you remain tidy as you prepare the dog for the ring. Your overnight case should include a small sewing kit for emergency repairs, bandaids, headache and indigestion remedies, and any personal products or medications you normally use.

In your car, you should always carry maps of the area where you are headed and an assortment of motel directories. Generally speaking, Holiday Inns have been found to be the nicest about taking dogs. Ramadas and Howard Johnsons generally do so cheerfully (with a few exceptions). Best Western generally frowns

Ed Jenner enjoys handling his Pekingese, too, upon occasion. Here he is handling Ch. Mei-Li Red Baron to a good Best of Breed in March 1984.

on pets (not always, but often enough to make it necessary to find out which do). Some of the smaller chains welcome pets; the majority of privately-owned motels do not.

Have everything prepared the night before the show to expedite your departure. Be sure that the dog's identification and your judging program and other show information are in your purse or briefcase. If you are taking sandwiches, have them ready. Anything that goes into the car the night before the show will be one thing less to remember in the morning. Decide upon what you will wear and have it out and ready. If there is any question in your mind about what to wear, try on the possibilities before the day of the show; don't risk feeling you may want to change when you see yourself dressed a few moments prior to departure time!

In planning your outfit, make it something simple that will not detract from your dog. Remember that a dark dog silhouettes attractively against a light background and vice-versa. Sport clothes always seem to look best at dog shows, preferably conservative in type and not overly "loud" as you do not want to detract from your dog, who should be the focus of interest at this point. What you wear on your feet is important. Many types of flooring can be hazardously slippery, as can wet grass. Make it a habit to wear rubber soles and low or flat heels in the ring for your own safety, especially if you are showing a dog that likes to move out smartly.

Your final step in pre-show preparation is to leave yourself plenty of time to reach the show that morning. Traffic can get amazingly heavy as one nears the immediate area of the show, finding a parking place can be difficult, and other delays may occur. You'll be in better humor to enjoy the day if your trip to the show is not fraught with panic over fear of not arriving in time!

ENJOYING THE DOG SHOW

From the moment of your arrival at the show until after your dog has been judged, keep foremost in your mind the fact that he is your reason for being there and that he should therefore be the center of your attention. Arrive early enough to have time for those last-minute touches that can make a great difference when he enters the ring. Be sure that he has ample time to exercise and that he attends to personal matters. A dog arriving in the ring and immediately using it as an exercise pen hardly makes a favorable impression on the judge.

When you reach ringside, ask the steward for your arm-card and anchor it firmly into place on your arm. Make sure that you are where you should be when your class is called. The fact that you have picked up your arm-card does not guarantee, as some seem to think, that the judge will wait for you. The judge has a full schedule which he wishes to complete on time. Even though you may be nervous, assume an air of calm self-confidence. Remember that this is a hobby to be enjoyed, so approach it in that state of mind. The dog will do better, too, as he will be quick to reflect your attitude.

Always show your dog with an air of pride. If you make mistakes in presenting him, don't worry about it. Next time you will do better. Do not permit the presence of more experienced exhibitors to intimidate you. After all, they, too, were once newcomers.

The judging routine usually starts when the judge asks that the dogs be gaited in a circle around the ring. During this period the judge is watching each dog as it moves, noting style, topline, reach and drive, head and tail carriage, and general balance. Keep your mind and your eye on your dog, moving him at his most becoming gait and keeping your place in line without coming too close to the exhibitor ahead of you. Always keep your dog on the inside of the circle, between yourself and the judge, so that the judge's view of the dog is unobstructed.

Calmly pose the dog when requested to set up for examination. If you are at the head of the line and many dogs are in the class, go all the way to the end of the ring before starting to stack the dog, leaving sufficient space for those behind you to line theirs up as well, as requested by the judge. If you are not at the head of the line but between other exhibitors, leave sufficient space ahead of your dog for the judge to examine him. The dogs should be spaced so that the judge is able to move among them to see them from all angles. In practicing to "set up" or "stack" your dog for the judge's examination, bear in mind the importance of doing so quickly and with dexterity. The judge has a schedule to meet and only a few moments in which to evaluate each dog. You will immeasurably help yours to make a favorable impression if you are able to "get it all together" in a minimum amount of time. Practice at home before a mirror can be a great help toward bringing this about, facing the dog so that you see him from the same side that the judge will and working to make him look right in the shortest length of time.

Listen carefully as the judge describes the manner in which the dog is to be gaited, whether it is straight down and straight back; down the ring, across, and back; or in a triangle. The latter has become the most popular pattern with the majority of judges. "In a triangle" means the dog should move down the outer side of the ring to the first corner, across that end of the ring to the second corner, and then back to the judge from the second corner, using the center of the ring in a diagonal line. Please learn to do this pattern without breaking at each corner to twirl the dog around you, a senseless maneuver that has been noticed on occasion. Judges like to see the dog in an uninterrupted triangle, as they are thus able to get a better idea of the dog's gait.

It is impossible to overemphasize that the gait at which you move your dog is tremendously important and considerable study and thought should be given to the matter. At home, have someone move the dog for you at different speeds so that you can tell which shows him off to best advantage. The most becoming action almost invariably is seen at a moderate gait, head up and topline holding. Do not gallop your dog around the ring or hurry him into a speed atypical of his breed. Nothing being rushed appears at its best; give your dog a chance to move along at his (and the breed's) natural gait. For a dog's action to be judged accurately, that dog should move with strength and power, but not excessive speed, holding a straight line as he goes to and from the judge.

As you bring the dog back to the judge, stop him a few feet away and be sure that he is standing in a becoming position. Bait him to show the judge an alert expression, using whatever tasty morsel he has been trained to expect for this purpose or, if that works better for you, use a small squeak-toy in your hand. A reminder, please, to those using liver or treats: take them with you when you leave the ring. Do not just drop them on the ground where they will be found by another dog.

When the awards have been made, accept yours graciously, no matter how you actually may feel about it. What's done is done, and arguing with a judge or stomping out of the ring is useless and a reflection on your sportsmanship. Be courteous, congratulate the winner if your dog was defeated, and try not to show your disappointment. By the same token, please be a gracious winner; this, surprisingly, sometimes seems to be still more difficult.

Ch. Ku Jin T'Sun of Chintoi, bred by Mrs. Ella Pilgrim in England, was jointly owned by Edward B. Jenner and Elaine Rigden, for whom he did considerable winning a couple of decades back. Handled by Mrs. Rigden.

Chimie Wheat, C.D.X. was 1978's Top Obedience Pekingese. Trained and handled by Miss Sandy Wheat, Phoenix, Arizona. Chimie's daughter also gained C.D.X. at this same period of time.

276

Chapter 11

Your Pekingese and Obedience

For its own protection and safety, every dog should be taught, at the very least, to recognize and obey the commands "Come," "Heel," "Down," "Sit," and "Stay." Doing so at some time might save the dog's life and in less extreme circumstances will certainly make him a better behaved, more pleasant member of society. If you are patient and enjoy working with your dog, study some of the excellent books available on the subject of obedience and then teach your canine friend these basic manners. If you need the stimulus of working with a group, find out where obedience training classes are held (usually your veterinarian, your dog's breeder, or a dog-owning friend can tell you) and you and your dog can join. Alternatively, you could let someone else do the training by sending the dog to class, but this is not very rewarding because you lose the opportunity of working with your dog and the pleasure of the rapport thus established.

If you are going to do it yourself, there are some basic rules which you should follow. You must remain calm and confident in attitude. Never lose your temper and frighten or punish your dog unjustly. Be quick and lavish with praise each time a command is correctly followed. Make it fun for the dog and he will be eager to please you by responding correctly. Repetition is the keynote, but it should not be continued without recess to the point of tedium. Limit the training sessions to ten- or fifteen-minute periods at a time.

Formal obedience training can be followed, and very frequently is, by entering the dog in obedience competition to work toward an obedience degree, or several of them, depending on the dog's aptitude and your own enjoyment. Obedience trials are held in conjunction with the majority of all-breed conformation dog shows, with Specialty shows, and frequently as separate Specialty events. If you are working alone with your dog, a list of trial dates might be obtained from your dog's veterinarian, your dog breeder, or a dog-owning friend; the AKC *Gazette* lists shows and trials to be scheduled in the coming months; and if you are a member of a training class, you will find the information readily available.

The goals for which one works in the formal AKC Member or Licensed Trials are the following titles: Companion Dog (C.D.), Companion Dog Excellent (C.D.X.), and Utility Dog (U.D.). These degrees are earned by receiving three "legs," or qualifying

Jai Mie Se Me Tu of Tujaks, U.D., practicing his jumps during a home-training session. Owned by Eleanor Lamb, trained and handled by Jim Lamb, Mi Gems Pekingese.

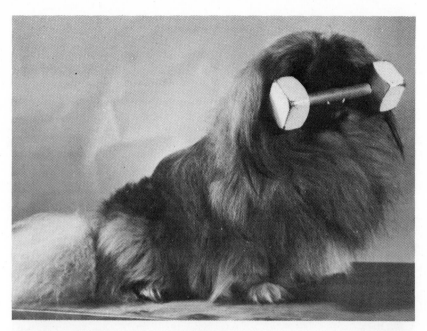

Jai Mie Se Me Tu of Tujaks, U.D., holding his dumb-bell. This noted Obedience winner is from the Mi Gems Pekingese owned by Mr. and Mrs. James P. Lamb, Sr., West Palm Beach, Florida.

scores, at each level of competition. The degrees must be earned in order, with one completed prior to starting work on the next. For example, a dog must have earned C.D. prior to starting work on C.D.X.; then C.D.X. must be completed before U.D. work begins. The ultimate title attainable in obedience work is Obedience Trial Champion (O.T.Ch.)

When you see the letters C.D. following a dog's name, you will know that this dog has satisfactorily completed the following exercises: heel on leash and figure eight, heel free, stand for examination, recall, long sit, and long down. C.D.X. means that tests have been passed on all of those just mentioned plus heel free and figure eight, drop on recall, retrieve on flat, retrieve over high jump, broad jump, long sit, and long down. U.D. indicates that the dog has additionally passed tests in scent discrimination (leather article), scent discrimination (metal article), signal exercise, directed retrieve, directed jumping, and group stand for examination. The letters O.T.Ch. are the abbreviation for the only obedience title which precedes rather than follows a dog's name. To gain an obedience trial championship, a dog who already holds a Utility Dog

Ch. Dragon Hai Fanfare at Bronx County in 1973. This handsome dog went on to three Bests in Show and nine Group Firsts. Owned by Mike-Mar Kennels, handled by Mr. Michael Wolf.

degree must win a total of one hundred points and must win three firsts, under three different judges, in Utility and Open B Classes.

There is also a Tracking Dog title (T.D.) which can be earned at tracking trials. In order to pass the tracking tests the dog must follow the trail of a stranger along a path on which the trail was laid between thirty minutes and two hours previously. Along this track there must be more than two right-angle turns, at least two of which are well out in the open where no fences or other boundaries exist for the guidance of the dog or the handler. The dog wears a harness and is connected to the handler by a lead twenty to forty feet in length. Inconspicuously dropped at the end of the track is an article to be retrieved, usually a glove or wallet, which the dog is expected to locate and the handler to pick up. The letters T.D.X. are the abbreviation for Tracking Dog Excellent, a more difficult version of the Tracking Dog test with a longer track and more turns to be worked through.

280

OBEDIENCE AND THE PEKINGESE
by James P. Lamb, Mi Gem's Pekingese

Pekingese are not a breed of dog usually associated with obedience training. Yet we understand that notable results can be gained in training the breed for this purpose. Jim Lamb is an expert on the subject, and thus we are delighted and honored to present this section which he so kindly has written for this book.

A.K.N.

The most often asked question is "at what age should I begin to train my dog?" My own preference is to start as soon as the puppy comes into the family, with the first lesson being the "come" experience. As soon as the puppy responds, pick him up and praise him. Pretty soon the puppy will come every time he is called, providing that he is praised every time he responds. Never call the puppy to punish him. Go to the puppy and then correct him.

One of the most exciting and rewarding activities a Pekingese owner or handler could possibly imagine involves the obedience training of our regal breed. As in all endeavors, the value of the reward is equal to the effort involved; or, bluntly speaking, you get what you put into it. The long hours of training are quickly forgotten when you suddenly realize that your animal is beginning to think and learn as impressively as any so-called "working dog." However, let it be known that obedience training of a Pekingese is similar to slipping sunrise past a rooster. It can be done, but one must be very patient and very untiring.

Let me assure you that *come, heel, down,* and stay are not the only four words you will learn in training your Pekingese. If you expect to make progress, you must also include "good boy," "fine job," and others of similar attitude, because praise, admiration, and affection are the motivating stimuli that keep the training from becoming boresome. Think how much harder you work when your efforts are praised and appreciated. The same is true with an animal, so don't be afraid to lavish many words of encouragement on the dog. Who cares what the neighbors think?

By now you most likely are wondering how to recognize a potential obedience candidate. Which of your dogs responds quickest when all are called at once? Which of your dogs seems most

281

active without being uncontrollable? Which of your dogs follows you around at your side? Should you be fortunate enough to have two or more of these traits in the same animal, you are well on your way.

Every time I hear that a Pekingese is not structurally built for obedience, I cringe. All that is required is to walk, run 20 feet at most, sit, lie in a prone position, and jump his/her own height at the shoulders. Personally, I have yet to see a Pekingese who couldn't do all of these without being prompted. These are all things your puppy does, or will soon do, as quickly as it is able to get around. Certainly, by 12 weeks of age, the puppy should be doing everything mentioned in the daily routine of playing and exercising. Remember, at 12 weeks the puppy is already brain-developed enough to comprehend the basics needed for obedience; but, please, save the jumping until your puppy has developed good, sound front legs and chest. In some lines this may be as early as 12-14 months, while in others it may be as late as 18-24 months. Remind yourself that two-thirds of your Peke's weight is in his/her head, shoulders and chest, and that this is the part the rear must make airborne. Also, with yet-to-develop front legs, the young puppy is landing on weak muscles and bones. Consequently, jumping could become very painful and even detrimental to your young Peke. A good rule of thumb is: do not jump your Peke until he has earned the Novice degree. Believe me, by the time you have earned this Novice degree (the Junior High equivalent) the dog will have you trained enough to know when to begin another routine. *No*, that was *not* a mistake! The dog will teach *you* many things, provided you are patient enough to learn. The more time spent together, the more you and your Peke begin to work togethr as one, with the primary objective to work as one moving body. When you can *feel* where your dog is, you will win.

In my opinion, the easiest way to train your dog is to join an obedience club. Every problem you may encounter has been experienced by another trainer, and the correction is there for the asking. The correction methods used on a Dobe may not be suitable for a Peke, but with proper modification, the result can be the same. Most obedience clubs have a beginners class with very competent instructors and a training program that will meet your needs. Don't panic if your "little darling" is placed alongside a Great Dane, because chances are you will have to encounter the

The top dog of the present at Saimaifun Kennels owned by Diane and Doug Kleinsorge, North Vancouver, Canada, is Am. and Can. Ch. Saimaifun Hot Shot, by the English import Ch. Bellerne's Yu Benito ex Can. and Am. Ch. Saimaifun Gay Dinamite. He is an all-breed Best in Show dog; a multiple Specialty winner; and a dog with numerous Bests of Breed, Group wins and placements. Now proving a stud dog of excellence.

same conditions at a trial. So why not get accustomed to it now?

In order to have a clear measure of achievement, I suggest picking the largest and best-performing dog in the class and striving to train your dog to out-perform the star pupil. Just remember, the larger dogs are higher from the ground, so they cannot turn as quickly as your dog, nor sit as straight as your dog. So go out there and use every advantage you have to make your dog work better. Without motivation, you will wind up just walking your dog with the group. This is not what inspires greatness; so go out

283

Ch. Elpha Sun Inquisition finishing title at seven months old. This handsome Peke is now Ch. Elpha Sun Inquisitor C.D. Owned by Peggy Reed of Wilton, Connecticut. Bred by Doll and McGinnis, Elpha Sun, Lakeland, Florida.

there and train to *win*. On graduation night (or whatever the final beginning class is called), when you and your dog are acknowledged as Best in Class, all those days of training and hours of walking are suddenly forgotten.

Unquestionably, the most famous and successful Pekingese to date in the obedience world would have to be my own Jai Mie See Me Tu of Tujaks, U.D. Jai Mie has been in first place among Pekingese in every pool and every American Kennel Club obedience rating for five consecutive years, proving that "once a bond has been established between dog and handler, a good dog can make an old man look *very* good."

Jai Mie began his career in Novice on November 8, 1980, on that occasion taking fourth place behind a Doberman, a Miniature Poodle, and a German Shepherd Dog. On November 9 and 16, he completed the requirements for his Companion Dog degree finishing second behind a Golden Retriever and gaining Highest Scoring Toy.

284

In April 1981, he was considered to be ready for Open in search of C.D.X. That, too, was an easily taken step. On April 25, Jai Mie's score was 189 in his first Open trial, and a week later, on May 2 and 3, he earned his other two legs for the title with a score of 191. That weekend he was Highest Scoring Toy both days, gaining himself the coveted "Excellent."

In September 1981, Jai Mie set off, along with five other dogs also selected for the honor, to represent the Obedience Training Club of Palm Beach County in the annual state competition of the Dog Obedience Clubs of Florida. The top obedience clubs in Florida each send a six member team (two members each from Novice, Open, and Utility), and the team garnering the most points at the trial is named State Champion.

Jai Mie kept his cool by capturing a third place in the Open Division for a score of 195 ½, thus anchoring the Palm Beach Club as they rolled to 1152 points. The Obedience Training Club of Palm Beach County became the State Champion in 1981, and an impressive little Pekingese had become the third-best Obedience Open Dog in Florida! In October, *Front*, the national obedience publication, listed Jai Mie as the No. 1 Pekingese in Obedience, figured from the results of all AKC Obedience Trials during 1980. Jai Mie still holds this record.

Utility came next, proving to be a bit more difficult for our furry little hero. But he made it, and in October 1982 Jai Mie was officially recorded Utility Dog. In 1983, he again represented Palm Beach County in the Florida State competition, in Utility this time. His score was 194; Palm Beach County again was the winner. Jai Mie competed in the 1983 Gaines Invitational Regional competition, the first Pekingese ever to have appeared in the Super Dog Obedience. On to Obedience Trial Championship!

Mi Gems has produced other obedience-winning Pekingese in addition to Jai Mie. These include Wendy's Pooh Bear, C.D. (No. 3, nationally, in 1982), owned by Wendy Johnston, US Navy; Paula Lings Tedi Bear, C.D.X. (No. 4 in 1982 and No. 3 in 1983), owned by Paula Summers; and Mi Gems Jamison Blueprint, C.D.X. (No. 4 in 1983 and No. 2 in 1984), Jim Lamb, owner.

Honorable mention must also go to Duke of Arca, American Canadian C.D.X., who is owned and exhibited by Delphine and Gancey of Detroit, Michigan. Moe Moe, as he is called, has been among the Top Ten for several years, and is still going strong.

285

Muhlin Most Royal, one of the foundation studs at O'Honeybear Kennels, Abilene, Texas. Annette L. Borders, owner. Royal has proven himself a sire of tremendous merit.

Chapter 12

Breeding Your Pekingese

The first responsibility of any person breeding dogs is to do so with care, forethought, and deliberation. It is inexcusable to breed more litters than you need to carry on your show program or to perpetuate your bloodlines. A responsible breeder should not cause a litter to be born without definite plans for the safe and happy disposition of the puppies.

A responsible dog breeder makes absolutely certain, so far as is humanly possible, that the home to which one of his puppies will go is a good home, one that offers proper care and an enthusiastic owner. To be admired are those breeders who insist on visiting (although doing so is not always feasible) the prospective owners of their puppies to see if they have suitable facilities for keeping a dog, to find out if they understand the responsibility involved, and to make certain if all members of the household are in accord regarding the desirability of owning one. All breeders should carefully check out the credentials of prospective purchasers to be sure that the puppy is being placed in responsible hands.

No breeder ever wants a puppy or grown dog he has raised to wind up in an animal shelter, in an experimental laboratory, or as a victim of a speeding car. While complete control of such a situation may be impossible, it is important to make every effort to turn over dogs to responsible people. When selling a puppy, it is a good idea to do so with the understanding that should it become necessary to place the dog in other hands, the purchaser will first contact you, the breeder. You may want to help in some way, possibly by buying or taking back the dog or placing it elsewhere. It is not fair to sell puppies and then never again give a thought to their welfare. Family problems arise, people may be forced to move where dogs are prohibited, or people just grow bored with a dog and its care. Thus the dog becomes a victim. You, as the dog's breeder, should concern yourself with the welfare of each of your dogs and see to it that the dog remains in good hands.

The final obligation every dog owner shares, be there just one dog or an entire kennel involved, is that of making detailed, explicit plans for the future of these dearly loved animals in the event of the owner's death. Far too many people are apt to procrastinate and leave this very important matter unattended to, feeling that everything will work out or that "someone will see to them." Neither is too likely, at least not to the benefit of the dogs, unless you have done some advance planning which will assure their future well-being.

Life is filled with the unexpected, and even the youngest, healthiest, most robust of us may be the victim of a fatal accident or sudden illness. The fate of your dogs, so entirely in your hands, should never be left to chance. If you have not already done so, please get together with your lawyer and set up a clause in your will specifying what you want done with each of your dogs, to whom they will be entrusted (after first making absolutely certain that the person selected is willing and able to assume the responsibility), and telling the locations of all registration papers, pedigrees, and kennel records. Just think of the possibilities which might happen otherwise! If there is another family member who shares your love of the dogs, that is good and you have less to worry about. But if your heirs are not dog-oriented, they will hardly know how to proceed or how to cope with the dogs themselves, and they may wind up disposing of or caring for your dogs in a manner that would break your heart were you around to know about it.

It is advisable to have in your will specific instructions concerning each of your dogs. A friend, also a dog person who regards his or her own dogs with the same concern and esteem as you do, may agree to take over their care until they can be placed accordingly

Back in 1968, St. Aubrey Glitters of Elsdon winning Best Bitch at the Progressive Dog Club under Mrs. Mary Brewster, handled by co-breeder owner Mr. Nigel Aubrey Jones. Later sold to Mrs. Fortune Roberts, Bronxville, New York.

and will make certain that all will work out as you have planned. This person's name and phone number can be prominently displayed in your van or car and in your wallet. Your lawyer can be made aware of this fact. This can be spelled out in your will. The friend can have a signed check of yours to be used in case of an emergency or accident when you are traveling with the dogs; this check can be used to cover his or her expense to come and take over the care of your dogs should anything happen to make it impossible for you to do so. This is the least any dog owner should do in preparation for the time their dogs suddenly find themselves alone. There have been so many sad cases of dogs unprovided for by their loving owners, left to heirs who couldn't care less and who disposed of them in any way at all to get rid of them, or left to heirs who kept and neglected them under the misguided idea that they were providing them "a fine home with lots of freedom." These misfortunes must be prevented from befalling your own dogs who have meant so much you!

Conscientious breeders feel quite strongly that the only possible reason for producing puppies is the ambition to improve and uphold quality and temperament within the breed—definitely *not* be-

Starduster O'Honeybear, gaining points in 1985, would seem destined for a bright future for his owner Annette L. Borders, Abilene, Texas.

Ch. Cee-Kae's Ying Hee with puppies by Ch. Cee-Kae's Bon's Fuh Fuh: *left*, Ama Star Luv Bug; *right* Ch. Cee-Kae's Silver Rocket. Cee-Kae Pekingese, Chuck and Kim Langley, Galt, California.

cause one hopes to make a quick cash profit on a mediocre litter, which never seems to work out that way in the long run and which accomplishes little beyond perhaps adding to the nation's heart-breaking number of unwanted canines. The only reason ever for breeding a litter is, with conscientious people, a desire to improve the quality of dogs in their own kennel or, as pet owners, to add to the number of dogs they themselves own with a puppy or two from their present favorites. In either case, breeding should not take place unless one definitely has prospective owners for as many puppies as the litter may contain, lest you find yourself with several fast-growing young dogs and no homes in which to place them.

THE BROOD BITCH

Bitches should not be mated earlier than their second season, by which time they should be from fifteen to eighteen months old. Many breeders prefer to wait and finish the championships of their show bitches before breeding them, as pregnancy can be a disaster to a show coat and getting the bitch back in shape again takes time. When you have decided what will be the proper time, start watching at least several months ahead for what you feel would be the perfect mate to best complement your bitch's quality and bloodlines. Subscribe to the magazines which feature your breed exclusively and to some which cover all breeds in order to familiarize yourself with outstanding stud dogs in areas other than your own, for there is no necessity nowadays to limit your choice to a local dog unless you truly like him and feel that he is the most suitable. It is quite usual to ship a bitch to a stud dog a distance away, and this generally works out with no ill effects. The important thing is that you need a stud dog strong in those features where your bitch is weak, a dog whose bloodlines are compatible with hers. Compare the background of both your bitch and the stud dog under consideration, paying particular attention to the quality of the puppies from bitches with backgrounds similar to your bitch's. If the puppies have been of the type and quality you admire, then this dog would seem a sensible choice for yours, too.

Stud fees may be a few hundred dollars, sometimes even more under special situations for a particularly successful sire. It is money well spent, however. *Do not* ever breed to a dog because he is less expensive than the others unless you honestly believe that he can sire the kind of puppies who will be a credit to your kennel and your breed.

Contacting the owners of the stud dogs you find interesting will bring you pedigrees and pictures which you can then study in relation to your bitch's pedigree and conformation. Discuss your plans with other breeders who are knowledgeable (including the one who bred your own bitch). You may not always receive an entirely unbiased opinion (particularly if the person giving it also has an available stud dog), but one learns by discussion so listen to what they say, consider their opinions, and then you may be better qualified to form your own opinion.

As soon as you have made a choice, phone the owner of the stud dog you wish to use to find out if this will be agreeable. You will be asked about the bitch's health, soundness, temperament, and freedom from serious faults. A copy of her pedigree may be requested, as might a picture of her. A discussion of her background over the telephone may be sufficient to assure the stud's owner that she is suitable for the stud dog and that she is of type, breeding, and quality herself, capable of producing the kind of puppies for which the stud is noted. The owner of a top-quality stud is often extremely selective in the bitches permitted to be bred to his dog, in an effort to keep the standard of his puppies high. The owner of a stud dog may require that the bitch be tested for brucellosis, which should be attended to not more than a month previous to the breeding.

Check out which airport will be most convenient for the person meeting and returning the bitch, if she is to be shipped, and also what airlines use that airport. You will find that the airlines are also apt to have special requirements concerning acceptance of animals for shipping. These include weather limitations and types of crates which are acceptable. The weather limits have to do with extreme heat and extreme cold at the point of destination, as some airlines will not fly dogs into temperatures above or below certain levels, fearing for their safety. The crate problem is a simple one, since, if your own crate is not suitable, most of the airlines have specially designed crates available for purchase at a fair and moderate price. It is a good plan to purchase one of these if you intend to be shipping dogs with any sort of frequency. They are made of fiberglass and are the safest type to use for shipping.

Normally you must notify the airline several days in advance to make a reservation, as they are able to accommodate only a certain number of dogs on each flight. Plan on shipping the bitch on about her eighth or ninth day of season, but be careful to avoid shipping her on a weekend when schedules often vary and freight offices are apt to be closed. Whenever you can, ship your bitch on a direct flight. Changing planes always carries a certain amount of risk of a dog being overlooked or wrongly routed at the middle stop, so avoid this danger if at all possible. The bitch must be accompanied by a health certificate which you must obtain from your veterinarian before taking her to the airport. Usually it will be necessary to have the bitch at the airport about two hours prior to flight time. Before finalizing arrangements, find out from the stud's owner at what time of day it will be most convenient to have the bitch picked up promptly upon arrival.

It is simpler if you can bring the bitch to the stud dog yourself. Some people feel that the trauma of the flight may cause the bitch to not conceive; and, of course, undeniably there is a slight risk in shipping which can be avoided if you are able to drive the bitch to her destination. Be sure to leave yourself sufficient time to assure your arrival at the right time for her for breeding (normally

Ch. Nagel's Hi Lisa of Woodlawn, by Ch. Jalna's Hi-Lite ex Bugatti Belle of Woodlawn, owned and handled by Mary McCracken, Jersey Shore, Pennsylvania.

294

the tenth to fourteenth day following the first signs of color); and remember that if you want the bitch bred twice, you should allow a day to elapse between the two matings. Do not expect the stud's owner to house you while you are there. Locate a nearby motel that takes dogs and make that your headquarters.

Just prior to the time your bitch is due in season, you should take her to visit your veterinarian. She should be checked for worms and should receive all the booster shots for which she is due plus one for parvovirus, unless she has had the latter shot fairly recently. The brucellosis test can also be done then, and the health certificate can be obtained for shipping if she is to travel by air. Should the bitch be at all overweight, now is the time to get the surplus off. She should be in good condition, neither underweight nor overweight, at the time of breeding.

The moment you notice the swelling of the vulva, for which you should be checking daily as the time for her season approaches, and the appearance of color, immediately contact the stud's owner and settle on the day for shipping or make the appointment for your arrival with the bitch for breeding. If you are shipping the bitch, the stud fee check should be mailed immediately, leaving ample time for it to have been received when the bitch arrives and the mating takes place. Be sure to call the airline, making her reservation at that time, too.

Do not feed the bitch within a few hours before shipping her. Be certain that she has had a drink of water and been well exercised before closing her in the crate. Several layers of newspapers, topped with some shredded newspaper, make a good bed and can be discarded when she arrives at her destination; these can be replaced with fresh newspapers for her return home. Remember that the bitch should be brought to the airport about two hours before flight time, as sometimes the airlines refuse to accept late arrivals.

If you are taking your bitch by car, be certain that you will arrive at a reasonable time of day. Do not appear late in the evening. If your arrival in town is not until late, get a good night's sleep at your motel and contact the stud's owner first thing in the morning. If possible, leave children and relatives at home, as they will only be in the way and perhaps unwelcome by the stud's owner. Most stud dog owners prefer not to have any unnecessary people on hand during the actual mating.

After the breeding has taken place, if you wish to sit and visit for awhile and the stud's owner has the time, return the bitch to her crate in your car (first ascertaining, of course, that the temperature is comfortable for her and that there is proper ventilation). She should not be permitted to urinate for at least one hour following the breeding. This is the time when you attend to the business part of the transaction. Pay the stud fee, upon which you should receive your breeding certificate and, if you do not already have it, a copy of the stud dog's pedigree. The owner of the stud dog does not sign or furnish a litter registration application until the puppies have been born.

Upon your return home, you can settle down and plan in happy anticipation a wonderful litter of puppies. A word of caution! Remember that although she has been bred, your bitch is still an interesting target for all male dogs, so guard her carefully for the next week or until you are absolutely certain that her season has entirely ended. This would be no time to have any unfortunate incident with another dog.

The multi-Best in Show winner and the Top Pekingese Sire of all time. With more than 100 Champions to his credit, Ch. St. Aubrey Laparata Dragon is still siring at age eleven years. Handled by Luc Boileau for owner Edward B. Jenner, Knolland Farm.

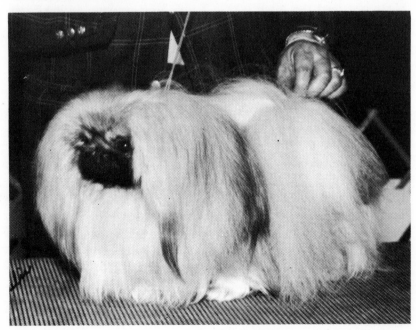

Eng. and Am. Ch. Goofus Bugatti, a fabulous English dog purchased by Nigel Aubrey Jones and R. William Taylor, Montreal, Quebec, Canada.

THE STUD DOG

Choosing the best stud dog to complement your bitch is often very difficult. The two principal factors to be considered should be the stud's conformation and his pedigree. Conformation is fairly obvious; you want a dog that is typical of the breed in the words of the Standard of perfection. Understanding pedigrees is a bit more subtle since the pedigree lists the ancestry of the dog and involves individuals and bloodlines with which you may not be entirely familiar.

To a novice in the breed, the correct interpretation of a pedigree may at first be difficult to grasp. Study the pictures and text of this book and you will find many names of important bloodlines and members of the breed. Also make an effort to discuss the various dogs behind the proposed stud with some of the more experienced breeders, starting with the breeder of your own bitch. Frequently these folks will be familiar with many of the dogs in question, will be able to offer opinions of them, and may have access to additional pictures which you would benefit by seeing. It is very important that the stud's pedigree be harmonious with that of the bitch you plan on breeding to him. Do not rush out and breed to the latest winner with no thought of whether or not he can produce true quality. By no means are all great show dogs great producers. It is the producing record of the dog in question, and the dogs and bitches from which he has come, that should be the basis on which you make your choice.

Breeding dogs is never a money-making operation. By the time you pay a stud fee, care for the bitch during pregnancy, whelp the litter, and rear the puppies through their early shots, worming, and so on, you will be fortunate to break even financially once the puppies have been sold. Your chances of doing this are greater if you are breeding for a show-quality litter which will bring you higher prices, as the pups are sold as show prospects. Therefore, your wisest investment is to use the best dog available for your bitch regardless of the cost; then you should wind up with more valuable puppies. Remember that it is equally costly to raise mediocre puppies as it is top ones, and your chances of financial return are better on the latter. Breeding to the most excellent, most suitable stud dog you can find is the only sensible thing to do, and it is poor economy to quibble over the amount you are paying in a stud fee.

It will be your decision as to which course you follow when you breed your bitch, as there are three options: linebreeding, inbreeding, and outcrossing. Each of these methods has its supporters and its detractors! Linebreeding is breeding a bitch to a dog belonging originally to the same canine family, being descended from the same ancestors, such as half brother to half sister, grandsire to granddaughter, niece to uncle (and vice-versa) or cousin to cousin. Inbreeding is breeding father to daughter, mother to son, or full brother to sister. Outcross breeding is breeding a dog and a bitch with no or only a few mutual ancestors.

Linebreeding is probably the safest course, and the one most likely to bring results, for the novice breeder. The more sophisticated inbreeding should be left to the experienced, longtime breeders who throroughly know and understand the risks and the possibilities involved with a particular line. It is usually done in an effort to intensify some ideal feature in that strain. Outcrossing is the reverse of inbreeding, an effort to introduce improvement in a specific feature needing correction, such as a shorter back, better movement, more correct head or coat, and so on.

It is the serious breeder's ambition to develop a strain or bloodline of their own, one strong in qualities for which their dogs will

298

become distinguished. However, it must be realized that this will involve time, patience, and at least several generations before the achievement can be claimed. The safest way to embark on this plan, as previously mentioned, is by the selection and breeding of one or two bitches, the best you can buy and from top-producing kennels. In the beginning you do *not* really have to own a stud dog. In the long run it is less expensive and sounder judgement to pay a stud fee when you are ready to breed a bitch than to purchase a stud dog and feed him all year; a stud dog does not win any popularity contests with owners of bitches to be bred until he becomes a champion, has been successfully Specialed for a while, and has been at least moderately advertised, all of which adds up to quite a healthy expenditure.

The wisest course for the inexperienced breeder just starting out in dogs is to keep the best bitch puppy from the first several litters. After that you may wish to consider keeping your own stud dog, if there has been a particularly handsome male in one of your litters that you feel has great potential or if you know where there is one available that you are interested in, with the feeling that he would work in nicely with the breeding program on which you have embarked. By this time, with several litters already born, your eye should have developed to a point enabling you to make a wise choice, either from one of your own litters or from among dogs you have seen that appear suitable.

The greatest care should be taken in the selection of your own stud dog. He must be of true type and highest quality as he may be responsible for siring many puppies each year, and he should come from a line of excellent dogs on both sides of his pedigree which themselves are, and which are descended from, successful producers. This dog should have no glaring faults in conformation; he should be of such quality that he can hold his own in keenest competition within his breed. He should be in good health, be virile and be a keen stud dog, a proven sire able to transmit his correct qualities to his puppies. Need one say that such a dog will be enormously expensive unless you have the good fortune to produce him in one of your own litters? To buy and use a lesser stud dog, however, is downgrading your breeding program unnecessarily since there are so many dogs fitting the description of a fine stud whose services can be used on payment of a stud fee.

You should *never* breed to an unsound dog or one with any serious disqualifying faults according to the breed's standard. Not all champions by any means pass along their best features; and by the same token, occasionally you will find a great one who can pass along his best features but never gained his championship title due to some unusual circumstances. The information you need about a stud dog is what type of puppies he has produced, and with what bloodlines, and whether or not he possesses the bloodlines and attributes considered characteristic of the best in your breed.

If you go out to buy a stud dog, obviously he will not be a puppy, but rather a fully mature and proven male with as many of the best attributes as possible. True, he will be an expensive investment, but if you choose and make his selection with care and forethought, he may well prove to be one of the best investments you have ever made.

Of course, the most exciting of all is when a young male you have decided to keep from one of your litters, due to his tremendous show potential, turns out to be a stud dog such as we have described. In this case he should be managed with care, for he is a valuable property that can contribute inestimably to this breed

Ch. Mar-Pat's Tiko's Juliet winning at Salina K.C. in 1963. Owned by Mar-Pat Pekingese, Martha Olmos-Ollivier and Patricia Miller, Gardena, California.

Can. Ch. Saimaifun Fair 'N' Square taking Best of Winners on way to title, Eugene, Oregon, 1984. Bred and owned by Diane and Doug Kleinsorge, North Vancouver, B.C., Canada.

as a whole and to your own kennel specifically.

Do not permit your stud dog to be used until he is about a year old, and even then he should be bred to a mature, proven matron accustomed to breeding who will make his first experience pleasant and easy. A young dog can be put off forever by a maiden bitch who fights and resists his advances. Never allow this to happen. Always start a stud dog out with a bitch who is mature, has been bred previously, and is of even temperament. The first breeding should be performed in quiet surroundings with only you and one other person to hold the bitch. Do not make it a circus, as the experience will determine the dog's outlook about future stud work. If he does not enjoy the first experience or associates it with any unpleasantness, you may well have a problem in the future.

Your young stud must permit help with the breeding, as later there will be bitches who will not be cooperative. If right from the beginning you are there helping him and praising him, whether or not your assistance is actually needed, he will expect and accept this as a matter of course when a difficult bitch comes along.

Things to have handy before introducing your dog and the bitch are K-Y jelly (the only lubricant which should be used) and a length of gauze with which to muzzle the bitch should it be necessary to keep her from biting you or the dog. Some bitches put up a fight; others are calm. It is best to be prepared.

At the time of the breeding, the stud fee comes due, and it is expected that it will be paid promptly. Normally a return service is offered in case the bitch misses or fails to produce one live puppy. Conditions of the service are what the stud dog's owner makes them, and there are no standard rules covering this. The stud fee is paid for the act, not the result. If the bitch fails to conceive, it is customary for the owner to offer a free return service; but this is a courtesy and not to be considered a right, particularly in the case of a proven stud who is siring consistently and whose fault the failure obviously is *not*. Stud dog owners are always anx-

Ch. Sherida of Essdee winning a 4-point major in 1969. One of the original English Pekingese on which the Toimanor Kennels were founded. By Oscar of Coughton ex Oysterhaven Pu Suki. Owned by Audrey Drake and Janet Drake Oxford, Fayetteville, Arkansas.

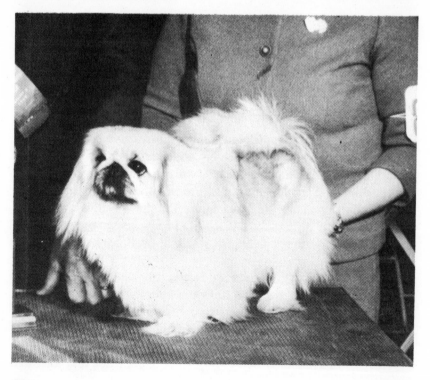

'Ch. Olga's Jill of Popa's, by Ch. Hydlewood Loo Foo Snow Sprite ex Beau-
pre's Snow Shani, was bred by Mrs. Olga FitzGerald and Mrs. Ruthe Painter
and is co-owned by Miss Audrey A. Atherton and Mrs. Norma Jean Popa.
Here taking Winners at South Jersey K.C.

ious to see their clients get good value and to have, in the ring,
winning young stock by their dog; therefore, very few refuse to
mate the second time. It is wise, however, for both parties to have
the terms of the transaction clearly understood at the time of the
breeding.

If the return service has been provided and the bitch has missed
a second time, that is considered to be the end of the matter and
the owner would be expected to pay a further fee if it is felt that
the bitch should be given a third chance with the stud dog. The
management of a stud dog and his visiting bitches is quite a task,
and a stud fee has usually been well earned when one service has
been achieved, let alone by repeated visits from the same bitch.

The accepted litter is one live puppy. It is wise to have printed
a breeding certificate which the owner of the stud dog and the

303

owner of the bitch both sign. This should list in detail the conditions of the breeding as well as the dates of the mating.

Upon occasion, arrangements other than a stud fee in cash are made for a breeding, such as the owner of the stud taking a pick-of-the-litter puppy in lieu of money. This should be clearly specified on the breeding certificate along with the terms of the age at which the stud's owner will select the puppy, whether it is to be a specific sex, or whether it is to be the pick of the entire litter.

The price of a stud fee varies according to circumstances. Usually, to prove a young stud dog, his owner will allow the first breeding to be quite inexpensive. Then, once a bitch has become pregnant by him, he becomes a "proven stud" and the fee rises accordingly for bitches that follow. The sire of championship quality puppies will bring a stud fee of at least the purchase price of one show puppy as the accepted "rule-of-thumb." Until at least one champion by your stud dog has finished, the fee will remain equal to the price of one pet puppy. When his list of champions starts to grow, so does the amount of the stud fee. For a top-producing sire of champions, the stud fee will rise accordingly.

Almost invariably it is the bitch who comes to the stud dog for the breeding. Immediately upon having selected the stud dog you wish to use, discuss the possibility with the owner of that dog. It is the stud dog owner's prerogative to refuse to breed any bitch deemed unsuitable for this dog. Stud fee and method of payment should be stated at this time and a decision reached on whether it is to be a full cash transaction at the time of the mating or a pick-of-the-litter puppy, usually at eight weeks of age.

If the owner of the stud dog must travel to an airport to meet the bitch and ship her for the flight home, an additional charge will be made for time, tolls, and gasoline based on the stud owner's proximity to the airport. The stud fee includes board for the day on the bitch's arrival through two days for breeding, with a day in between. If it is necessary that the bitch remain longer, it is very likely that additional board will be charged at the normal per-day rate for the breed.

Be sure to advise the stud's owner as soon as you know that your bitch is in season so that the stud dog will be available. This is especially important because if he is a dog being shown, he and his owner may be unavailable, owing to the dog's absence from home.

As the owner of a stud dog being offered to the public, it is essential that you have proper facilities for the care of visiting bitches. Nothing can be worse than a bitch being insecurely housed and slipping out to become lost or bred by the wrong dog. If you are taking people's valued bitches into your kennel or home, it is imperative that you provide them with comfortable, secure housing and good care while they are your responsibility.

There is no dog more valuable than the proven sire of champions, Group winners, and Best in Show dogs. Once you have such an animal, guard his reputation well and do *not* permit him to be bred to just any bitch that comes along. It takes two to make the puppies; even the most dominant stud cannot do it all himself, so never permit him to breed a bitch you consider unworthy. Remember that when the puppies arrive, it will be your stud dog who will be blamed for any lack of quality, while the bitch's shortcomings will be quickly and conveniently overlooked.

Going into the actual management of the mating is a bit superfluous here. If you have had previous experience in breeding a dog and bitch, you will know how the mating is done. If you do not have such experience, you should not attempt to follow directions given in a book but should have a veterinarian, breeder friend, or handler there to help you with the first few times. You do not turn the dog and bitch loose together and await developments, as too many things can go wrong and you may altogether miss getting the bitch bred. Someone should hold the dog and the bitch (one person each) until the "tie" is made and these two people should stay with them during the entire act.

If you get a complete tie, probably only the one mating is absolutely necessary. However, especially with a maiden bitch or one that has come a long distance for this breeding, a follow-up with a second breeding is preferred, leaving one day in between the two matings. In this way there will be little or no chance of the bitch missing.

Once the tie has been completed and the dogs release, be certain that the male's penis goes completely back within its sheath. He should be allowed a drink of water and a short walk, and then he should be put into his crate or somewhere alone where he can settle down. Do not allow him to be with other dogs for a while as they will notice the odor of the bitch on him, and, particularly with other males present, he may become involved in a fight.

305

PREGNANCY, WHELPING, AND THE LITTER

Once the bitch has been bred and is back at home, remember to keep an ever watchful eye that no other males get to her until at least the twenty-second day of her season has passed. Until then, it will still be possible for an unwanted breeding to take place, which at this point would be catastrophic. Remember that she actually can have two separate litters by two different dogs, so take care.

In other ways, she should be treated normally. Controlled exercise is good and necessary for the bitch throughout her pregnancy, tapering it off to just several short walks daily, preferably on lead, as she reaches her seventh week. As her time grows close, be careful about her jumping or playing too roughly.

The theory that a bitch should be overstuffed with food when pregnant is a poor one. A fat bitch is never an easy whelper, so the overfeeding you consider good for her may well turn out to be a hindrance later on. During the first few weeks of pregnancy, your bitch should be fed her normal diet. At four to five weeks along, calcium should be added to her food. At seven weeks her

Ch. Raffles Jubilation Sing Lee, by Ch. Sungarth Raffkes Sing Lee ex Ch. Dockleaf's Ming Cherry Sing Lee, is a Best in Show winner at both all-breed shows and Specialty Shows, including the Pekingese Club of America in 1984. Bred, owned, and handled by J. Robert Jacobsen, Sing Lee Pekingese, Pt. Reyes Station, California.

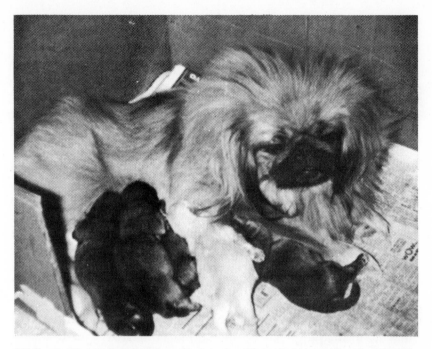

Mi Gems Ting Lee of Lyt-ton with her first litter of six puppies sired by Ch. Micklee Travis. One male attained his C.D., another male attained both C.D. and C.D.X., and two females produced champions. Two were sold but never shown. Eleanor Lamb, Mi Gems Pekingese, West Palm Beach, Florida.

food may be increased if she seems to crave more than she is getting, and a meal of canned milk (mixed with an equal amount of water) should be introduced. If she is fed just once a day, add another meal rather than overload her with too much at one time. If twice a day is her schedule, then a bit more food can be added to each feeding.

A week before the pups are due, your bitch should be introduced to her whelping box so that she will be accustomed to it and feel at home there when the puppies arrive. She should be encouraged to sleep there but permitted to come and go as she wishes. The box should be roomy enough for her to lie down and stretch out in but not too large, lest the pups have more room than is needed in which to roam and possibly get chilled by going too far away from their mother. Be sure that the box has a "pig rail"; this will prevent the puppies from being crushed against the sides. The room in which the box is placed, either in your home or in the kennel, should be kept at about 70 degrees Fahrenheit. In winter

307

it may be necessary to have an infrared lamp over the whelping box, in which case be careful not to place it too low or close to the puppies.

Newspapers will become a very important commodity, so start collecting them well in advance to have a big pile handy for the whelping box. With a litter of puppies, one never seems to have papers enough, so the higher pile to start with, the better off you will be. Other necessities for whelping time are clean, soft turkish towels, scissors, and a bottle of alcohol.

You will know that her time is very near when your bitch becomes restless, wandering in and out of her box and out of the room. She may refuse food, and at that point her temperature will start to drop. She will dig at and tear up the newspapers in her box, shiver, and generally look uncomfortable. Only you should be with your bitch at this time. She does not need spectators; and several people hanging over her, even though they may be family members whom she knows, may upset her to the point where she may harm the puppies. You should remain nearby, quietly watching, not fussing or hovering; speak calmly and frequently to her to instill confidence. Eventually she will settle down in her box and begin panting; contractions will follow. Soon thereafter a puppy will start to emerge, sliding out with the contractions. The mother immediately should open the sac, sever the cord with her teeth, and then clean up the puppy. She will also eat the placenta, which you should permit. Once the puppy is cleaned, it should be placed next to the bitch unless she is showing signs of having the next one immediately. Almost at once the puppy will start looking for a nipple on which to nurse, and you should ascertain that it is able to latch on successfully.

If the puppy is a breech (*i.e.*, born feet first), you must watch carefully for it to be completely delivered as quickly as possible and for the sac to be removed quickly so that the puppy does not drown. Sometimes even a normally positioned birth will seem extremely slow in coming. Should this occur, you might take a clean towel, and as the bitch contracts, pull the puppy out, doing so gently and with utmost care. If, once the puppy is delivered, it shows little signs of life, take a rough turkish towel and massage the puppy's chest by rubbing quite briskly back and forth. Continue this for about fifteen minutes, and be sure that the mouth is free of liquid. It may be necessary to try mouth-to-mouth breathing, which is begun by pressing the puppy's jaws open and, using a finger, depressing the tongue which may be stuck to the roof of the mouth. Then place your mouth against the puppy's and blow hard down the puppy's throat. Rub the puppy's chest with the towel again and try artificial respiration, pressing the sides of the chest together slowly and rhythmically—in and out, in and out. Keep trying one method or the other for at least twenty minutes before giving up. You may be rewarded with a live puppy who otherwise would not have made it.

If you are successful in bringing the puppy around, do not immediately put it back with the mother as it should be kept extra warm. Put it in a cardboard box on an electric heating pad or, if it is the time of year when your heat is running, near a radiator or near the fireplace or stove. As soon as the rest of the litter has been born, it then can join the others.

An hour or more may elapse between puppies, which is fine so long as the bitch seems comfortable and is neither straining nor contracting. She should not be permitted to remain unassisted for more than an hour if she does continue to contract. This is when you should get her to your veterinarian, whom you should already have alerted to the possibility of a problem existing. He should examine her and perhaps give her a shot of Pituitrin. In some cases the veterinarian may find that a Caesarean section is necessary due to a puppy being lodged in a manner making normal delivery impossible. Sometimes this is caused by an abnormally large puppy, or it may just be that the puppy is simply turned in the wrong position. If the bitch does require a Caesarean section, the puppies already born must be kept warm in their cardboard box with a heating pad under the box.

Once the section is done, get the bitch and the puppies home. Do not attempt to put the puppies in with the bitch until she has regained consciousness, as she may unknowingly hurt them. But do get them back to her as soon as possible for them to start nursing.

Should the mother lack milk at this time, the puppies must be fed by hand, kept very warm, and held onto the mother's teats several times a day in order to stimulate and encourage the secretion of milk, which should start shortly.

Assuming that there has been no problem and that the bitch has whelped naturally, you should insist that she go out to exercise, staying just long enough to make herself comfortable. She can be offered a bowl of milk and a biscuit, but then she should settle down with her family. Freshen the whelping box for her with newspapers while she is taking this respite so that she and the puppies will have a clean bed.

Unless some problem arises, there is little you must do for the puppies until they become three to four weeks old. Keep the box clean and supplied with fresh newspapers the first few days, but then turkish towels should be tacked down to the bottom of the box so that the puppies will have traction as they move about.

If the bitch has difficulties with her milk supply, or if you should be so unfortunate as to lose her, then you must be prepared to either hand-feed or tube-feed the puppies if they are to survive. Tube-feeding is so much faster and easier. If the bitch is available, it is best that she continues to clean and care for the puppies in the normal manner, excepting for the food supplements you will provide. If it is impossible for her to do this, then

Mary McCracken takes Winners Dog with Mike-Mar's China Boi of Wyn-D-Hill; Monica McCracken takes Winners Bitch with Ch. Wyn-D-Hill's Dragon Puff. Both owned by Mary McCracken, Wyn-D-Hill Pekingese, Jersey Shore, Pennsylvania. China Boi co-owned by Michael Wolf. Mrs. Anne Clark judging.

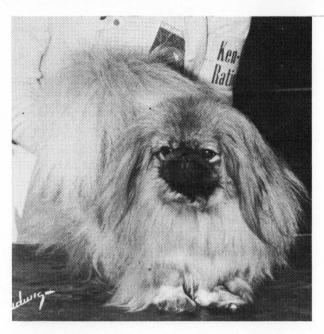

Ch. Mar-Pat Tiko's Jade, by Ch. Tiko of Pekeboro, is typical of the splendid Pekes bred at Mar-Pat Kennels.

after every feeding you must gently rub each puppy's abdomen with wet cotton to make it urinate, and the rectum should be gently rubbed to open the bowels.

Newborn puppies must be fed every three to four hours around the clock. The puppies must be kept warm during this time. Have your veterinarian teach you how to tube-feed. You will find that it is really quite simple.

After a normal whelping, the bitch will require additional food to enable her to produce sufficient milk. In addition to being fed twice daily, she should be given some canned milk several times each day.

When the puppies are two weeks old, their nails should be clipped, as they are needle sharp at this age and can hurt or damage the mother's teats and stomach as the pups hold on to nurse.

Between three and four weeks of age, the puppies should begin to be weaned. Scraped beef (prepared by scraping it off slices of beef with a spoon so that none of the gristle is included) may be offered in very small quantities a couple of times daily for the first few days. Then by the third day you can mix puppy chow with warm water as directed on the package, offering it four times daily. By now the mother should be kept away from the puppies and out of the box for several hours at a time so that when they have reached five weeks of age she is left in with them only over-

311

night. By the time the puppies are six weeks old, they should be entirely weaned and receiving only occasional visits from their mother.

Most veterinarians recommend a temporary DHL (distemper, hepatitis, leptospirosis) shot when the puppies are six weeks of age. This remains effective for about two weeks. Then at eight weeks of age, the puppies should receive the series of permanent shots for DHL protection. It is also a good idea to discuss with your vet the advisability of having your puppies inoculated against the dreaded parvovirus at the same time. Each time the pups go to the vet for shots, you should bring stool samples so that they can be examined for worms. Worms go through various stages of development and may be present in a stool sample even though the sample does not test positive in every checkup. So do not neglect to keep careful watch on this.

The puppies should be fed four times daily until they are three months old. Then you can cut back to three feedings daily. By the time the puppies are six months of age, two meals daily are sufficient. Some people feed their dogs twice daily throughout their

Ch. Windemere's Dauntless Dragon taking his first points, age 11 months, from Bred-by Class. Owned and handled by Joy Thoms, Mololla, Oregon.

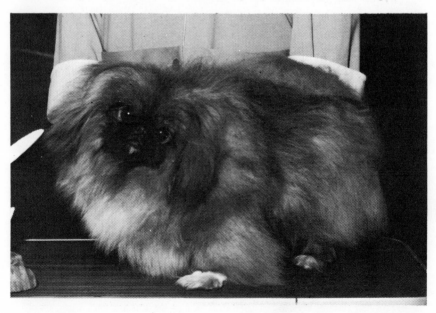

Ch. Mahjong Karoline, by Aust. Ch. Yamagee Keis Son ex Mahjong Karan, owner-handled by Mrs. Joan Mylchreest, Yardley, Pennsylvania, to Best of Winners at the Progressive Dog Club 1985.

lifetime; others go to one meal daily when the puppy becomes one year of age.

The ideal age for puppies to go to their new homes is between eight and twelve weeks, although some puppies successfully adjust to a new home when they are six weeks old. Be sure that they go to their new owners accompanied by a description of the diet you've been feeding them and a schedule of the shots they have already received and those they still need. These should be included with the registration application and a copy of the pedigree.

A WORD OF CAUTION

With Pekingese being one of the larger-headed breeds, there is always the risk of a problem in whelping. This should be discussed with your veterinarian, and plans should be made for a Caesarean should it appear that any difficulty is developing. Do not leave this to chance; make certain that your vet is available, should the need arise.

Chapter 13

Traveling with Your Pekingese

When you travel with your dog, to shows or on vacation or wherever, remember that everyone does not share your enthusiasm or love for dogs and that those who do not, strange creatures though they seem to us, have their rights too. These rights, on which you should not encroach, include not being disturbed, annoyed, or made uncomfortable by the presence and behavior of other people's pets. Your dog should be kept on lead in public places and should recognize and promptly obey the commands: "Down," "Come," "Sit," and "Stay."

Take along his crate if you are going any distance with your dog, and keep him in it when riding in the car. A crated dog has a far better chance of escaping injury than one riding loose in the car, should an accident occur or an emergency arise. If you do permit your dog to ride loose, never allow him to hang out a window, ears blowing in the breeze. An injury to his eyes could occur in this manner. He could also become overly excited by something he sees and jump out, or he could lose his balance and fall out.

Never, ever, under any circumstances, should a dog be permitted to ride loose in the back of a pick-up truck. Some people do transport dogs in this manner, which is cruel and shocking. How easily such a dog can be thrown out of the truck by sudden jolts or an impact! Doubtless many dogs have jumped out at the

John B. Royce, owner of Dah Lyn Pekingese, as judge placed Am. and Can. Ch. St. Aubrey Tinkabelle of Elsdon Best of Opposite Sex at the 1962 Pekingese Club of America Specialty at Westchester. R. William Taylor, co-owner with Nigel Aubrey Jones, handled at this event.

sight of something exciting along the way. Some unthinking individuals tie the dog, probably not realizing that were he to jump under those circumstances, his neck would be broken, he could be dragged alongside the vehicle, or he could be hit by another vehicle. If for any reason you are taking your dog in an open-back truck, please have sufficient regard for that dog to at least provide a crate for him; and then remember that, in or out of a crate, a dog riding under the direct rays of the sun in hot weather can suffer and have his life endangered by the heat.

If you are staying at a hotel or motel with your dog, exercise him somewhere other than in the flower beds and parking lot of the property. People walking to and from their cars really are not thrilled at "stepping in something" left by your dog. Should an accident occur, pick it up with a tissue or paper towel and deposit it in a proper receptacle; do not just walk off, leaving it to remain there. Usually there are grassy areas on the sides of and behind motels where dogs can be exercised. Use them rather than the more conspicuous, usually carefully tended, front areas or those close to the rooms. If you are becoming a dog show enthusiast, you will eventually need an exercise pen to take with you to the show. Exercise pens are ideal to use when staying at motels, too, as they permit you to limit the dog's roaming space and to pick up after him more easily.

Never leave your dog unattended in the room of a motel unless you are absolutely certain that he will stay there quietly and not

315

damage or destroy anything. You do not want a long list of complaints from irate guests, caused by the annoying barking or whining of a lonesome dog in strange surroundings, or an overzealous watch dog barking furiously each time a footstep passes the door or he hears a sound from an adjoining room. And you certainly do not want to return to torn curtains or bedspreads, soiled rugs, or other embarrassing evidence of the fact that your dog is not really house-reliable after all.

If yours is a dog accustomed to traveling with you and you are positive that his behavior will be acceptable when left alone, that is fine. But if the slightest uncertainty exists, the wise course is to leave him in the car while you go to dinner or elsewhere; then bring him into the room when you are ready to retire for the night.

When you travel with a dog, it is often simpler to take along from home the food and water he will need rather than to buy food and look for water while you travel. In this way he will have the rations to which he is accustomed and which you know agree with him, and there will be no fear of problems due to different drinking water. Feeding on the road is quite easy now, at least for short trips, with all the splendid dry foods and high-quality canned meats available. A variety of lightweight, refillable water containers can be bought at many types of stores.

Always be careful to leave sufficient openings to ventilate your car when the dog will be alone in it. Remember that during the summer, the rays of the sun can make an inferno of a closed car within only a few minutes, so leave enough window space open to provide air circulation. Again, if your dog is in a crate, this can be done quite safely. The fact that you have left the car in a shady spot is not always a guarantee that you will find conditions the same when you return. Don't forget that the position of the sun changes in a matter of minutes, and the car you left nicely shaded half an hour ago can be getting full sunlight far more quickly than you may realize. So, if you leave a dog in the car, make sure there is sufficient ventilation and check back frequently to ascertain that all is well.

If you are going to another country, you will need a health certificate from your veterinarian for each dog you are taking with you, certifying that each has had rabies shots within the required time preceding your visit.

316

Index

318